Your Successful Career as a

Mortgage Broker

Your Successful Career as a

Mortgage Broker

David Reed

AMACOM

American Management Association

New York • Atlanta • Brussels • Chicago • Mexico City • San Francisco
Shanghai • Tokyo • Toronto • Washington, D.C.

This publication is designed to provide accurate and authoritative information in regard to the subject matter covered. It is sold with the understanding that the publisher is not engaged in rendering legal, accounting, or other professional service. If legal advice or other expert assistance is required, the services of a competent professional person should be sought.

Library of Congress Cataloging-in-Publication Data

Reed, David, 1957 Oct. 1–
        Your successful career as a mortgage broker / David Reed.
            p.   cm.
        ISBN-13: 978-0-8144-7370-2
        ISBN-10: 0-8144-7370-9
        1. Mortgage brokers—United States—Vocational guidance.   I. Title.

    HG2040.5.U5R433   2007
    332.7'202373—dc22

                                                            2006100279

Printing number

10   9   8   7   6   5   4   3   2

Contents

Appendix F
State Licensing Chart

Appendix G
Payments Per Thousand Dollars Financed

Preface

When I first started in the mortgage business way back in 1989, I had absolutely no clue what I was getting into. I had some solid sales experience, but I was anything but a "numbers" person.

Being a mortgage loan officer never, ever crossed my mind. Heck, I honestly didn't know they existed. I thought perhaps the closest thing I could relate to might be a teller in my local bank.

I had no idea how much money I could make. I also had no idea how fun the business actually is. Yes, I said fun! The mortgage market can be a roller-coaster ride, with rates moving up, then down, then sideways. It can really keep you on your toes, meaning you'll never have a boring day.

I have seen the mortgage market mature into something hardly recognizable. Just as with any industry, the Internet has created remarkable changes. You still need basic mortgage skills, but the mortgage business has changed. It's dynamic. And one of the neatest things about this business is that there's no "one way" to be successful. Yes, there are certainly core requirements you need to master—ones you'll learn in this book—but there are different paths to success.

The very first thing I did in the mortgage business was process loans. This is sometimes a mundane activity, collecting information from borrowers, appraisers, and bank accounts and sticking it in a loan file. I did this to learn how loans were approved.

Later I became a loan officer, and through hard work and selling skills I was eventually promoted to vice president of sales at my mortgage company in San Diego, California.

I got my mortgage business by calling on Realtor offices. Later, as I built a database of clients, I began concentrating more on marketing to them. In 1996, I was one of the first to venture into cyberspace by creating one of the first mortgage websites in the country and originating mortgage loans via the Internet.

I've trained many loan officers over the course of my career, and I focus on how to make them successful—very successful. I don't train them for a living or have a website that sells training material. In this book I identify various resources that sell products to help loan officers, but I don't make any money from doing that.

Everything I have learned in the mortgage business I am about to share with you. Good luck, and here's to an exciting new career!

David Reed 2007

Getting Started

The Mortgage Loan Officer and His Team

A loan officer is an individual who assists those who need or want to borrow money in order to buy real estate. Loan officers take loan applications, counsel clients on the types of loans that best suit their needs, and help them with other mortgage-related questions about loan qualifications, closing costs, monthly payments, and credit issues.

A loan officer can be an employee of a national bank or a "mom and pop" mortgage-broker organization. Regardless of who employs them, all loan officers provide the same basic customer-service functions.

There are numerous advantages to being a mortgage loan officer, including these:

You can make a lot of money as a mortgage loan officer. Lots of it. According to the CNNMoney.com annual salary survey, the average loan officer makes over $76,000 per year. Make it to the top 5 percent of the industry and you'll make over $360,000 per year. Not bad for a day's work, is it?

There are no college degrees required to be a loan officer, nor do you have to have any special education requirements. Although there are various state licensing laws that you need to comply with, you don't have to amass any special formal education. Okay, you need to read and know how to work a calculator, but that's about it.

You help people. In fact, you help people with one of the biggest decisions they'll ever make. Your counsel and advice, along with your encouragement, get people into their own homes.

If you do your job right, you will get a sense of accomplishment found in few other careers. Helping people get into their first homes or being the person responsible for helping someone repair his or her damaged credit in order to buy a home is a feeling hard to find elsewhere. I remember one young lady several years ago that actually broke down in tears when I told her she qualified to buy her very own home. Go ahead, find something else like that in the financial world. I dare you.

You can telecommute. You can be a mortgage loan officer anywhere. If you decide that the Southern California lifestyle is no longer for you and you yearn to live on a ranch in west Texas, then by gosh unpack those boots and do it. You're not stuck with a career that only works in major cities. You can go anywhere you please.

The skills are transferable. Mortgage loans are approved in the very same fashion in Miami as they are in Mobile. Geography does not distinguish a 30-year fixed-rate conventional mortgage. That means the skills you've learned in one part of the country will be the very same skills you rely on in other parts of the country. If you're a good loan officer in Seattle, you'll be a good loan officer in Schenectady. Many jobs don't allow you the luxuries that being a loan officer does.

You work your own hours. You can sleep late if you want. Or not. Successful loan officers treat their loan businesses as seriously as any other professionals. If you want to start your day at 10:00 a.m., you can. If you want to begin work before the sun comes up, you can do that too. Some loan officers take a day off during the week so they can work Saturdays. Some loan officers work Sunday afternoons. Some loan officers work in the evenings. Most successful loan officers work a combination thereof.

You will become more financially savvy. Becoming a loan officer gives you a better sense of the importance of financial well-being. There are few high school or college courses that teach the importance of credit and financial responsibility. Most of us learn it just by living every day, paying our bills when they're due. Others may not understand how late payments on a credit report can affect their financial futures. By being a mortgage loan officer, you're knee-deep in the world of credit and how it affects consumers. You will understand how financial responsibility can reap rewards such as being able to borrow money at a cheaper rate than someone with less-than-stellar credit.

As a mortgage loan officer, you will be able to share the knowledge that owning a home is perhaps the single greatest way for someone to achieve financial independence. Building equity in a house can mean an easier retirement or an easier time paying for other things such as college tuition or home improvements.

You can be a part of all that. You can become a successful mortgage loan officer and make a lot of money if you follow the instructions outlined in this book.

Characteristics of Good Loan Officers

Okay, so now that you know what a loan officer does, do you have the tools necessary to be a loan officer? Maybe. Maybe not. The fact is there are not any "core" requirements to be a loan officer. There are, however, certain characteristics that will certainly help you succeed in this career.

You Are Responsible Enough To Be Your Own Boss

This is probably the hardest component for a lot of people. Some need to have an eight-to-five job—they simply need to have structure that is sometimes attained only through a time clock.

Don't take this the wrong way, but some people in their work lives need to be told what to do. They perform better when someone else sets the objectives and goals for the day.

As a loan officer who gets paid primarily on commission, you will determine your own success or failure. You have to be a self-starter and be able to stay on top of all aspects of your job.

Many loan officers starting out are fortunate enough to have bosses who help steer their career paths in the right direction. Still other lenders simply say to the loan officer newbie, "Okay, we're going to pay you a big commission to bring in these deals, but you have to bring them in!"

Being your own boss means that, whether you're self-employed or not, you must have the ability to establish and follow a marketing plan as well as adapt easily to the constant changes in business climates that directly affect your plan. Knowing these changes will occur will make them easier to accept.

You Are Comfortable Crunching Numbers

You don't need to be able to do calculus, but you do need to understand numbers. Mortgage loans don't involve quantum theory, but you must be able to comfortably add up numbers, divide that number by another number or two, and be able to use a financial calculator.

When I was in school, math was never my best subject. I was definitely a "right brain" guy who could handle the abstract and present it in a coherent way, but often certain calculations would leave me dry. I didn't necessarily struggle with math, but it was definitely harder to execute than, say, writing or giving speeches.

Before I entered the mortgage field, I had a good friend who owned a mortgage company. I would go over to his house and see him work off a funny calculator that had a bunch of odd, numbered keys on it. This funny calculator was the famed Hewlett-Packard 12C, or HP12C, as it's known in the financial world.

A regular hand-held calculator would let you type in "12 + 10 = 22" or some simple process. A 12C financial calculator would give you an unintelligible answer when you tried to enter in the very same 12 + 10 sequence. It was weird.

After I became a loan officer, I used the 12C every day, all day. And now, I honestly find it difficult to use any "normal" calculator. It frustrates me. My 10-year-old son can use one with ease, but I can't seem to make it work and I usually throw it aside.

Although I talk about the 12C, it is certainly not the only financial calculator on the market. The point here is you need to be able to comfortably work with a handheld financial calculator. There are a variety of online calculators and even some you can run on your computer, but be wary. You will need to be able to figure payments by yourself, without the aid of a computer.

Whether you need to accomplish that feat often is not as important as knowing how to do it. You will, someday, need to calculate payments. You will, some day, impress your potential client when he or she sees that you know how to figure payments with a calculator and not rely on a computer or website. It makes them think you're a financial genius. And like me, who was math-challenged, that's a big plus.

You Are Capable of Explaining Things

The mortgage business has so many foreign terms that most consumers never run across them until they buy a house. And even if someone buys three or four houses in his lifetime, he still might not get the lingo down.

It's your responsibility as a loan officer to explain the entire mortgage process in language borrowers understand. Mortgages aren't necessarily complex, it's just that the language inherent in the process can make them so.

If you're able to explain things, you won't get your feathers ruffled when someone asks a question or gets frustrated with you when she's hit with a bunch of numbers that don't quite mean much. Your customers will be happy and will refer you to their friends.

The Loan Officer's Team

A *mortgage* is a loan, and the property bought with the loan is the collateral. If the borrower defaults on the loan or otherwise doesn't make the payments, then the lender will take the property back.

Mortgages come from lenders. Eventually, anyway. But lenders don't make mortgages by loaning the money in their bank vaults. Instead, they usually issue mortgages through special credit lines they have established for the sole purpose of making mortgages. For example, a lender might borrow money at 5.00% and issue mortgages at 7.00%.

A loan officer shepherds her clients, the borrowers, through the mortgage process from start to finish. There are many others involved in the loan process as well, but it's the loan officer who is the primary contact person for the borrowers.

Who are all these other important people and what do they do?

The Loan Processor

As a loan officer, the loan processor will be your best friend. If you haven't made best friends with the loan processor, you're making a huge mistake. This person assembles the borrower's documentation for the loan application. The processor will collect things such as paycheck stubs, bank statements, or income-tax returns from the borrowers. This person will also cover your rear end when, not if, you make a mistake.

The processor will also interact with every other player in the approval process. He or she will collect information from the insurance agent about insurance coverage for the property. The processor will talk to the title company to get the report on title.

The processor will have a checklist of all the things needed to close the loan and will order them. If something hasn't arrived, the processor will track it down and get it.

Your processor is your partner doing the paperwork while you're out getting new business or making sales calls. It's a lot of work and sometimes thankless. The loan application itself doesn't get to an underwriter until the file is completely documented.

The processor is your face to the rest of the world—he's the one who talks to your clients nearly every day while keeping track of all of your loan files in process. He works on loan conditions, fixes mistakes on applications, and works on anything else required to close the loan. It's much like spinning plates sometimes. And if there's one person you must absolutely be nice to all the time, it's the loan processor.

The Loan Underwriter

The loan underwriter is the person who makes the final determination about whether your borrowers meet the criteria for the loan they've applied for. If the loan guidelines say your borrowers must be at their current jobs for at least two years, the underwriter will review the documentation from the processor and make sure that they have in fact been at their jobs for two years (i.e., do the last two years of W-2s have the same company name as the paycheck stubs?). If the borrowers meet the criteria, the underwriter can sign off on the loan requirement.

The underwriter interprets lending guidelines and reviews documentation. If your loan processor has done his job correctly, the underwriter simply goes down the submission sheet and checks things off as they're submitted.

If the loan requires $10,000 in the bank, the loan processor documents $10,000 in your client's application via recent bank statements and puts the documents in your borrower's file for the underwriter to review. If the bank statements show $10,000 in the bank, then that requirement has been fulfilled. If the bank statements show $9,999, then regardless of how close $9,999 is to $10,000, the underwriter can't approve the loan. It doesn't meet the guidelines.

Underwriters can also make judgment calls about a loan application as long as the calls are within bounds of the loan guidelines. There are *requirements* and there are *guidelines*. A requirement is a "must," but a guideline might have some latitude.

For instance, you might have a borrower who can't show that she has been self-employed for two years, a common requirement. Typically, a condition to prove self-employment for two years is to provide two years of tax returns. Sometimes though, the borrower hasn't filed on time or has filed for extensions.

So the underwriter might waive the requirement for two years of tax returns if there is another method the underwriter feels is appropriate to verify the two years of self-employment. I recall a client a few years ago who had placed an ad in the yellow pages. The telephone book was published more than two years ago, so I forwarded the phone book to the underwriter. It worked. The underwriter used her latitude to document a lending guideline.

The Inspector

There are two types of inspectors: pest inspectors and building inspectors. One person can most usually do both types of inspections, but they are in fact different.

A building inspector checks for structural or operational problems by scouring the prospective property from top to bottom for current or potential problems. It's the inspector who will walk into the basement and look for water seepage or cracks in the foundation.

The inspector will look at the roof to check for damage and will crawl into the attic to look for problems. The inspector will run the dishwasher or the garbage disposal to make sure those work. The inspector will even flush toilets and flip light switches, then provide a final report to the customer.

A pest inspector typically searches for termites—either active or signs of previous termite damage. A pest inspector will also look for other property-damaging pests and report them. Some states require a termite report before the loan closes, but others do not.

The Surveyor

The surveyor physically measures the property to see where the property lines are and determines where any structures sit on the property. The surveyor can determine if a neighbor's fence accidentally crosses your own property lines. Or vice versa.

A surveyor will indicate, by drawing, any other permanent structures such as a pool or a storage shed. The survey will also show any easements that appear. An easement is a legal right of access to your property.

Typical easements are usually provided for utility companies or cable companies. For example, an employee of the electrical utility has a legal right to access your property to read meters or repair electrical lines. This is usually also the case for the telephone, water, or cable company.

The survey will show where those lines are on the property in relation to the other buildings on the lot. As buyers, your clients want to know about such easements. As an agent for the lender, you will want to know that as well. Is there a telephone line that runs right underneath the living room floor? An easement will allow the phone company to access that line, even tear up the floor, if it needs to repair it.

The Appraiser

The appraiser is also someone who inspects the property, but not for structural damage, pests, or where the property is located. The ap-

praiser helps to establish the value of the home, and part of the evaluation process is a physical inspection.

Sometimes the general public (and even those in the real estate
industry) confuses the roles of appraisers and inspectors, but in fact
they do perform different duties.

An appraiser's job is to justify the sales price of a home, or in the
case of a refinance, to determine the approximate market value of the
existing home. An appraiser's market-value determination is done in
two ways; the first uses the cost approach and the second uses the
market approach.

The cost approach measures the square footage of a house, estimates the costs needed to build that house, then adds the value of that
house to the value of the land the house sits on. This is not the value
the lender uses for the loan. The lender uses the market value.

An appraiser will determine the market value of the home by first
taking the sales contract on the property as the basis for value determination. The appraiser will then visit the neighborhood and identify recently sold homes from that area. These homes are called *comparable
sales* or simply *comps*. The appraiser will look for a minimum of three,
sometimes four, comps that have sold within the most recent 12-month
period, then compare those sales with your subject property.

Generally, the appraiser will access the Multiple Listing Service, or
MLS used by Realtors to list homes and look at the sales prices of
homes in the subject property's area. The appraisal will only reflect
closed deals, not homes that are currently listed.

The appraiser will then compare the most recent home sales that
are closest to the subject property. If a 2,000-square-foot home sold
for $200,000, then that would imply the house was worth approxi-
mately $100 per square foot. If the subject property was 2,200 square
feet, then at $100 per square foot the appraiser would begin making a
market determination. The house should sell for somewhere around
$220,000.

Remember, the appraiser will use a minimum of three comps to justify the sales price. After determining the sales prices and comparing square footages, the appraiser will then make certain "adjustments" to the subject property, based upon other features of the homes being used for comps. Adjustments can be added to or subtracted from the subject for items such as a swimming pool or a deck or even a nice view.

The Attorney

The attorney can play various roles depending upon which state the property is in. In some states, attorneys play no role whatsoever. In California, for instance, there is no attorney involved unless the buyers or sellers hire one to review sales contracts or other pertinent documents.

In other states, Texas, for example, attorneys must review all loan papers before any closing can occur. This is the case for every single mortgage there. But an attorney in Texas won't be at a closing. In Illinois, however, attorneys hold the closings. They also review contracts on behalf of the buyer and seller.

In Oklahoma, attorneys are involved but they provide information about liens, title, and surveys for the subject property. There is no universal performance requirement for attorneys, and their responsibilities can vary from state to state. And in some cases they aren't required at all.

The Title Agent

The title agent is responsible for delivering the title-insurance policy to the closing. In real estate, a *title* is written and legally recorded evidence of ownership. Every piece of property has a written ownership history, including when it was sold, and who it was sold to. The title can also show where the property is located via a written description.

The title agent will research the historical ownership of the property and make sure it was legally transferred from all the previous parties. The title agent also ensures there are no other claims to the property that would prevent the current owners from selling. For instance, the homeowners may have had some roof work done years back but never paid the roofer—it's likely the roofer placed a mechanic's lien on the property so that he would eventually get paid if the home ever got sold.

Title insurance is insurance that protects the new lender and new owners from any previous claims or defects that might appear. For example, say a long-lost heir of a previous seller claims that he was awarded part of that property when his uncle died but he was never paid. Or say, during a divorce settlement, one of the ex-spouses wasn't satisfied with the divorce settlement and never properly awarded the property.

Again, depending upon your state laws, various people can produce a title insurance policy. Sometimes it's the title company itself, sometimes it's an attorney, or sometimes it's a combination whereby the title company produces the insurance but the attorney is responsible for the physical delivery.

The Settlement Agent

The settlement agent can be one of many different people—it can be an attorney, or a title agency representative, or it might be someone else called an *escrow agent*. The settlement agent is the person who handles the closing for the buyers and the sellers. He or she witnesses the buyers and sellers sign this and sign that, verifies the identity of all parties, collects money from the buyers, and disburses money to the sellers.

The Closer

The closer works for the lender. The closer makes certain everything the lender asked the settlement agent to do was done correctly. After everything is completed, the loan goes into funding.

Funding is the term used to describe the transfer of money from the lender's account to the seller's account. If the sellers had a mortgage on their home, the settlement agent will transfer those funds from the sellers' account to the old mortgage company.

After the loan funds, that's when you make your money. Then you go on to the next one.

How Do I Get Started?

D octors need licenses. Contractors need licenses. Real estate agents need licenses. Granted, it took quite some time for mortgage brokers to become licensed, but eventually nearly every state in the union established licensing requirements for brokers and bankers. And this is not a bad thing. So the first thing to do is make sure you know if you're legally operating in your state.

When you issue mortgage loans, you're not talking about 10 or 20 bucks here or there. No, you're talking a few million dollars of money changing hands each and every month. So the community as a whole, including mortgage lenders, would like to know a little bit about you before you take on this new endeavor, which is why you need a license. Licensing is also not free—you'll have to pay some money to the state or to whichever organization regulates your new career.

Getting Licensed

What is required? Licensing requirements vary from state to state. Not only that, but state legislatures seem to find it a good habit to find new ways to regulate you. That means licensing requirements may in fact change from year to year. And you can bet those changes don't mean less regulation . . . but more. (See Appendix F.)

You will also find out that states regulate mortgage brokers and mortgage bankers differently. Many times states will have two separate regulatory agencies, one for bankers and one for brokers. Whichever path you take, you will have certain requirements to fulfill.

Those requirements are just too varied to list in this book. Regulatory requirements for each state take up hundreds of pages of printed text. Regardless, most states ask that you pass some tests on real estate and real estate finance, get fingerprinted, and pass a background check ensuring that you haven't been a serial loan-fraud expert. Most usually also require annual continued education credits, or CEs. For some reason, 15 hours of CE per year is a common standard.

When I got my first mortgage-broker license in California, I was required to be a licensed real estate agent. That meant I took the very same test that real estate agents took when they wanted to be agents. I also had to take continuing education classes every so often to make sure I was sharp and up-to-date on all the latest real estate practices, trends, and laws. At that time, and as of this writing, the California Department of Real Estate, or DRE, licenses and monitors mortgage brokers.

For mortgage bankers, licensing is typically less stringent but still required. Mortgage bankers already are licensed, audited, and monitored by the Department of Housing and Urban Development (HUD) as well as a host of other agencies.

The way to find out which agency you need to contact is to simply call or use Google to learn about your state government. Your government is there to help you and it'll point you in the right direction.

Your employer is typically responsible for monitoring your licensing, so when your license is getting ready to come up for renewal or a CE class comes up and you need some hours, usually it's your employer that lets you know your status.

Licensing is a big issue. If you want to work for a broker, the broker will want to see your license first. In the unlikely event that you arrange a loan and you're not licensed, the broker will probably lose his license, shutting down the entire operation.

In addition to government-required licensing and CEs, it's important that you go outside what's required by the government and start your own education routine.

First, join local or regional associations. There's a wealth of information at your disposal, most often issued every month at association meetings. I have been a member of mortgage broker associations and served as an officer in various capacities for mortgage banking associations. In fact, as I write this book I am the president of the Austin Mortgage Bankers Association.

Each month, our association and other mortgage bankers offer different training programs for people who want to learn more about the business. One month there may be a half-day seminar on VA mortgages. The next month, loans for first time homebuyers might be the topic. Or construction loans. Both lenders who want to educate their brokers as well as lenders who want to educate their employees offer continuing education outside of the "school of hard knocks."

Attend as many educational and social sessions as you can. Not only will you meet new people, you'll also get to hear real examples of how loans work, and don't work, in the real world.

Another added benefit? When you attend such functions, you're getting known in the community. You're also meeting new people. This is where you might meet a future employer, or find a new appraiser, or get a better deal with a credit-reporting company. Networking with those in the business is absolutely, positively a requirement. Be active. Be seen. Be there.

Getting Started

People who are thinking about getting into the business often ask me, "How do I start?" That's a very good question. And I have a very good answer. Find someone who will spend time with you, mentor you, and help you with problems as they arise.

You'd be surprised at how many mortgage operations hire straight-commission loan officers who could care less about their training and focus only on how many deals they might bring in that month.

"Welcome to our mortgage company . . . here's the phone book, now go find some business," is how it might go. You can't afford to work with a company that doesn't have the resources to train you, especially if you're brand-new in the business. It doesn't matter that a company offers a bigger commission structure if you have no idea how to find a loan in the first place.

The advice I've given over the years is to find a major mortgage banker, bank, or credit union that can pay you a base salary with a smaller commission structure while you train. This might take a couple of years. The mortgage business is in fact a definite science; there are lots of things to learn and often the hardest lessons are those learned from mistakes. When you have a company willing to pay you while it trains you, that means you can afford to make mistakes and gain valuable experience. This means that unless you've got tons of experience in mortgage lending, you should find someone to work for as you learn. The mortgage business is not the place to learn "on the job," and in fact most states will require that you have a minimum number of mortgage years under your belt before allowing you to open your own mortgage business.

Get some solid mortgage experience before you open up your own operation.

Mortgage Banker vs. Mortgage Broker

You've heard these terms before: *mortgage banker, broker, mortgage broker, mortgage lender.* But the truth is that a loan officer performs the very same or similar duties no matter what type of mortgage company he or she works for. There are differences, however, and each role has its own advantages. It's up to you to determine what you want to be and whom you want to work for. And hey, you can always change your mind.

I started in the mortgage business as a mortgage broker. The company was me, the owner, and two loan processors. It was small. And that's where I learned the business. Later on in my lending career I worked for a small mortgage banker. Still later, that company was bought by a regional bank. Still later, we were swallowed up again by a national bank.

So I've been on all sides of the origination business, from broker to banker to bank. I know firsthand the advantages and disadvantages of being a mortgage broker and a mortgage banker, and I will explain them here.

By definition, there is one distinct difference. A broker does not make mortgage loans. A broker does not have a vault full of money all lined up to issue home loans.

A banker on the other hand, does make mortgage loans. A banker does have a vault full of money (or perhaps more accurately, a credit line) all lined up to make home loans.

You can't tell the difference among a loan officer, a banker, or a broker if you just watched them work, as they perform essentially the very same functions. But there are certainly differences—differences that you need to evaluate before you decide which path to take.

Being a broker has the benefits of:

- Shopping different lenders for the best rate
- Shopping different lenders for a qualifying loan program
- Getting underwriting opinions from different sources
- Moving your clients' loans in times of dramatic rate moves

Being a banker has the benefits of:

- Having more control over the lending process
- Having full access to government programs such as Federal Housing Administration (FHA) loans
- Negotiating underwriting guidelines

At first glance you might say, "Whoa! Hands down, broker!" But there's a little more to it than that.

Shopping Different Lenders for the Best Rate

This is the single biggest advantage a broker has. A mortgage broker has access to as many lenders as the broker can stand.

You may have seen advertisements from mortgage companies stating, "We have access to over 100 banks and national lenders!" or some similar quote. That kind of quote is from a broker.

Consider an independent insurance agent. She doesn't issue the policy, but instead has access to competing insurance companies all vying for her, and ultimately her clients' insurance policies.

And that's what a broker does: she shops the bevy of lenders to find the absolute best rate available. Where do brokers find all these lenders? Most often, it's the lender that finds the mortgage broker first.

Most every mortgage lender and bank you've ever heard of (and still more you've never heard of) use mortgage brokers. These lenders operate separate mortgage divisions, called "wholesale" departments, that find mortgage brokers who will send borrowers to them.

Just as with any other wholesale-retail arrangement, wholesale lenders distribute their mortgages via mortgage brokers. The wholesale lender usually reduces the interest rate on a typical mortgage by 1/8 to 1/4 percent for the broker. The broker then marks that mortgage up to "retail" by that same 1/8 to 1/4 percent and pockets the difference.

That's how mortgage brokers get paid: they get loans cheaper than the consumer can get them from wholesale lenders, then they find borrowers, and then they mark up the loan to make their profits.

Wholesale lending is a very competitive business. Wholesale lenders hire marketing executives whose only job is to find mortgage brokers who will market their loans for them. And it makes a lot of sense—there's a lot of overhead involved in running any business, and a mortgage operation is no different. Most mortgage companies need office space, employees, telephones, computers, utilities, insurance, employment taxes, compliance issues . . . well, there's a lot.

But a wholesale lender doesn't need offices. Instead, a wholesale lender will find a mortgage broker who is willing to use his own office, computers, and marketing expertise in exchange for a wholesale loan. There are advantages to both parties.

Each and every morning, a broker gets rate sheets via fax or e-mail from wholesale lenders, usually by about 11:00 a.m. EST, when the markets have opened and lenders have figured out what rates to send out.

Brokers then review the various rate sheets, compare rates, how much those rates cost, and lender fees. We'll discuss rate quotes in more detail in chapter 9, but this is where the broker has an advantage. A broker can give his or her clients quotes from more than just one company because he or she has access to hundreds of them.

Shopping Different Lenders for a Qualifying Loan Program

Just as a broker can shop around for a competitive rate quote, a broker can also shop around for a specific loan program that not all lenders carry.

Most lenders offer the very same staple of mortgage programs. For example, almost every lender will offer 30-year and 15-year fixed-rate or adjustable-rate mortgages and hybrids. Some lenders will also have alternative loan programs designed for specific lending circumstances.

Some lenders offer loans designed for people having difficulty documenting their income or those who simply don't wish to disclose how much money they make. Other loan programs are for those with damaged credit or for people fresh out of a bankruptcy. Although most lenders will offer the same core loan programs, no one lender has all programs.

In fact, mortgage companies spend tons of money on marketing just to try and differentiate themselves from other mortgage firms. After all, a 30-year fixed-rate mortgage is a 30-year fixed-rate mortgage. There's just not a lot one can do to make something that is exactly the same appear different and more appealing without some savvy marketing.

Sometimes though, a lender introduces a product no one else has. If you work for a bank and don't have that product, you're stuck without that product. If, however, you're a broker, you simply call the lender offering the new loan program and voilà! New competitive edge!

I first experienced this advantage several years ago when I was working as a broker in Southern California. There was a rumor about a special loan program designed specifically for medical students just out of college.

You see, recent medical-school graduates don't have a two-year history of employment and are at the very beginning of their earning years. They'll make a decent income right out of the gate, but they'll typically make a heck of a lot more in a very short time.

Med students also often have debt when they graduate, having amassed their fair share of student loans. Both high debt load and marginal income result in higher-than-normal debt-to-income ratios.

Finally, med graduates, being poor, often don't have any money for down payments. They're broke from spending all their money in school. No money, marginal incomes, and high debt loads—a scenario lenders would walk away from. But one lender didn't.

One lender identified this problem and understood that it was temporary. Doctors make a lot of money, so why not relax some of the standard lending guidelines and offer a special loan program that accommodates high debt loads, no money down, and no job history? Just show the lender a transcript proving the student has graduated from medical school, show the lender proof of a new job, and don't require a down payment. Good credit was required, yes, but everything else was adjusted to accommodate the graduates.

The deal made sense. What better way to amass a ton of loyalty from young doctors, considering their future needs for credit cards, luxury automobile loans, and expensive houses?

But there was only one lender who offered this program. Most others were either too small to underwrite such a deal or didn't want to start lending outside of the box. Suddenly, I had a loan program most of my competitors did not.

I next contacted various hospitals and clinics and asked if I could drop some information about this new program off at their human resources department. Of course I could, they said. It was also a great way to introduce myself to nondoctors as well.

Soon I began getting phone calls from these new professionals and soon I closed a lot of loans. It was extra special knowing that I had a product my competitor at the bank down the street simply did not have.

And marketing my access to this special loan program gave the impression that not only was I different than everyone else, but I had programs no one else had. Yeah, that might have been the only loan program that was different, but it worked.

Another advantage brokers have is the ability to find loans for those with damaged credit. A mortgage banker may not have the right product for someone who is currently in financial straits or who has recently experienced bad times, but there are lenders, sometimes called "subprime lenders," that specialize in nothing but loans for people with bad credit.

If you as a broker can't get your client approved at one lender, you might be able to get him or her approved by another lender that offers a product that fits your buyers' profile.

Getting Underwriting Opinions from Different Sources

Even though most loan programs are the same, they can be interpreted differently, even under the very same guidelines. If you're a broker and you don't agree with the underwriter's interpretation of a lending requirement, then you can get another lender's take on it.

These interpretations are called underwriting scenarios. Your client might have special circumstances that don't lead to a definitive yes or no but rather a "this is how I interpret this guideline."

If you're a banker and your underwriter turns down your client's loan because of a guideline interpretation, you're stuck. A broker isn't.

A broker picks up the phone and asks for a second, third, or even a fourth opinion.

I recall a lender that wouldn't approve a loan because of my client's job status. There is a common underwriting guideline that requires the borrower have a full month's worth of pay stubs ("two most recent pay stubs covering 30 days" is how the guideline reads). The borrower was transferring to another city but wasn't able to close on the house under that time frame.

The borrower wouldn't have pay stubs covering the most recent 30 days. He would only have one, and that one would be less than a week old. The underwriter wouldn't budge. I called another lender and explained my scenario. The lender said, "provide me a letter of employment from the new employer outlining the terms of the new job and give me one pay stub and I'll approve the loan."

Having the ability to get varying opinions can be a deal-saver. Brokers have that ability.

Moving Your Clients' Loans in Times of Dramatic Rate Moves

As a broker, you have options on which lender to send your client's loan to. You also can choose which lenders to avoid, and you might even ask a lender to return a loan before the loan has closed.

Mind you, wholesale lenders don't appreciate this very much. But sometimes it's necessary to keep a deal in house. You don't pull a loan because the lender won't approve it; instead, the lender sends it back as unapproved. You pull the loan because rates have moved down after you locked in the loan. A rate lock is an interest-rate guarantee, but the significance is that if you locked in your client's rate at 7.00% at ABC Lender and rates move down in the meantime to 6.50%, you're stuck.

If you lock in a loan for a customer, you're really locking in that loan not necessarily with you but with ABC Lender. And, if you lock, you lock. If rates move up or down, you get what you locked in at.

Locks simply mean your client's mortgage interest rate is guaranteed; it doesn't mean the loan is approvable or that you must close a loan with the lender once you lock. It means that if the loan is approved and you do close the loan, the rate is guaranteed at what you locked.

For example, let's say that the lock at 7.00% is no longer attractive because rates moved lower. ABC Lender won't let you change that rate. You have no choice. You locked in on your client's behalf. Meanwhile, your client is reading the newspapers and the Internet and sees that rates are going down after he locked in his loan. Now he either wants you to honor the lower rates that are currently available or he is going to find another mortgage company.

You in turn make your formal request to ABC Lender for a new rate lock at 6.50%. They politely tell you no, so you have no choice except to pull the loan, find another lender offering 6.50%, and resubmit the loan application. Your customer is now happy that you honored the new lower rate, ABC Lender is not very happy because you locked in a loan and then pulled it, and the new lender is happy that you sent it a loan.

As a broker, you have the ability to transfer loans from one wholesale lender to another. This is something you should rarely practice, as it will damage the relationship you had with ABC Lender, but it is still an option you have that a mortgage banker does not have.

If a mortgage banker locks in a loan with her company and rates move down, it's pretty much "tough cookies" and the loan officer watches her client go to another mortgage company to get the new lower rates. The client probably goes to you, if you're a market-savvy mortgage broker.

But it's not hands-down a better deal to always be a mortgage broker. Hardly. I've been both and I can say that although I may not have always had the lowest rates on the planet, I did have one huge advantage: control.

Having More Control Over the Lending Process

When a broker submits a mortgage loan, she loses control of the loan file. Up until the point of loan submission, the broker is collecting data and organizing documents for the sole purpose of submitting the file to another entity: the wholesale lender.

When there are problems or questions after the loan is submitted to the lender, there is both a time and communication lag between the lender's underwriter and the borrower.

If the underwriter looks at a file and has a question or a concern, the underwriter e-mails or faxes the loan processor with his question. The question can also sometimes go from the underwriter to the underwriter's assistant, the loan manager, or even the wholesale lender's account executive. A really problematic question can go through up to five people, then back again before a decision is made. And what if the answer raises more questions?

If an underwriter sees an application reporting $500 per month in income but does not have any supporting documentation in the file (which is the processor's fault) the underwriter stops the approval process altogether until the question is answered.

Could the underwriter continue to underwrite the rest of the file while he's waiting on clarification of the $500? Sure, but he won't. No, he'll put the file aside and start working on someone else's loan. That means the broker's customer will have to wait until there is an answer to the question.

A question from the underwriter can be about anything. It doesn't have to be a processor's mistake. There are questions on nearly every single loan file, and the loans are conditional upon their answers.

Now the underwriter starts on another loan, while you or your loan processor track down your borrower to ask about the $500. If you're lucky, you'll get the answer the same day, such as, "That's additional money I make from consulting," or some other response from your borrower.

So your processor e-mails, calls, or faxes the underwriter, loan assistant, or account executive and says, "It's from his consulting business."

Then there's a new question from the underwriter: "But I don't see anything about a new business in the loan file, so we'll need tax returns. Please provide tax returns for the previous two years." So the process begins again. The loan processor again finds your client and asks for tax returns.

In reality, this scenario plays out every single day somewhere and eats up precious time—maybe about a week of phone calls, finding tax returns, and overnighting or faxing documents. And still, the underwriter is working on other files.

A mortgage banker, on the other hand, has direct access. The underwriter, the loan processor, and the loan officer work for the same company. If a processor has a question about how to submit a loan, he simply asks the underwriter, "Hey, I've got a problem; how can we fix it before we submit the loan so it conforms to underwriting guidelines?"

If there's a question on a loan file, it goes directly to the loan processor or loan officer. There is no hand-off from one company to another. Well, there's a hand-off, but because it's done internally there are inherent time savings.

Is time an important element when buying a house? You better believe it. The sales contract determines when the sale is supposed to close. If the buyer can't qualify in time or the settlement agent doesn't receive the loan documents before the scheduled closing date, the buyers run the risk of losing their deposit money. That can mean thousands of dollars lost, upset clients, and very, very mad Realtors.

As a mortgage banker, you may also have access to special government programs that mortgage brokers may simply not be qualified to offer. Being an FHA lender for example, requires significant audits, compliance, and reserves. Mortgage brokers can't originate such loans because the Department of Housing and Urban Development, or

HUD, requires that loan officers who originate FHA loans be employees of FHA lenders, not mortgage brokers.

Having Full Access to Government Programs Such as FHA Loans

FHA lending is a great resource for those who have little or nothing for a down payment, who might need the debt-ratio guidelines relaxed, or might have some credit challenges. Anyone who has ever done FHA loans as any significant part of his or her lending portfolio will tell you that these loans are a huge benefit both to their income and to their clients.

The Veterans Administration (VA) also has special advantages for mortgage bankers but not mortgage brokers. Appraisal procedures, for instance, are significantly streamlined for lenders that make VA loans.

Negotiating Underwriting Guidelines

Any reasonable underwriter can interpret mortgage-approval guidelines, and these interpretations can help loans close. In fact, experienced loan officers who also understand many of these guidelines can discuss loan qualifications directly with an underwriter to come to a consensus and approve the loan. Thus, a mortgage banker has a better ability to negotiate guidelines with an underwriter.

And when problems arise, and they do, a banker can have an edge.

Why can bankers fix problems quicker than a broker? First, they have direct access to their own files. A broker does not—she has to call the wholesale lender to get things fixed, all the while going through additional channels.

For example, consider a loan submitted for approval. Everything is going well. Then there's a problem. The underwriter notices that the borrower has two last names in her credit report. This might indicate that she was previously married. Or it could be nothing more than a mistake on the report . . . but nobody knows. So the underwriter stops what he's doing and e-mails, calls, or contacts the wholesale lender's account executive for that particular mortgage broker.

The account executive then calls the loan processor and says, "Your applicant has two last names on her credit report, do you know if she's been married before or known by any other name, so we can get that cleared up?"

At first glance, this isn't any big deal, right? So what if she had two last names? What does that matter; she still qualifies for the loan, right?

Two names on a credit report for a female can indicate a previous marriage. Was she married to Mr. Smith, got divorced, and now uses her maiden name, Ms. Jones? Or because Ms. Jones is such a common name, could the credit report also simply be wrong?

Here's another example. Perhaps there is an income issue. Maybe the borrower took some vacation time and the pay isn't reflected on the pay stub. There's some income missing and the underwriter needs to document it in the file. Or perhaps there's not enough insurance coverage on the home and the borrower needs more.

I'm not kidding here, this happens every day somewhere in the lending business.

But the communication chain to get all this accomplished is jumbled up. First, the underwriter calls the account exec, and the account exec calls the loan processor or loan officer. The loan officer tracks down the borrower and asks her, "Were you known as Mrs. Smith at some point or are you divorced?" or "Your reported income doesn't match your pay stub, what gives?" or some such question.

Remember the telephone game, where one child whispers something to another and those words are "repeated" until the very last person tries to get the original statement correct? Did "My mother wears a big pink ribbon in her hair" turn out to be "My brother has pink underwear"?

Like the game, the more channels information goes through, the more likely the request and the final information will get jumbled. Not just jumbled, but delayed.

In our example, the loan officer finally gets the request from the underwriter and phones the client. Ms. Jones answers. "Yes, I was married to that idiot, what's wrong now?"

The broker says, "We need a copy of your divorce decree so we can establish that you have no financial obligations to your ex."

"That was six years ago; I don't have that decree and don't know where to get it."

"We'll have to find the judge, the court records, your attorney, just someone who might have a copy of it. There's no way around this."

"Okay," says Ms. Jones and hangs up the phone. Now things come to a screeching halt. Gotta find that divorce decree. After several days and more than a few phone calls, Ms. Jones calls back and says, "Okay, I found a copy, I'm going to bring it over."

She delivers the divorce decree to the mortgage broker. The broker then sends it via overnight courier to the lender, who logs it in (along with all the other new loan files received from other mortgage brokers), and puts it in line for the underwriter who originally asked to clear up the name discrepancy.

So far, this has taken several days—not just because the borrower had to track down old papers, but because there is an ongoing time lag between the mortgage broker and the underwriter. When there are problems with a loan file, this "wall" between a broker and a lender can be a challenge. And it can mean your deal falling through or not.

*   *   *

This same scenario with a banker works a little differently.

First the loan is submitted to the underwriter, typically meaning the loan moves from one part of the office to another. If not, then it goes to another building, maybe another town, but it still is with the same lender.

The underwriter picks up the file and begins underwriting. He sees there's a discrepancy in the credit file. Instead of putting everything on hold, he calls the loan officer directly.

"David, your client has two last names on her credit report. What gives?"

"I didn't notice that. I'll call her. Hold on."

After David contacts the borrower, he calls the underwriter back and says, "She's been divorced, but she doesn't have a copy of her divorce decree to establish whether she has additional monthly obligations. We do have tax returns showing no income or support payments being made. This should work, shouldn't it?" David asks.

"Great," says the underwriter. "We're good to go."

* * *

I can relate this story because it happened to me several years ago. Because I was the loan officer with the mortgage banker, I was able to discuss an alternative loan condition directly with the underwriter.

If I had been a broker trying to do the same thing, it would have taken days just to get a copy of the divorce decree. I wouldn't have had direct access to the underwriter to get the problems worked out. I would have had to go through the system to get my documentation in front of the lender for review.

Although the mortgage broker may have more access to loan pricing and loan programs, the mortgage banker hands down has his or her finger on the loan's pulse. I've been both, I know. Sometimes having the absolute lowest rate on the planet doesn't matter if the loan can't close on time.

Because in lending, reputation is everything. Never forget that.

Training and Career Development

Another consideration of becoming a mortgage broker or mortgage banking loan officer is both training and capital. If you don't know anything at all about the business, you'll want some type of hands-on training. This book will give you the groundwork and inside tips, but you'll still need a mentor who can show you the ropes.

I started out in the mortgage business as a mortgage broker. Although I had some sales experience, I had absolutely zero experience in the mortgage industry. Zero. I could barely use a calculator.

I had a draw at first while I learned the mortgage business, and although I had a good boss who helped teach me, I still had to learn on my own. My boss owned the company, and there were two loan officers—me and him.

At the same time, I also had the advantage of making a better commission when I closed a loan—I split everything I brought in. If a loan brought in $4,000, I made $2,000. Not bad work. Especially in Southern California, where the home prices were higher than in most parts of the country.

But my mortgage learning experience was truly trial by fire. I made mistakes. I learned from them and moved on.

Potential loan officers often say to me, "Hey Dave, I'd like to get into the mortgage business, but don't want to starve to death while I'm learning."

Fair enough. But if a company is going to train you, then don't expect the high commission split an experienced mortgage broker can enjoy. Smaller mortgage operations may not have the resources to properly train you. Nor will they be able to provide you with ongoing support when you have problems or questions. Although this is not the case in every broker shop, it's the most common scenario.

Usually banks or national mortgage-banking chains offer a salary and training. In fact, some mortgage bankers provide a series of mortgage classes that provide continuous training. The trade-off?

Mortgage bankers who provide training and continuous support may also pay you less money. Mortgage brokers who do not train or support you on a daily basis may also pay you more. In fact, good mortgage-broker loan officers can command a 70% percent and even an 80% percent commission split.

The bigger the company, the more training you can expect . . . and lower commissions.

Financial Differences

If you want to work for a mortgage broker or start your own mortgage brokerage, you need to pony up for all the hardware, software, and supplies on your own. Major lenders and mortgage bankers who have their own lending credit line will typically provide you with everything you need to get started in the business.

You might expect at minimum a computer and/or laptop to use, your own office, copier, fax machine, etc., and also maybe an expense account to entertain clients.

A mortgage-broker operation, however, may or may not be able to provide you with those things. But you can also expect a higher commission split. In fact, some of the highest-paid loan officers in the country aren't mortgage bankers, they're mortgage brokers. Good mortgage brokers can work wherever and whenever they want. Think of them sometimes as hired guns. . . . they bring in a ton of business and give their employers a nice income.

Do I have a preference? I liked the control of a mortgage banker first and foremost. That control is invaluable when problems arise. But the independence and marketing possibilities of being a mortgage broker also carry huge advantages. Right now, it's a push.

· C H A P T E R ·

The Loan Application and Process

Way before you get to the money part, where you get your payday, you originate the loan. *Origination* is the term given to actually producing a loan application for a borrower.

For instance, if a Realtor refers a client to you and that client fills out a loan application with you, you've just originated that loan. Makes sense, actually.

But that's the key in originating: You have to get a completed loan application. The loan application is sometimes called the "1003" or "ten-oh-three," which is the corresponding form number issued by Fannie Mae. This application covers any type of residential mortgage or construction loan. It's five pages long and divided into 10 sections, and there is a copy of it in Appendix A, Figure A-1.

Understanding the 1003

There are ten sections to the 1003:

1. Type of Mortgage and Terms of Loan
2. Property Information and Purpose of Loan

3. Borrower Information

4. Employment Information

5. Monthly Income and Housing Expense Information

6. Assets and Liabilities

7. Details of Transaction

8. Declarations

9. Acknowledgment and Agreement

10. Information for Government Monitoring Purposes

Section I: Type of Mortgage and Terms of Loan

The very first thing the 1003 asks is what type of mortgage your clients are applying for, be it conventional, FHA, VA, or other. Many consumers won't know which type they need or if they're eligible for one or more of these types. That's okay, just put in the loan type you're more inclined to if they haven't decided. If your client is eligible for a VA loan, there will be a tad more paperwork to complete, with "VA" stamped all over it. There are also two boxes labeled "Agency Case Number" and "Lender Case Number" These boxes are reserved for FHA use, and the lender will fill them in later on. They're really of no significance to you.

This section also has places for you to note whether the interest rate on the loan is fixed or adjustable (or, of course, "other"), the term of the loan (how many months or years), and the requested loan amount. This part of the 1003, as is true of the other sections, can be changed throughout the application process, so if your borrowers check the "fixed rate" box and change their minds later, you won't need to complete a new application. Just make the changes needed.

Section II: Property Information and Purpose of Loan

This section asks for details about the property your clients want to buy. First is the address of the property. You can leave it blank if your borrowers haven't found a house yet, or you can put in something like "123 Main Street" just to get an address into the system. This section also asks for the number of "units" the property has (i.e., if the property is a single-family house or if it's a multiunit property, like a duplex) and the year in which the property was built. There is an area for the legal description of the property. The borrower or lender typically doesn't know the "legal" early on, so you'll probably leave this box blank. A legal reads something like "Lot II, Section A, 123 Main Subdivision." You will get this information from the agents, from the title company, or from an attorney involved in the transaction. Some Automated Underwriting System (AUS) programs require a property address to get a preapproval; if this is your case, use a simple "123 Main Street, Anywhere USA."

This section also asks if the borrowers will use the loan to refinance another loan, purchase property, or even fund construction. The borrowers must also indicate whether they will live in the property, use it as a second home, or use it as a rental or other investment property.

If the borrowers need the loan to fund construction, they must disclose the costs of the land and the improvements as well as the amount of any liens on the property. If the borrowers are refinancing an existing loan, they must disclose when they bought the property, what they paid for it, the amounts of any existing liens, why they're refinancing, what improvements were or will be made to the property, and the cost of those improvements.

The final part of this section asks how your clients are going to hold title, be it individually or along with someone else, and if they're going to own the property "fee simple" (which is outright ownership of both the land and the home), or "leasehold" (where they may own the home but the land is being leased).

How can someone buy a home on someone else's land? Well, leaseholds can benefit both parties when the lease period is for an extended period of time, say 99 years or so. This sounds odd, but it is not as uncommon as you think in areas where Native American tribes may own land that has been developed with houses, shopping malls, and the like. More than likely this will never be an issue for you.

The last thing to fill out in this section is the borrower's source of the down payment and other key up-front costs.

Section III: Borrower Information

This section is about the borrower. It is the "meat" of the application and identifies who your clients are—their legal names, social security numbers, and where they live. This is the most personal part of the application because it's used to check the client's credit and verify the client's address, age, marital status, and phone number. Your client's age is important because people have to reach a certain age before they can execute sales contracts. Age can also help identify a borrower (someone who is 18 years old shouldn't have credit lines on his credit report that are 20 years old, for example). Sometimes the age question sounds like a loan-approval question, but the fact is that it's illegal to discriminate based upon how old a borrower is.

This section also asks how many years of school your clients have had. For the life of me I've never understood why this is part of the 1003, and I've never been given any good reason. It seems to be a carryover from older loan applications used to predict future earnings. If an applicant has graduated from law school, for example, an underwriter might let the new graduate borrow a little more money because of his or her earnings potential. But is a person with a GED somehow less creditworthy than someone with a Ph.D. and an MBA? Hardly. But this box is still there; you or your clients can fill in that information if you want to, but it really doesn't matter one way or the other. It might mean something if you put in just 12 years of school but claim that your borrower is a doctor or a dentist—the borrower would need to explain how he accomplished such a feat. Don't worry that your clients will be rejected based upon the number of years they've gone to school.

The final section is reserved for the number of dependents. This information really only applies to VA loans that require household and residual income calculations, but again it isn't something that is used to approve or deny a loan request.

If your clients have lived at their current address for less than two years, you'll need to ask them to provide a previous address. But that's really about it. No pint of blood or first-born offspring required, but this section nails down exactly who your clients are and where they've lived.

Section IV: Employment Information

Now that you know who you your clients are, you want to make sure they have a job and a good work history that details how long they've been working and for whom they work (or whether they're self-employed). This section asks for their employers' names, addresses, and phone numbers. You or your loan processor will contact them—either by telephone, by letter, or even by e-mail as long as the e-mail addresses can be verified—and ask them to verify how long your clients have worked there, what their job descriptions are, and how much money they make.

You'll notice there are two separate boxes about length of employment; one box asks for "Years on this job" and the other asks for "Years employed in this line of work or profession." Lenders look for a minimum of two years at the same job as a sign of job stability. They also like to see someone in the same line of work for more than two years for the very same reason. But don't worry if your clients have not held the same job for two years as long as they've done the same or similar line of work somewhere else.

Has your borrower been laid off because of an economic downturn? Document the dates and reasons for the time not worked. If she's been a store manager at her current job for six months, all you need to do is document the previous jobs for at least another 18 months to make up the two-year minimum. There are additional boxes for previous employers, their contact information, and the borrower's earnings from these old jobs. Finally, the borrower must provide information about his or her job title, the type of business he or she is in, and whether he or she is self-employed.

Section V: Monthly Income and Housing Expense Information

This section is easy enough. It asks how much money your clients make and how much they are paying for housing now (whether it's rent, mortgage, or living payment-free). The income portion is divided into six sections plus the now-famous "other." Here you enter the borrower's base salary, commissions, bonuses, interest or dividend income from investments, overtime earnings, and any rental income the borrower might have from other real estate. Below this section there is an area to describe "other" income. This could be anything that's verifiable, such as child support or alimony payments, interest income, or lottery winnings.

The housing expense portion asks about the borrower's current rent or mortgage payment, monthly property taxes, hazard insurance payments, homeowners association dues, or mortgage insurance. It also asks for the same information on the property the borrower is attempting to purchase.

Section VI: Assets and Liabilities

This section covers the borrower's bank accounts, investment accounts, IRAs, or whatever other financial assets the borrower might have. Don't let this section intimidate you. Just because there's a space for "Life Insurance Net Cash Value" or "Vested Interest in Retirement Fund" doesn't mean that borrowers have to have either of these to get a home loan. They don't. They simply need enough money to close the deal.

The very first box describes the borrower's very first asset involved in the transaction: the "earnest money" or deposit money that he or she gave along with the sales contract. If the borrower gave $2,000 as earnest money, this will be the first money put into the deal. The lender wants to know how much your client gave as earnest money and who has it. It'll include those funds in the borrower's down payment.

The next four sections are for the borrower's bank accounts, be it checking or savings, and for related account information, such as account numbers and current balances. It's not necessary to complete every single box or divulge every single account the borrower might have. Typically lenders only care about having enough money to close the deal and less about what the borrower's IRA balance is. The only time other balances come into question is if the lender asks for them as a condition of the loan approval. These extra funds are called *reserves*.

Reserves are best described as money left in various accounts after all the dust has settled, including the down payment and closing costs. Reserves can sometimes be a multiple of the monthly mortgage payment, such as "six months worth of housing payments," and they must be in accounts separate and apart from the transaction.

Reserves can also beef up a borrower's application if he or she is on the border of obtaining a loan approval. A lender who is a little squishy on a loan may want to see some other aspects of the borrower's financial picture before issuing an approval. Reserves are an important criterion for many loans, but it's up to you to ask the lender if your borrowers in fact need to document absolutely everything in their financial portfolios or just enough to close the deal.

This section also asks for other real estate the borrowers might own, and there is even an area to list the type and value of their cars. I'm serious. Again, this is a holdover from earlier loan applications, but if you leave this section blank, an underwriter might want to know how your clients get to work and back. Finally there are the "other" assets. Historically this might mean expensive artwork or jewelry, but this too is an unnecessary question, so don't worry about leaving this box blank as well.

Next to the assets is the liabilities section, where the borrower lists his or her monthly bills. This section is only for items that might show up on a credit report, such as a car loan or credit card bill. It doesn't include such items as electricity or telephone bills. Don't worry if your client can't remember the exact balances or minimum monthly payments required, just tell the client to give a best estimate. The lender will fill in the application with information taken from the credit bureau later on. If the borrower owes child support or alimony, there's a place for that, too.

Section VII: Details of Transaction

This is the most confusing piece of the application, so much so that most borrowers leave it blank and let a lender or loan officer fill it in. In fact, most loan officers don't fill it in; they let their computer programs do the work for them.

This section provides an overview of your particular deal, showing the sales price of the home, the down payment amount (if any), the closing costs, and any earnest money held anywhere. It then shows how much money your client is supposed to bring to the closing table.

Note that this is just an overview and not the final word on the loan amount, costs, etc. It's simply a brief snapshot of the transaction. Believe me, you'll get reams of paper on this topic in other documents.

Section VIII: Declarations

These are 13 statements to which the borrower answers yes or no. They ask such things as, "Are there any outstanding judgments against you?" and, "Are you a party to a lawsuit?" and so on. Here the borrower will also state whether he or she has declared bankruptcy or had a foreclosure in the past seven years. (Actually, there is no such thing as a seven-year requirement for bankruptcies and foreclosures for conventional or government loans anymore; this is another carryover from older application processes. Nowadays, bankruptcies and foreclosures generally affect loan applications only if they're two to four years old.)

Section IX: Acknowledgement and Agreement

This is a long-winded, obviously lawyer-written area where borrowers cross their hearts and hope to die that what they put on the application is true, that they agree to have the home secured by a first mortgage or deed of trust, that they won't use the property for illegal purposes, that they didn't lie, and so on. They sign the loan application in this section and date it.

Section X: Information for Government Monitoring Purposes

This optional area exists thanks to the Home Mortgage Disclosure Act—or HMDA (HUM-duh)—and is referred to as the *HMDA monitoring section*. It asks optional questions about the borrower's race, national origin, and gender. The answers don't affect loan approval, and borrowers don't have to fill this out if they don't want to. However, the government requires loan officers to make a best guess as to "guy or girl" or "black, white, Pacific Islander" or whatever if a borrower opts not to provide this information. The information helps the federal government monitor the approval rates for various classes and races of borrowers to see if a bank or lender is discriminating based upon race, color, or creed. After all, how does the government know such things if it's not told?

For example, the Community Reinvestment Act, or CRA, requires lenders to make a certain percentage of their mortgages in specific geographic areas. The HMDA disclosures might identify certain lenders that aren't making loans where the community may need them most.

That's it. Now you need to put all of that in your Loan Origination Software, or LOS.

Setting Up an Office

One of the first things you'll need to work on mortgages is loan-origination software, also called loan software, or an LOS. An LOS puts all your application information in a clean, printed format and will fill in the most-looked-at document in your file: the 1003.

The LOS will also get your borrowers' credit information and will be the basis for getting preliminary loan approval. But to run an LOS, you'll need a computer—and a printer, and a few other "must haves" to be a loan officer.

Hardware

Most likely, your LOS will run on the computer you're using now, unless you're using an old clunker that's slower than slow. Personally I prefer a laptop over a desktop computer—there are times when you'll want to take an application remotely or at a client's location, and you'll want the portability of a laptop. If you have the luxury of both, then that's even better.

You should have a laser printer, not an inkjet one. The mortgage business still relies on mounds of paper sometimes, and you'll want to print things out faster than an inkjet can print, plus the ink can get expensive. When you're printing out a loan package or you have several loans to print at once, you'll want and need the speed of a laser.

You'll also need a cable or digital-subscriber line (DSL) connection for quick Internet connections. When you submit a loan application for approval or obtain credit reports online, you don't want the slower transmission times of dial-up telephone modems. Too often the files can get too big, which can result in dropped calls.

You also need to invest in a scanner, a copier, and a fax machine. Probably the best investment if you're on your own is some type of combination fax/scanner/copy product. People use fax/scanner/copy equipment less and less these days due to the Internet, but it is still required in many instances.

From a hardware perspective, that's about all you really need.

Software? You'll need special software to input all the information from your loan application. You've got several choices, but perhaps the two most common LOS products are Calyx Point (Point is the product name and Calyx is the company) and Encompass. Encompass is developed by a company called Ellie Mae, which also owns other LOS applications.

Neither is very expensive—both cost around $500 and both are very good. There are other solid LOS, but these two are the most common. Don't discount other LOS systems—certainly look at others—but if you get either one of these you're okay.

You can purchase Calyx Point at www.calyxsoftware.com and Encompass at www.elliemae.com. Ellie Mae also sells two other LOS applications, Genesis and Contour, that you should review, but if you're starting out on your own, I think Encompass or Calyx Point is the way to go.

After you install your LOS, you'll need to activate your other services, primarily your automated underwriting system (AUS), flood certification service, and credit reporting service. Your LOS will have instructions built into its system; you'll simply need to select which credit reporting agency you want to use, which lenders you'd like to use, and so on. Don't worry at this stage about which ones to select and which ones not to select. You can make changes any time you want, but the important thing is to get up and running right away.

Setting Up a Website

Finally, do you need a website? Yes. But the complexity of your website is up to you. There are differing opinions on the value of a website, but the bottom line is that these days consumers simply expect you to have one. What you put on it is up to you, but there are two main considerations when building a site.

1. Do you want consumers to apply online?
2. Do you want to advertise your interest rates?

What happens when consumers apply online?

First, it saves you time. Instead of making an appointment and showing up at someone's home or office, you instead direct your customers to your website and have them apply online. More and more people are comfortable with putting sensitive information on a website—so much so that many don't think twice about it.

Online applications work like this: A consumer goes to your website and completes an application online. The file is saved in a special "vault" that you have an access code for. You later log on to your site, open up your vault, click on your customers' files, and download the customers' loan applications. You will then open up your LOS, find the files you downloaded, and open them. You now have your clients' loan applications in hand.

You will find consumers who still aren't comfortable putting their social security numbers and bank account numbers on a website, and frankly I don't blame them, so don't think you'll never have to take a loan application face-to-face—you will. But having an online application is convenient both for you and your client. Face it, there are a lot more things your borrowers would rather be doing than sitting down at a desk with you and filling out all sorts of paperwork.

The downside to having an online application is that it adds to your overhead. A standard website with nothing more than your logo, information about you and your company, and a few paragraphs about how great you are might cost $30 per month for design and hosting. Or less.

Ask around to find a good Web designer near you or check Google for "Web designer." They're everywhere. But having an online loan application takes some specific skills that everyday Web designers don't have.

An online application must be secure and compatible with your LOS. Remember, there are a couple of hundred fields that consumers can complete on a 1003, and online applications need to fill those fields in the right order. You don't want to try and build one of these yourself—you probably can't even if you tried, and there's no need to.

One of the two best resources for Web design for mortgage loan officers is www.meyersinternet.com. Meyers has been around for years and will give you both a plethora of design templates to choose from as well as provide all the expertise needed to provide a secure online application. Another good choice for Web design and online applications is etrafficers.com. This is my favorite and who I use.

Both companies will give you different choices as to design, features, and functionality along with various price ranges, but expect to pay a couple of hundred dollars for setup and a minimum of $30 per month for maintenance.

Posting Rates on the Internet

There are those on both sides of this issue. One side says, "You need to post excellent rates on your website in order to get new customers," while another side says, "Don't post rates at all but instead encourage consumers to call you for a rate quote."

Both make valid points. I, however, don't agree that putting rates on a website is a good thing. I designed one of the industry's first Web pages for my company back in 1996. We were one of the first to be online, and I updated our website daily with fresh information, rate info, and loan product information.

But the dynamics work this way: no consumer is going to choose you simply because of an interest rate. You won't find casual Internet prospects filling out a loan application just because of your rates.

First, your rates can't be that much lower than anyone else's to prompt a random loan application. We'll discuss why more in depth in chapter 9. Second, no one is going to give you personal data without knowing who you are, talking to you, and essentially making sure you're not a "pfisher" who is trying to steal personal information.

Second, rates can change throughout the day. On volatile trading days, rates can move two, three, or even four times. In fact, sometimes lenders simply quit quoting rates when the rate market is that hectic. That doesn't happen very often, but it happens.

That means that during rate moves, you need to update your rates. If you quote 5.00% on a loan program but rates go up one-quarter percent one morning and a consumer calls you about your 5.00% rate, you'll be forced to say that the website is wrong, that rates actually went up, and that 5.00% is no longer available.

Consumers don't typically understand that rates can move like that, so they think you're lying or doing the old "bait and switch" tactic. If you want rates online, be prepared to move with the market.

What if you put rates on your website, kept up with them, and now they're too high? Then no one will call you. Besides, there are simply so many variables in rate quotes that online rates simply bring too many negatives to the table. There are others who will disagree with that point—in fact, you might—but I've been in the business too long, have had websites with and without rates, and can tell you that sites without rates are both more trustworthy to the consumer and easier to maintain.

When You Get an Application

Now let's pretend you have your first loan application. Hooray! A happy new client walks into your office and wants you to provide him or her with financing. In chapter 5, we'll address how to counsel your clients as to which type of loan works best for them, but you need to under-stand the basic process, especially the amount of government-required paperwork you'll be generating.

When you meet with a client and complete the application, the next thing you will do is provide the client with a Good Faith Estimate of Settlement Charges. The federal government requires you to give the applicant this estimate immediately if you meet with the applicant face-to-face.

The Good Faith Estimate

The Good Faith Estimate, or GFE, is a list of all the potential charges that your clients will incur and who will pay them. Your clients will review the GFE, sign it, and give it back to you. You will make a copy and hand one to the client. You must keep the GFE with the loan file throughout the life of the loan. Forever.

If your applicant applies online, faxes the application in, or mails it, then you must provide the GFE within three business days (and Saturday counts as a business day). The date on the GFE must be no more than three days after you have received the application. See Appendix A, Figure A-2, for a copy of a Good Faith Estimate form.

The GFE has six distinct sections, beginning with section 800 (I'm not kidding), 900, 1000, and then of course 1100, 1200, and 1300. Each line item within that series applies to a particular fee.

The 800 section is reserved for the lender and its service partners. Those service partners include credit-report companies, appraisers, flood certifiers, and tax service companies. Any charges issued by any of those firms will fall into this section. Line item 801, for example, is reserved for the lender's origination fee, and line 803 is for the ap-praisal fee. Don't be scared, there aren't 100 line items in section 800, but you probably won't see more than seven or eight entries. Section 800 is where you'll find all the lender "junk" fees.

Section 900 is for anything that needs to be paid up front or in advance. These are often called *prepaid items*, and they include home-owners insurance premiums and any taxes that are due.

In section 1000 you'll see line items for funds collected to establish insurance, tax, and homeowners association impound or escrow accounts.

Section 1100 is reserved for all title charges, including escrow fees, attorney's fees, and fees for closing. Anything that is generated by and on the behalf of the title company will show up here.

Section 1200 contains fees associated with the government. Recording fees, tax stamps, and similar charges are listed here.

Finally, section 1300 is mostly for anything else. You'll find pest-inspection charges, survey and abstract fees here, and anything else that doesn't have a place.

I'll break the charges down into lender and nonlender charges. In most any real estate transaction, most of these businesses will charge for:

Appraiser	$300–$500. More if the value is more than $1 million.
Attorney	$100–$500. Price will vary depending upon section of the country.
Escrow	$150–$300. Escrow can mean different things in different parts of the country—it can be a closing cost or it can be taxes and insurance payments to an account.
Title Ins.	$300 and higher. Many states regulate this fee, sometimes as high as one percent of the loan amount.
Survey	$300–$500. Again, this can be higher for complicated or bigger properties.
Tax Cert.	$70.
Flood Cert.	$20.
Credit Report	$20.
Intangible Tax	1–3% of the loan amount or sales price.
Documents	$200.
Recording	$100.

Closing costs are a broad swath of fees, terms, and customs. Many in the real estate business who read this list will no doubt see some omissions or errors. And they'd be right. Closing costs vary from one state to the next, even sometimes in one county or parish to the next. But this will give you some general guidelines. You will be able to get specific pricing from your local providers.

You should take these fees and make a template in your LOS. Each time a customer asks for a rate quote, a list of fees, or a new GFE, then all you need to do is open up your LOS and print one out with the defaulted fees already entered.

Now let's look at possible lender fees. These can be fees that your wholesale lender charges you, or they can be fees from your mortgage company and fees you want to add. Lenders can charge, just like anyone else, whatever they can get away with legally and in a free market.

Discount Fees (Points)	1% of the loan amount
Origination Fee	1% of the loan amount
Processing	$200–$500
Administration	$200–$500
Document Prep.	$200–$500
Funding Fee	$200–$500
Underwriting	$200–$500
Commitment	$200–$500
Anything Else	$200–$500

Truth in Lending Disclosure

The GFE also provides the necessary data to generate another form required by the government: the Truth in Lending disclosure (sometimes called the "TIL" or "till"). It's this form that attempts (and I mean *attempts*) to explain to the borrower the impact of all those fees on the loan amount, the amount of interest paid over the life of the loan, and other loan details. See Appendix A, Figure A-3 for this form.

This form can be very confusing, but it is also a required form and you should be able to understand it as well as explain it. The TIL takes the loan amount, the interest rate, term, and closing fees and arrives at four very important numbers:

1. The annual percentage rate
2. Finance charges
3. Amount financed
4. Total of payments

Annual Percentage Rate. The annual percentage rate, or APR, is the cost of money borrowed expressed as an annual rate. It's also the number you must use whenever and wherever you advertise your interest rates.

When someone gets a mortgage, she gets an interest rate. But she also gets some other things associated with that rate, primarily closing costs. The APR number adds the closing charges, such as points or processing fees, to the sum of the interest payments on the loan and calculates the "true" interest rate on the loan. This helps the consumer understand the impact of closing costs on a mortgage.

Borrowers don't make payments based upon an APR rate; they still make payments based upon the stated interest rate. But because of the additional costs associated with the mortgage, the APR number will always be higher than the note rate.

For instance, if you quoted 6.00% to your clients but didn't quote your closing costs of $5,000, then your consumer couldn't make a fair comparison between you and a competitor offering 6.125% with no closing costs. That's a stretch, but it's an example.

To calculate APR, add the lender closing costs to the loan amount, and calculate what the monthly payment on that higher balance would be at the loan's original interest rate. Using that monthly payment, find the interest rate that would create that monthly payment on the original principal amount. It's this new interest rate that is the APR.

The higher the APR, the more closing costs your client is paying.

You can play with the APR number with your calculator, but I'll give you a couple of examples.

The monthly payment on a $200,000 mortgage that has a 7.00% fixed interest rate for 30 years is about $1,330. Now consider the effects of one point, or $2,000; a $300 appraisal; and a $400 processing fee. Those charges add up to $2,700, and if they were added to the original loan amount, the payment would increase to about $1,349. So what is the interest rate that creates a $1,349 payment on a $200,000 loan? The APR number works out to about 7.13%. Under that same example, if you charged two points instead of one and the total costs rose to $4,700, the APR would jump to 7.23%.

The APR number is helpful to consumers because it helps identify lender charges. The greater the disparity between the note rate of 7.00% and the APR numbers of 7.13% and 7.23% tells the consumer which is the better deal.

Finance Charges. The next field on the TIL is labeled Finance Charge. The finance charge is the dollar amount the loan will cost your client, and it is arrived at by subtracting the original loan amount from the sum of the payments.

For a $200,000 30-year loan at 7.00%, your client will pay $479,018 over 30 years. By subtracting the $200,000 loan, the finance charge works out to $279,018. That is the amount of interest charged to your client over 30 years. If, of course, your client kept the loan that long.

Amount Financed. The next box on the TIL is labeled Amount Financed, and it discloses the original loan amount.

Total of Payments. The next box, Total Number of Payments, is the sum of all the payments. In our example, it's $479,018. The TIL will also show the number of payments required on the loan, if there is any prepayment penalty, when a payment would be considered late, and what the late-payment fee is.

You now know more about the Truth in Lending disclosure than most loan officers. The TIL is confusing at first glance, so many loan officers simply ignore it, get the consumer to sign it without fully explaining it, and move forward.

Other Disclosures You Must Provide

Borrowers need to sign other disclosures when they apply for mortgage loans, and these disclosures vary from state to state. But there are some universally required disclosures and forms:

Borrowers' Certification and Authorization form

Equal Credit Opportunity disclosure

Standard Flood Hazard Determination form

Patriot Act disclosures

Privacy policy disclosures

Notice of Right to Receive an Appraisal

Servicing disclosure

Examples of all of these forms are in Appendix A.

Then there are all the other state-required disclosures. As you set up your LOS, set up these disclosures to automatically print each time you enter a new loan application, so you won't forget them.

After you've taken the loan application and fulfilled your legal requirements with regard to disclosures, you document the loan file.

Documenting the Loan File

Documenting the loan file means providing written or other forms of third-party evidence to prove what a borrower put on his or her loan application. For example, if the borrower reported $5,000 per month of income, you would document that by obtaining last year's W-2 or a recent pay stub or both. We'll discuss documentation levels in chapter 6.

You'll also need evidence of the money reported in various accounts by collecting bank statements from your clients and essentially anything else in the application that needs to be verified.

Preapproving a Loan

The next step in the process is one of the most important: preapproving a loan application before the borrowers go house shopping. You'll get better at this as time goes on and your experience grows, but your clients will rely on you to tell them whether they can qualify for a home loan.

After you review your client's credit report, determine whether the client's income can handle the debt load, and ascertain whether the client has enough money to close on a prospective purchase, you issue a preapproval letter.

You can manually preapprove a client by reviewing the credit report, income, and asset information yourself. Or you can input your client's loan application into an Automated Underwriting System, or AUS, that will electronically review the application and credit and issue an approval all within a matter of minutes.

This approval letter (see Figure 4-1) will be on your letterhead. It will include your client's name and address, and the client will use it when a seller entertains an offer from your client. A preapproval letter is a bargaining chip for your clients. It tells the sellers of the property, as well as their Realtors, that a lender has already reviewed your client and it's simply a matter of finding the right house to buy.

If your client has a preapproval letter in hand and a competing offer also comes to the sellers from people who do not have a preap-

Figure 4-1. A sample preapproval letter.

YOUR MORTGAGE COMPANY

January 1, 2010

Mr. And Mrs. Borrower
123 Main Street, Apt. A
Anytown, USA

Re: Mortgage Approval

Dear Mr. And Mrs. Borrower,

Congratulations, we at CD Reed Mortgage Company are happy to extend this letter of approval for the amount requested. Your loan application has been submitted and approved under Fannie Mae's Desktop Underwriter Automated Underwriting System. Your approval was based upon the following:

Credit Report
Credit Score
Income Verification
Asset Verification
Mortgage Application

Additional items including but not limited to clear Title, Appraisal, and Survey will be required prior to final funding. We anticipate a quick close.

Congratulations, it's been a real pleasure working with you on your first home!

Sincerely,

David Reed
CD Reed Mortgage Company
111 Broadway Apt. XYZ
Anytown, USA
(555) 555-1212

cc: Joe Realtor

proval letter, your clients will win the deal. After all, if you were selling a home, you'd want to know if the buyers can get financing, right?

Besides your computer, your laptop, and other business necessities, you'll also need wholesale lenders if you're going to be a mortgage broker. You can't just shake a tree and find them. Yes, you can search for them on the Internet but wholesale lenders aren't found in the phone book.

How to Find Mortgage Wholesale Lenders

Sometimes you don't have to find wholesale lenders, they find you. Mortgage wholesalers often find mortgage brokers on their own by researching mortgage-broker licensing lists or other broker reservoirs.

In fact, that's primarily how you're going to get started in the mortgage business—by having wholesale lenders find you. Depending upon how you're regulated by your state, wholesalers might be able to scour new broker-licensing lists. If you're a brand-new broker, simply wait a few months for someone to find you. Don't worry, it'll happen. Lenders you've never heard of will magically begin appearing at your door.

But you can't wait that long, right? That's okay. You can find them first. Simply use Google to find any national or regional bank with the word "wholesale lending" in it and you'll find yourself flooded with contact information.

But simply putting your name into the hat to be a broker for a wholesale lender isn't how it works. Wholesale lenders are making mortgage loans, not throwing newspapers. You'll need to apply with them and get approved. So how do you get approved?

Wholesale lenders have different approval requirements, but they typically ask that you:

Be duly licensed and bonded per your state laws

Complete the wholesale-lenders broker application

Provide names, social security numbers, and resumes of the principals of your business

Explain your company structure documentation, i.e. corporation, sole proprietorship, etc.

Provide a list of current wholesale lenders that you do business with

Provide a list of references

Authorize the wholesale lender to contact your references and review the credit reports of your principals

This is not the only list, and various wholesale lenders might have a few twists and turns, but this is standard information you can expect to provide when you begin contacting wholesale lending companies.

One item might stand out: the list of current wholesale lenders you do business with. What if you're just starting out and don't have any wholesale lenders? You start small.

It's true that most of your recognized wholesale lenders may not approve you if you've never done business before. But that's okay, you'll probably end up with someone you may not recognize at the very beginning, and that's not a bad thing by any stretch.

These wholesale lenders all must underwrite and approve loans in the very same fashion as the Big Dogs do; it's just that the larger wholesale lenders want to see some sort of track record before working with you. They want to see if you can not only run your business but also originate quality loans. They do that by getting references from other lenders.

Don't worry if you don't start off with all the national players. In fact, it's likely you'll end up sending most of your business to a wholesale lender you have never heard of. When I started out, I didn't send loans to Countrywide or Bank of America at first. I sent them to a company called Dollar Mortgage.

Later, as our company grew, account executives from wholesale lenders eventually beat down our door to do business with us. We gained a good reputation of sending good loans and lots of them. But much of my loyalty stayed with Dollar Mortgage, who was willing to sign us up as a broker when others might not have.

Your Responsibilities to Wholesalers

Lenders like to see a track record because they are actually putting their money where their mouth is. It's not your money you're loaning, it belongs to the wholesale lender. And if something bad happens on a loan, the lender loses money. If something bad happens after the loan is only 90 days old or less, you might in fact owe that lender some money.

There is a term called *first payment default.* It means that no matter what, if your borrower doesn't make his or her first payment on time, the wholesale lender could ask you to send back all the money it gave you for originating the loan. On a $300,000 loan, that could be $3,000 to $5,000 or more, depending upon how you priced the loan to your client.

Another instance in which you could owe the wholesale lender money is if the loan is retired via a refinance or flat-out sold to someone else within the first 90 days.

You can also owe money to the lender if the lender requires more documentation after the loan closes and you don't provide it. Sometimes a lender simply makes a mistake when it approves a loan, and it may ask you to help fix the mistake.

For instance, a lender might see that the insurance policy is short on the amount of coverage needed so it asks you to get another policy showing the correct amount. The lender will usually give you enough time to do this, such as 30 days, and as part of your broker agreement you agree to help them.

If the lender suspects loan fraud or that documents in the file are forged, not only will you owe money, it's likely you will go to jail. Loan fraud is something lenders and the FBI jump on.

All that being said, your mortgage broker agreement is simply part of becoming a mortgage broker. If you do everything you're supposed to do and the lender does everything it's supposed to do, you'll soon establish a mutually beneficial relationship. You need good wholesale lenders just as much as wholesale lenders need good brokers.

Good cooperation works both ways.

Qualities of Good Wholesalers

When looking at wholesalers, you want a company that has good:

Service

Price

Product

What? Isn't the mortgage broker's best asset her access to both the best price and best selection of loan products? Sure. But what if the wholesale lender can't deliver?

Mortgage brokers are totally dependent upon the performance of their wholesale lenders. Period. If the wholesale lender makes a mistake on a loan or if an interest rate shows up wrong at the closing table, it's not the wholesale lender that gets yelled at by the borrowers or trashed by the Realtors sitting at the same table.

It's the broker.

Forget about having the best rate and the best loan program; none of it matters if the loan doesn't get delivered on time. I'll give you a real-world example that happened to me several years ago when I first got into the business, but it's a story that happens with regularity still to this day. Some wholesale lenders simply never learn.

Every now and then, a wholesale lender will do something dramatic to help spur loan volume. If its wholesale account representatives aren't bringing in enough loans from the vast world of mortgage brokers, then the wholesale lender has a fire sale. It slashes rates.

How much? Rates can't vary much from one lender to another, so a "fire sale" in rate may mean something like a quarter of a percent. That equates to $2,000 on a $200,000 loan. A wholesale lender will drop its rates by that much to attract loan volume.

In the meantime, mortgage brokers who get those rate sheets advertising those new, lower rates, immediately see somewhat of a price war. So naturally, a loan officer who is trying to get new loans by offering the lowest rates will begin quoting lower rates offered by the lender conducting the sale.

But that loan officer isn't the only one. Every other loan officer on the wholesale lender's mailing list sees the very same thing. So what happens? The wholesale lender gets its prayer answered: lots and lots of loans.

Suddenly, all those idle loan underwriters, closers, and account executives are very, very busy. In fact, too busy. Now, a staff that is prepared to handle 100 loans per day is presented with 500. Or 1,000. And there's a train wreck ahead.

Meanwhile, your clients are bragging to their buddies about what a low rate they got with you, and how smart they were to find you, and what idiots their friends were for not using you. Then you begin to sweat.

Even though you submitted your loan to the underwriter last week, you still haven't heard anything regarding an approval. You place calls. E-mails. You track down your account executive and say, "Where is my loan approval and why won't anyone return my calls?"

But guess what? You're not the only loan officer yelling the same things. The lender spurred loan volume by dropping rates, but instead of closing more loans, it began to close fewer. And there's nothing you can do about it.

There is absolutely nothing you can do if the lender is late. There is nothing in your broker agreement that says, "If the wholesale lender is slow in approving the loan, then the mortgage broker gets a ton of money," or something to that effect. Your only choice is to not send any more loans to that wholesale lender.

That's all you can do about it. Yeah, you got the lowest rate on the planet, but the papers never made it to closing. You lose.

Your communication with the wholesale lender is paramount. I've run across wholesale lenders that had some of the best account reps that could be found. They were nice, attractive, smart, dressed well, and said all the right things. But when your clients' loan actually gets submitted to the wholesale lender, suddenly everything changes. The underwriter is a complete jerk. Uppity. Knows everything. Doesn't speak to anyone. Won't work out problems. Expects you to bow down to him and forgets that his job is to get people into homes.

If you go to the grocery store and get poor customer service, you'll probably try and find another grocery store if it's not too far away. If the lawnmower guy does a crappy job of mowing your lawn, you find another landscaper.

If you find a bad wholesale lender, it doesn't matter what its rates are, it can destroy your reputation. Service is paramount in wholesale lending. Price and product are secondary.

Most wholesale lenders will have similar rates. You won't find one that is consistently a quarter percent better than everyone else. At least not for very long. So the key is less price and more service.

The better service a wholesale lender provides you, the better service you in turn provide your borrowers. They are one in the same. But that begs the question: how do you know in advance if a wholesale lender has good customer service or not?

First, you can ask your colleagues. Account reps aren't the best source of which wholesale lenders are doing well and which ones aren't; you need to talk to other loan officers in the business. We'll talk about marketing and building your business in chapters 11 and 12.

But here's where it gets a little tricky, and this is a big secret: other mortgage brokers won't tell you which is the best wholesale lender, but they'll tell you which isn't.

Think about that for a moment. If one of your worthy competitors has a favorite wholesale lender, she's not going to readily tell you about it. Why should she? Why should she have still another mortgage broker tie up her underwriters' precious time with your loans? She won't.

Instead of asking, "Whom do you think I should send my loans to?" ask "So, who's been making you mad lately?" If you get a response, that's a lender you should avoid. At least at present. That same wholesale lender could also simply be experiencing a personnel shortage due to a fire sale.

Although you will never truly know if a wholesale lender gives good customer service until after you've submitted a few loans, a little research on your part can help ease the pain of guessing.

Your main contact with your wholesale lender is your account executive. Whenever you have a question or a problem, this is the person you always call first. Think of a wholesale rep as a loan officer for you, the loan officer. This person will handle your questions regarding loan programs and qualifications and will be the one who will come by your office to review a possible loan file.

For instance, if you've received a loan application and have some questions about the loan approval, or potential lack thereof, you first call your wholesale rep and say, "David, I've got a loan here that I'm not sure about. The ratios are a little high and I'm not clear on his tax returns. Can you come by my office and help me out?"

This is a key part of a wholesale rep's job: to evaluate "loan scenarios" to see if you have an approvable loan. If the rep answers your calls quickly, answers your questions correctly, and is available when you need him or her, keep this in mind when deciding where to send your loan. If you try time and time again with certain wholesale reps and only get their voice mail or don't get your calls returned, how do you think they'll be when you have a loan that has some problems?

Again, customer service is king.

You need to establish your relationship with a wholesale lender. Too often, mortgage brokers send their loans to whomever has the best price for the day. One lender might pay $100 more on a file than another. So the broker sends the file to someone who has the absolute best price without regard to service or any history with that wholesale lender.

If you keep hopping from one lender to the next, you'll make each relationship difficult to establish. You need these relationships. You will need favors. A mortgage banker has an advantage in this regard; the relationship between loan approval and the loan officer is built-in: Everyone works for the same company and everyone generally knows everyone else.

But as a mortgage broker, you may only be a file number. Loan # 1433, or some other intangible identification. When there are problems or questions and you need some help, you don't want to be a number, you want to be recognized by the account exec and the underwriter as someone who knows what he's talking about.

You don't want to ever be perceived as a screaming, whining loan officer who doesn't understand the lending process and is quick to call people names and pull files. You do however want to be known as someone who understands the drill and is a known commodity . . . in a good sense.

Loyalty to Lenders Pays Off When You're a Broker

Don't "lender hop." Instead, keep three or four lenders handy and use them. Wholesale lenders also want this relationship. They want loyalty. They want loan officers who will send them loans on a regular basis, and in exchange they will cater to you in a more special way than someone who sends in a random deal every now and then.

When I first became a broker, I found out how important this relationship is. I began to send loans to a particular mortgage company and liked its service, liked its account execs, and overall enjoyed the experience.

That of course made me look good in front of my borrowers. Nothing ever went wrong. When there were problems, they were fixed. Because I had established myself as a loyal customer and didn't shop my loans around for an extra couple of hundred bucks, I was treated better, which was a good thing because I soon reaped those rewards.

Soon thereafter, mortgage rates began to move downward, so lots of folks wanted to refinance their loans at the new lower rates. This lasted for a couple of years, and loan officers were falling from trees. They were everywhere. And so were customers. There was no end in sight for loan applications from people who wanted to get a lower monthly payment. Heck, all some loan companies had to do was place an ad in the newspaper and wait for the phone to start ringing off the hook.

Eventually, rates began to go up. Fewer loan applications came, and when rates move up, they can move up quickly. Because I always sent my loans to this one particular lender, I had a special status. Even when that same wholesale lender was being inundated with new loans from people it had never heard of.

The wholesale lender, along with every other wholesale lender, got overbooked. It had too many loans and not enough people or time to close the deals. It was swamped. That meant that loans that normally took one or two days to approve were now taking one or two weeks—not because the deals were hard to approve, but because there were so darned many of them.

Then something else happened. Rate locks began to expire. Borrowers were yelling at their loan officers for taking so long. Those loan officers lost business and tarnished their reputations.

But not me. As a long-time client and loyal mortgage broker, my loans always sailed through. I was rewarded for my loyalty. Think of it as an eternal first-class upgrade on American Airlines. I was rewarded with more business and an enhanced reputation.

Wholesale lenders understand this, and you should too. Find a couple of lenders and stick with them. Even if they don't offer the lowest rate on the planet every day, your chosen lenders will always be competitive. Providing you with superior service is more important than $200.

When the Clients Have Found a House

After a few weeks of work with their Realtors, your customers will have found the perfect home. Now the fun begins.

You'll first get the sales contract from the Realtor to include with your file. The sales contract will have the correct street address, the official sales price, the names and phone numbers of all the Realtors involved, and how they will be handling the closing.

Before your clients get too far, they will most likely first order a home inspection. Most contracts allow for a buyer to back out of a deal if something is wrong with the home and the seller can't or won't fix it. It's also a good idea to make sure there's a sound house before doing too many things on your end.

After the house passes the inspection with flying colors, you begin your work in earnest. Many existing-home sales close within a 30-day period, so you'll need to start work immediately.

First, call your appraiser and order an appraisal. The appraiser will want you to fax or e-mail the sales contract to her for her files, and she will schedule an appointment with either the sellers or the sellers' Realtor. The appraiser will need to have physical access to the property for such things as observing the overall condition of the home, measuring square footage, and calculating the value of improvements made to the home.

In the meantime, your loan processor is updating the loan file. All credit documents in the file need to be less than 90 days old. This means if a credit report is more than three months old, a new or an updated one must be ordered. Paycheck stubs and bank statements that are in the file will also have to be updated if they are more than 30 days old.

The processor will contact the closing agent and order a copy of the title report. The processor will also order documentation that your AUS has asked for, such as tax returns or other requirements, and will contact the settlement agent, insurance agent, the surveyor, etc. Your processor does a lot. Now you know why you need to make this person your very best friend.

The file slowly builds by adding various pieces of paper and documents. The appraisal arrives, along with the title report. Then your client's insurance agent writes a policy for the new home and sends a copy of the policy to your processor.

Once everything is submitted to you and your processor, you essentially have a complete loan file and your client's loan goes to an underwriter. If you work directly for a lender, the file goes to your underwriting department. If you're a mortgage broker, the file goes to the underwriter who works for the mortgage company you selected on behalf of your clients.

The underwriter will review the entire file to ensure that everything submitted agrees with the application. The underwriter evaluates whether the appraisal meets appraisal standards and that nothing is old, expired, or contradicts something else.

When the underwriter signs off on the loan, the loan goes to the closing department. The department prints and delivers the closing documents to the settlement agent, who gets all the signatures, collects all the funds, and sends the loan back to the lender.

Then the lender funds your loan, money is exchanged, and you get your check. All of that typically takes about three weeks. But then of course, you're not closing just one loan. You're closing about 10 per month and making about $20,000 per month.

· C H A P T E R ·

5

Types of Mortgage Loans

Mortgages come in all shapes and sizes. You can see the ads on television or read about them in the newspaper. Many of them shout, "We have over 500 loans programs from which to choose!" I can recall working for a mortgage company that had eight-page rate sheets for its customers and over 125 different loan programs. Why all the loans?

It can be overwhelming to anyone new in the mortgage business. Loan programs are everywhere, and they all have different rates and different prices. Wholesale lenders will even give special "names" to their loan offerings to make them appear different than everyone else's.

Instead of a "Stated Income 30-Year Fixed," the lender might give it a name such as "Speedy Loan" or "Fast Funds" or something similar. In addition, lenders will also confuse a rate sheet by adding different loan-pricing "adjustments" that clutter the page.

Don't get too confused. It's really very easy to read all these rate sheets once you understand that there are really only two kinds of mortgages, not 125. Those two kinds are fixed and adjustable. The rest are nothing more than a few variations on those themes.

Fixed-Rate Mortgages

Fixed-rate mortgages are easy to explain. You get an interest rate for a mortgage and it's fixed. It doesn't change. Ever. Easy enough, right? The only thing you and the clients need to decide about a fixed rate is what the rate will be and over what period to amortize the loan. Amortization is the fixed period during which the borrower repays the loan. If the amortization period is 20 years, then the loan will be paid off in exactly 20 years. The monthly payments remain the same, fixed, throughout the life of the mortgage.

Amortization periods can be mostly whatever the lender offers, but if a lender wants to sell the loan to Fannie Mae or Freddie Mac, then the loan must conform to Fannie Mae or Freddie Mac standards and amortize over 10, 15, 20, 25, 30, or sometimes 40 years. The interest rates and how much interest the borrowers will pay throughout the lives of these loans differ. The longer the loan term, the lower the payment simply because the payback period is longer.

For example, on a $200,000 15-year fixed-rate mortgage, you might find a 6.00% rate. That payments calculates to about $1,688 per month. Over 15 years, the clients will have paid the lender a total of $303,788. That means the lender made $103,788 in interest charges.

That same amount on a 30-year loan at 5.50% works out to a $1,136 monthly amount. Over 30 years that adds up to $408,808. The lender makes $208,808. Yes, the monthly payments are lower with a 30-year loan, but over the long haul that's twice the amount of interest.

The time over which a loan amortizes affects how much of each monthly payment applies to interest or principal. In fixed-rate mortgages, most of the initial payments go to interest and very little goes toward repaying the principal. But when the loan term is shortened, say from 30 to 15 years, the note is paid down quicker.

Using the same example as above, after five years the principal balance on the 30-year loan is $184,921. The original mortgage is paid down only by $15,079. With the 15-year example, the loan balance is

$152,018, a difference of $47,982 after just five years. So there's a tradeoff with amortization. Lower payments also mean slower loan pay down.

Fixed loans can also have another feature called a *balloon*. A balloon is a loan that comes due in full after a predetermined period has elapsed. Many conventional balloons come due after five years and are called "thirty-due-in-five" and written as "30/5." Again using the above example, after five years the 30-year loan's outstanding balance of $184,921 becomes due—all of it. The loan has to be refinanced or the property otherwise sold off to avoid the balloon payment. Who would want a balloon payment?

Lenders offer balloons because they can offer a reduced interest rate. And they're particularly attractive if borrowers don't think they'll have the mortgage that long anyway. A 30/5 interest rate might be 5.25% instead of 5.55%.

There's another version of a fixed-rate, sometimes called a *two-step* or a 5/25. This loan offers a reduced rate for the first five years, then makes a one-time adjustment to another rate for the remaining 25 years. There are also two-step loans called 7/23s that work similarly.

Adjustable-Rate Mortgages

The interest rates on adjustable-rate mortgages, or ARMs, adjust. They can change. Fortunately there's a rhyme and a reason regarding when and how much they change. There are ARMs that change twice per year, once per year, once per month, and so on. The ARM will have those preset change options built into the note, and those change options are called the *index, margin*, and *cap*.

An index is the benchmark the interest rate on the adjustable-rate mortgage is associated with or tied to. Common indexes are the interest rates on the one-year Treasury bill or a six-month CD, but the index can be mostly whatever the lender wants it to be. Other indexes are the prime rate, the six-month Treasury bill, and the London Interbank Offered Rate, or LIBOR.

The second component of an ARM is the margin. Think "profit margin" and you'll get the idea. The lender adds the margin to the index to arrive at the loan's interest rate. For example, consider an ARM based on the interest rates on the six-month Treasury bill. That rate, which can fluctuate with the economy, could be 3.61% on the date the loan is set. Next add the margin—a common one is 2.75%—to the 3.61% index rate for a total 6.36% interest rate on the loan.

The adjustment period is another feature of an ARM. This is the exact date that the loan's interest rate can adjust. The lender recalculates the rate by taking the index at the time of adjustment and adding the margin. Often the adjustment time coincides with changes in the index itself. For example, if the index is a one-year Treasury bill, then the loan might adjust once per year, every year. For a six-month CD index, the rate might adjust every six months. But it doesn't necessarily follow with all ARMs; it's just how most are calculated.

But what happens, you may ask, if the index goes from 2.50% in year one to 10.00% in year two? Big changes in payment, right? Wrong. Built into the ARM are neat things called *adjustment caps* or *caps*. A cap protects the client from an index's mood swings by limiting the degree to which a loan's interest rate can change. Most caps prohibit a loan's interest rate from changing more than one percent every six months or 2 percent per year. But not all are that way. Government ARMs, for example, have a one-percent cap every 12 months.

Here's an example. Let's assume that $200,000 30-year loan has an adjustable rate. If the index on which the loan is based started at 2.00%, by adding a 2.50% margin, the mortgage rate is a whopping 4.50%. That works out to a monthly payment of $1,013. Now let's assume weird things happen over the next year and the index rises significantly to 10.00%. Add the 2.50% margin and the new loan rate is 12.50%, resulting in a new monthly payment of $2,134 per month—more than twice what the borrower was paying.

But if there is an adjustment cap of two percentage points, the interest rate on the loan can never go more than two percentage points higher or lower than the previous year's rate. So even though the ARM wanted to go to 12.50%, due to the cap, it couldn't. It could only go up two percent, or to 6.50%. Now the payment adjusts to $1,264. It's higher than before but nothing like what your borrower would have had without an adjustment cap.

Another cap friend is the lifetime cap, which dictates the highest interest rate the loan can ever carry. Most lifetime caps are 6.00% over the rate you started at, so in this example the maximum rate would never be higher than 4.50% + 6.00% , or 10.50%. Yeah, that's high, but because of the two-point annual adjustment cap, it will take at least three years to get there.

Hybrids

I told you that fixed-rate and adjustable-rate mortgages are essentially the only kinds of mortgages out there, but there's also an "in-between" choice. It's called a hybrid. A hybrid is a cross between a fixed-rate mortgage and an adjustable-rate mortgage in that the rate is fixed for a preset period, but then the loan turns into an annual or semiannual ARM. One common form of hybrid mortgage carries a fixed rate for five years and then turns into an ARM that adjusts every year. This is called a 5/1 ("five one") mortgage. Another common hybrid, called a 7/1 ("seven one"), carries a fixed rate for seven years and then turns into an ARM that adjusts every year.

Hybrids can also morph into six-month ARMs or have different initial rates. If you can figure out what a 5/6 ARM is or a 3/1 ARM, then you get the picture.

Helping People Decide Among Fixed Rates, ARMs, and Hybrids

Generally speaking, a borrower will select an ARM if fixed rates are much higher and interest rates are at historical or cyclical highs.

Choosing an ARM implicitly means that the borrower believes recent history and economic trends indicate that rates in general are more likely to go lower rather than higher. People who don't plan to own a home for very long might also choose an ARM.

People who choose a fixed rate do so when rates are at historical lows or they plan on owning the home for a very long time. It's your job to suggest proper loan options by asking the correct questions.

Hybrids are more popular for those who are fairly certain they're not going to have a mortgage on the property for very long. If a home-buyer is certain she is going to get a job transfer within five years, she might choose a 5/1 or 5/6 ARM. The rates are often lower than a standard 30-year fixed and for a time she avoids the annual adjustments that can occur with ARMs. In fact, hybrids have become the loan program du jour for short-termers.

Interest-Only Loans

One type of ARM that has regained its fame is called an interest-only loan. With this type of program, the monthly payment is composed of interest only. The loan does not amortize. To calculate the monthly payment on an interest-only loan, simply multiply the annual interest rate by the loan amount. The result is the annual amount of interest due on that loan. Now divide that amount by 12 (months in a year) to arrive at the interest rate payment for the loan.

When you compare the monthly payments on a fully amortizing loan with the payments on an interest-only loan, the difference is noticeable. For a 30-year fixed-rate loan, a 5.5% interest-only payment on $100,000 is:

$$5.5\% \times \$100,000 = \$5,500$$

Divide that amount by 12 and the monthly payment is $458. Compare that with a fully amortized payment of $568 and you can really see the difference in payment.

Amortizing negatively is a nice way of saying that the loan actually gets bigger over time, not smaller.

Advising Clients About Option ARM Loans

If you are pushing this type of loan to your clients, be very, very aware of what you're doing and be even more careful that they understand what they're getting into. These types of loans are a benefit to only a few people, and the lower payments associated with some ARMs should never be used to simply get someone qualified.

There are places for option ARMs. They can work well for borrowers who get paid infrequently or who plan on keeping a property only for a very short period. However, using an option arm just to qualify for the mortgage in the first place is irresponsible for the loan officer and a very bad mistake by the consumer. There are simply too many choices in the mortgage market without having to resort to a loan program that inherently has potential foreclosure built right into it. Especially when the borrower has done nothing wrong except pay the amount required by the note.

Conventional and Government Loans

Now that you have a handle on the different types of loan programs, you next need to understand the differences between conventional and government loans. Both conventional and government loans can be fixed-rate, ARMs, or hybrids, but there are some unique qualifications for certain loan types that you need to understand.

A *conventional loan* is a mortgage that meets Fannie Mae or Freddie Mac guidelines but is guaranteed by the mortgage banker. That means that if the loan goes bad, it's the lender that gets hit with the foreclosure.

A government loan is called that because it is guaranteed by the government. These loans are VA and FHA loans.

The federal government has programs designed to get your clients into a home. And although it might sound obvious that you should start out with government loans, all too often people who are eligible for such programs don't apply either because they don't think they qualify or because they aren't aware of the loan programs.

VA Loan Programs

In 1939, the federal government did a very good thing. To reward their service to the country, qualified veterans received lots of new benefits. One of those benefits was being able to buy a home without any money down.

Back then, no-money-down loans were few and far between. Down payments on loans varied depending primarily on regional factors such as which bank was the biggest or which savings and loan was making home loans. Down payments of up to 50 percent of the sales price were not uncommon. Imagine that. Half down and the home was theirs.

But the Veterans Administration came up with a stellar plan to thank qualified veterans and active-duty personnel in the form of housing assistance. The VA doesn't actually make a VA loan, a lender does. But if the loan goes into default, the VA will refund the mortgage loss to the lender. Thus, the VA guarantees the mortgage instead of issuing it.

People who qualify for VA home benefits are:

Veterans

Active-duty personnel

Reserve troops with qualifying service

Surviving spouses of servicemen or women who have died in combat

For some reason, maybe because they are in fact a government product, VA loans are a complicated lot. There are so many more gov-

ernment forms the borrower must complete, and the loans are under-
written in a slightly different manner. That's why there are so many
misunderstood items about VA loans. Here are some of those confusing items.

Types of VA loans

VA loans come in two types, much like any other loan program: fixed
and adjustable hybrid. Suggest a fixed-rate VA loan if your clients anticipate being in the home for several years. Choose a hybrid if they're
planning on owning the home for a shorter period of time. It's really
that simple. One note: ARMs may not be available every year, as Congress legislates available VA loan choices.

One of the features of VA loans is that the closing costs are limited—it's an added benefit that other conventional or government loans
don't have. Veterans are only allowed to pay for appraisals, credit reports, title and title-related charges, origination fees, discount points,
recording fees, and surveys where required. The lender or the seller
must absorb or pay everything else. An easy way to remember which
fees veterans are allowed to pay is to remember the acronym ACTORS:
appraisal, credit, title, origination, recording, and survey.

There is also one other fee that the veteran must pay, but it's a fee
that can be rolled into the loan amount. This fee is called the funding
fee, and it is 2 percent of the loan amount. Lenders waive this fee for
veterans who have service-connected disabilities.

For example, consider a home for sale at $300,000. A qualifying
veteran wants to buy that home and put no money down. By including
the funding fee of 2 percent, the loan amount then becomes $306,000.

There are in fact closing costs, although limited, that the veteran
pays for, or at least "may" pay for. Let's look at the typical closing costs
on a $300,000 VA loan:

Appraisal	$350
Credit Report	$20

Title Ins.	$500
Origination	$3,000
Recording	$100
Survey	$300

That adds up to $4,270. That's a lot of money. So instead of a zero-money-down VA loan, it becomes a zero-money-down VA loan with closing costs. A true zero-down home loan also means no closing costs. Nothing.

If the borrower has no money for the down payment or closing costs, or maybe the borrower does but doesn't want to use it, there is no better loan program available. Period. VA loans are as competitive as any conventional loan in terms of rates and fees and are easy to qualify for.

If your client is VA eligible, this is the first program you should explore. And it will probably be the program he ends up with.

FHA Loan Programs

In 1934, Congress formed the Federal Housing Administration, or FHA, to foster home ownership. The country wasn't long out of the Depression, so the federal government embarked on a series of efforts to help the country's economy get moving. By helping people buy homes, one of the expected benefits was the homeowner would also buy other things—couches, beds, pillows, drapes, paint, and other such housing-related items. That would spur the economy and make everyone a happy homeowner.

The FHA allowed for, among other things, a method similar to the VA's. If an FHA loan went bad, the government would pay back the defaulted lender. Just like a VA loan, the FHA doesn't make the loan, it simply guarantees it as long as the lender issued the loan under FHA guidelines.

Although FHA loans aren't "zero down" in and of themselves, they are nearly so. Three percent is all that the FHA borrower needs to have in a purchase transaction. Note that I said *transaction* and not *down payment*. There are closing costs, insurance policies, and the FHA's version of the VA funding fee (it's called the mortgage insurance premium, or MIP) along with a down payment.

Now, instead of trying to calculate a 3 percent down payment plus closing fees plus seller-paid costs plus the mortgage-insurance premium, the FHA simply requires a 3 percent minimum investment by the borrower. If a home sells for $200,000, then the buyer is required to come to the closing table with at least 3 percent, or $6,000. That $6,000 can be applied to any part of the buyer's liability in the purchase, but at the end of the closing, the buyer has still put only 3 percent into the deal.

Who is a good candidate for FHA loans? Those with little money for a down payment who might have trouble qualifying for a conventional loan due to damaged credit or high debt ratios. Note that FHA loans aren't for people with bad credit, but in many instances FHA does allow for a few more credit "dings" than a conventional loan can.

Recent changes in FHA lending have actually made them more competitive. It used to be that the FHA restricted certain of the buyer's closing costs, meaning that if the buyer took out an FHA loan, then someone else was going to have to pay the extra $1,000 or so of lender junk fees and other settlement costs. Now, however, the FHA has determined that borrowers can pay "usual and customary" charges just like conventional borrowers. This has made FHA loans a bit more competitive in the mortgage market. Not that FHA loans were a hardship by any stretch, it was just that if given a choice, conventional lending was almost always slightly better.

Tweaking FHA Loans

You'll be surprised at how a little tweaking can affect a loan approval. *Tweaking* means adjusting certain factors in the loan to score an approval for your client. If the client's credit score is low, say below 620, then try raising the down payment. A 620 score with 5 percent down might be difficult for many conventional lenders, but it might just be the ticket for an FHA loan.

If it's not quite the ticket for an FHA loan, try putting 10 percent or 15 percent down. High-down-payment FHA loans are much more forgiving when it comes to loan approval. If you've got some credit issues and FHA loan limits are right for the area, I'd look at putting 10-15 percent down on an FHA loan if you have those resources available.

Subprime Loans

Subprime loans, sometimes also called *nonprime loans,* are for clients with credit that has been damaged to the point where they can't qualify for any FHA, VA, or conventional mortgage.

Bad credit happens. Lenders typically won't make a mortgage loan to someone who simply doesn't care about paying anything back whatsoever, but they do like to make loans to people who have temporarily had some type of financial disaster in their lives.

In the olden days, say in the mid-to-late 1980s, it used to be that someone who had bad credit would simply be shut out of homebuying altogether. The borrower would have to wait, sometimes as long as seven years or more, before a lender would make him or her a mortgage loan.

Now though, subprime loans make up nearly a quarter of all mortgage loans issued in the United States. And that number could be even higher if others tried to buy a home instead of not applying because of their own assumptions about loan qualification.

So how and when do you send the buyer to a subprime lender or provide a subprime loan?

First, don't prejudge the client's credit situation unless you've been in the business for a few years. Heck, don't even do it then. The very first thing you should do after taking a loan application and running a credit report is to submit the loan to an automated underwriting system (AUS) to get a decision.

Let's first use a little common sense here. If the client's credit is really bad (i.e., the client's FICO score is in the 500s and he has less than 20 percent down), don't get too excited about providing a conventional loan. Go ahead first and try for an automated decision. If you don't get the result you want, then take the next step and go subprime.

Subprime loans can come in most any mortgage type, including fixed-rate and adjustable-rate programs, but most often the subprime loan of choice is the hybrid. Hybrid ARMs provide a fixed, below-market rate for the first few years then turn into an adjustable-rate loan that resets annually or periodically. Most of the subprime loans I've seen are either the 2/28 or 3/27 version of the hybrid.

The trick with subprime loans is to understand specifically what they're designed for. They're designed to help your clients get back on their feet and into homeownership. With a subprime loan, your clients will want to do everything they can to repair and reestablish their credit scores. One of the best ways to improve a score is to make mortgage payments on time. This can be done with a subprime loan.

It can take two to three years of responsible credit history to improve a credit rating. By getting a subprime loan, a borrower can reestablish his or her credit by the time the initial hybrid period ends and then refinance into a lower-rate conventional loan.

Don't think of a subprime loan as a bitter pill your borrowers must swallow due to their credit situations. They should instead see the loan as "mortgage medicine" that will help them get better soon.

Sure, subprime loans come in many flavors, but their rates can be 2–4 percent higher, or more, than conventional loans. The trick with subprime loans is to take the hybrid, pay close attention to the credit patterns, and refinance your clients out of the higher-rate loan as the hybrid adjusts. Subprime ARMs can have some pretty nasty margins, some as high as 5 percent or more.

You don't want your client's interest rate to jump from 6.00% to

11.00% after the first 36 months. The subprime loan is a Band-Aid and is not to be used for the rest of his or her life. Also make sure that if you plan to refinance the client later on that you are being realistic. You should realize that if a subprime loan is the only loan the client qualifies for at the time of application, then the client won't be in a position to refinance until after two or three years anyway. That's about how long it will take to reestablish good credit, which is necessary before you can refinance into a fixed-rate conventional mortgage.

Most subprime loans carry, where allowed, a prepayment penalty as well. If the loan has a prepayment penalty, I wouldn't worry about it too much. Most prepayment penalties coincide with the fixed portion of the hybrid ARM. For example, if your borrowers have chosen a 3/27 hybrid, the prepayment period will usually last three years, or two years on a 2/28. Most loans of this type also offer the option of "buying out" the prepayment penalty either in points—usually one year of buyout will cost one-half to one percent of the original principal—or by increasing the rate. If your client buys out one year of the prepayment penalty, the client can anticipate a quarter-point rate increase for each year bought out.

On a side note, it's very important your clients not pay discount points when taking a subprime loan. A discount point is a fee equal to one percent of the loan amount, and for every point paid up front, the lender reduces the interest rate on the loan. If the goal is to refinance in two to three years, then it doesn't make any sense to pay a fee to get a lower rate—the client won't be keeping that subprime mortgage long enough to garner the full benefit of the lower rate.

For example, a $300,000 subprime loan may be offered at 7.50% for a 2/28 hybrid. That works out to a $2,097 monthly payment. Remember that the goal is to refinance in 24 months after the client has repaired his credit. The lender offers to reduce the rate to 7.00% if you pay two points, or $6,000. That's a common spread.

The monthly payment using 7.00% on $300,000 is $1,995. Yes, the monthly payment is now over $100 lower. But your clients paid

$6,000 for that privilege. It will take them 59 months ($6,000 divided by $100) to recoup that money. If in 24 months they refinance into a conventional loan, they would have saved just over $2,400 but in effect lost $3,600 because they "bought down" the rate.

There are "zero-point" subprime loans just as there are zero-point conventional or FHA loans. Keep the loan costs low on a subprime loan if the goal is to refinance after a short period or right at the end of the hybrid term. The math rarely works out.

Subprime loans offer more variables than conventional or government loans do. Although a conventional loan might offer 5.50% on a 30-year fixed with 10 percent down, most likely that's the rate offered if the borrower put 20, 30, or even 40 percent down. But not with subprime loans. Subprime lending makes allowances for different variables:

Down payment
Debt ratios
Credit scores

A subprime lender will offer better deals if any of those three variables are adjusted. Still even better if all three are improved.

For example, let's say that the client's credit score is 590, his debt ratios are at 50%, and the lender's minimum down payment is 10 percent. You might get a 2/28 subprime offering of 8.00%. But if you put down 20 percent instead of 10, the rate might be reduced another quarter point.

If the client chooses to put down more money, say 30 percent, which also reduces the debt ratios further to 44, you'll find that the rate might go down further—perhaps by another percent.

Subprime lenders are fairly strict about such guidelines. You'll see that on their rate sheets. In these cases, credit scores, loan-to-value ratios, and debt ratios are in fact set in stone. In subprime lending, the rate in fact goes up by a quarter point if the borrower's credit score is

589 and not 590, or if the debt ratio is 46 instead of 45. Unlike conventional lending, which rarely has such requirements, subprime lending doesn't allow for many exceptions.

Advising Clients About Subprime Loans

How can you determine which combination of variables is best for your clients? That depends. Does the client in fact have enough money to make a larger down payment? Can she get it from somewhere? If she doesn't, then she'll have to borrow less to keep the ratios down. Or she'll need to find some more income in the form of a new job, a raise, or another borrower who will live in the house with her.

Determining Which Loan Is Right for Your Client

Okay, now that you know the different types of loans, how do you know which is best for the borrowers? Good question, and one that should always be in the forefront of the mind.

Generally speaking, if the borrowers are keeping the mortgage for longer than five years, it's usually best they take a fixed rate. If it'll be less than five years, consider an adjustable mortgage or a hybrid.

The hybrids you will most often select will be the 3/1 and 5/1 variety. But there is one caveat with such loans: they're still adjustable mortgages.

There are hybrids that extend far beyond five years, usually a 7/1 or 10/1 time frame, but you'll find these extended hybrids are less competitive and in some instances actually higher than similar fixed-rate fare.

So, what do you suggest? Keep it simple. It's tempting when a borrower looks you in the eye and says, "What kind of loans are there?" to show your loan prowess and answer the question in detail.

About an hour later, when the borrower's eyes have glazed over long ago, you might finish explaining the loan choices. Don't do that. Keep it simple.

Ask, "How long do you anticipate keeping this mortgage on this house?" Don't ask, "How long are you going to keep this house?" Remember, people can get a home loan, pay off the mortgage, and still keep the house. If you ask, "How long are you going to keep the house?" the borrowers might simply reply, "Till we die," and you might then offer something long-term like a 30-year fixed-rate. But they may simply be planning on paying off the mortgage in two years with a bonus from work, funds from a pension plan, or they're going to buy lotto tickets until they hit the perfect scratcher.

If they intend to keep the mortgage for a long time, suggest a fixed-rate mortgage. If it's a shorter term, as is the case with someone who anticipates moving or being transferred for a job or some other life issue, then suggest an ARM or a hybrid.

Better yet, have the borrowers tell you what they want. Here's why: If the borrower tells you what he wants and you provide it, then the next thing to do is simply provide a competitive rate and fee structure and you're done.

But if you want to start acting like a financial wizard and bombard your clients with so many numbers they get dizzy, then that's certainly your call. The job as a loan officer is to find clients, provide them with what they need or want, and close the loan. Next client.

However, if you are in fact comfortable with numbers and you do have a client who will not only understand but appreciate comparative numbers, then you should provide as many choices as possible.

The problem with that scenario is that unless the clients are not only committed to you as a loan officer but also actually want that data, it's likely that you'll confuse the process for the clients so much that they'll leave you and go somewhere less intimidating.

In fact, the first mortgage company I ever worked for had a neat little spreadsheet it developed internally that would show all the possible loan choices based upon such things as paying points or not paying points, length of time carrying the mortgage, and other life issues. The spreadsheet would compare the choices and highlight the best ones.

It was a great program and many an accountant enjoyed it. But that approach is for a select audience. The mortgage-approval process can be intimidating to people simply at face value; don't make it more so by muddying the waters.

If the borrowers want a fixed rate, provide them with a fixed. If they want an ARM, give them an ARM. But do borrowers automatically get the mortgages they ask for? If they want a 15-year fixed, do they automatically qualify for that loan? No. And it's your job to shepherd them through the process—from prequalification to preapproval to loan commitment.

Refinancing

If you did what you were supposed to do with all of your previous leads and closed loans, you have a regular database of people to market to: happy customers. Because you kept in touch and they were happy with your work, they are a prime market for refinances. They used you once and they'll use you again.

A refinance is not a new loan type, such as a fixed or an ARM, but a process using a particular loan program. Interest rates will move up and down. And they'll take their time doing so. One of the reasons the mortgage business is such a good business to be in is that you're often bulletproof during economic slowdowns.

Remember how the Fed attempts to keep the economy in check by adjusting the cost of money. In good economic times, people feel confident. They've got lots of money in the bank, so they go buy houses. Lots of them. When the economy is moving along at a steady clip, rates are higher, including mortgage rates. Soon, the economy slows down and like all normal economic cycles people get laid off at work, fewer jobs are created, and fewer people buy things, which keeps the cost of goods and services low, and so on.

That means interest rates will begin to move downward. Mortgage rates will drop because investors will put more money into less-risky bonds, including mortgage bonds, which drives up bond prices and reduces mortgage rates. And lower rates encourage people to refinance.

And guess what—you make the very same amount of money on a refinance as a purchase. Or at least you have the opportunity to do so. Refinancing is a brand-new loan that replaces any current loans on the property and at a lower rate.

That's typically why people refinance—they can get a lower monthly payment. For example, on a 30-year $300,000 mortgage loan fixed at 7.50%, the monthly payment is $2,097. If rates begin to fall, say to 6.25%, the monthly payment on that same loan is now $1,847 . . . a difference of nearly $250. That's a good deal.

I bought a house in 1998 and the rate was 6.875%. I later refinanced that note to 6.00%. A couple of years later I refinanced yet again and my rate was 5.00%. There's nothing to stop someone from refinancing over and over again. In fact, a person can refinance as many times as he wants as long as it makes sense to refinance. Just as there are closing costs with a purchase mortgage, there are the same costs with a refinance. The borrower needs a new appraisal and new title insurance, and there are new processing fees, new underwriting fees, new intangible taxes, new everything.

That costs money. On a $300,000 refinance mortgage, closing costs could be nearly $4,000. Your borrower has to pay that all over again. But with a refinance, the borrower can pay those costs out of pocket or roll those fees directly into the loan amount and borrow them. Or, the borrower could pay a 1.5-point premium for a lower interest rate and have the lender pay the closing costs.

How do you determine if a refinance makes sense or not? First, take the dollar amount of closing costs and divide the new monthly savings into the closing costs. The result is the number of months it will take to "recover" the closing costs associated with refinancing the mortgage.

Let's use the $300,000 loan with $4,000 in closing costs and a $250 monthly savings as an example. By dividing $4,000 by $250, you get 16. Thus, it takes 16 months to recover the refinancing fees. Not bad. As long as your client keeps the mortgage longer than 16 months, it's something to consider.

It is important to note that lenders set maximum loan amounts on refinancings. Refinanced loans can typically go no higher than 90 percent of the value of the home based upon the new appraisal.

Your clients can pull equity out of their homes if they want with one big mortgage. This is called a *cash out* refinance. Refinancing a mortgage without pulling cash out is called *rate and term* refinance. Not a bad deal if the numbers work. Reduce the interest rate and get some cheap cash at the same time. Here's an example of a cash out refinance.

Appraised value	$500,000
Current loan balance	$250,000
Closing costs	$4,000
Cash out	$20,000

The total refinanced loan amount equals the loan balance plus closing costs and cash out, or:

$$250,000 + \$4,000 + \$20,000 = \$274,000$$

The old rate of 7.50% on $250,000 gave us a monthly payment of $1,748. The new lower rate of 6.25% on the same 30-year fixed-rate note with the higher loan amount of $274,000 yields a $1,687 monthly payment.

Not bad. Your client's monthly payment dropped by about $60 per month and she walked away with $20,000 in her pocket to make home improvements, send kids to college, or invest in mortgage bonds. Or whatever.

Cash-out loans are restricted to 80 percent of the value of the property, but you'll find the pricing much more competitive for your client if you keep the loan at 75 percent or below.

Another reason people refinance is not just to get a lower rate but also to get out of an adjustable-rate mortgage and get a fixed-rate loan. Or the client may have originally thought he would only have a mortgage for a couple of years so he got a hybrid.

It's important that you keep track of your previous clients and always look for opportunities that could help them out. If rates are at historic lows, it's probably time for every single one of your past clients who have ARMs or hybrids to consider refinancing into a fixed-rate mortgage.

Be Aware of Restrictions on Marketing to Past Clients

One important note: As a mortgage broker, every single wholesale lender agreement you sign asks that you not solicit their borrowers for refinancing. Some have a requirement that you stay away from your clients for a year or so, others flat-out ban it.

But that doesn't mean you can't keep in touch with them on a regular basis. I send out a regular e-newsletter packed with articles about homes and personal finance—it keeps me in front of my past clients without directly asking, "Hey, can I refinance your loan?" You can log on to www.realtytimes.com and get more information on how to create those newsletters—the tool is called The Financial Wire.

By marketing to your database, you'll be doing what successful loan officers have always done—building and marketing to their past customers. When you get to that stage, you're well on your way to a successful, satisfying, and lucrative career.

The Basics of the Job

· C H A P T E R ·

Loan Prequalification and Approval

Prequalification, sometimes called "prequal," is the process of determining the borrower's eligibility for a mortgage loan. During prequalification, the borrower's income is compared to the borrower's debts. Historical "ratios" are referenced, and voila—instant prequalification.

A borrower's debt ratio equals the borrower's total house payment divided by his or her gross monthly income. The house payment, for purposes of calculating the ratio, is the principal and interest payment on the mortgage plus 1/12th the annual property tax payment and 1/12th the annual homeowners-insurance payment.

For instance, on a $400,000, 30-year, fixed-rate mortgage at 7.00%, the monthly principal and interest payment on that loan is $2,661. If property taxes are 2 percent of the home's value (based on a sales price of $500,000), then the annual taxes are $10,000 or $833 per month. Now add a hazard-insurance premium of perhaps $2,000 per year or $167 per month. The principal and interest, taxes, and insurance (or PITI), is $2,661 plus $833 plus $167 = $3,661.

There are two debt ratios, sometimes called the "front" and the "back" ratio. The front ratio uses the PITI number and second ratio uses the PITI number plus the borrower's other monthly debt payments, such as automobile payments, student loans, and/or credit cards.

If the borrower's gross monthly income, which is the income before all taxes and withholdings are deducted, is $15,000, then to figure the front ratio you divide the PITI of $3,661 by the gross monthly income of $15,000. This works out to .244, or 24.4 percent, meaning that the borrower's front ratio is 24.4.

Now add the borrower's two automobile payments totaling $800, minimum credit card payments of $500, and $600 worth of monthly student loan payments to the PITI number to get $5,561. When you divide $5,561 by $15,000 the answer, the back ratio, is .37, or 37 percent.

So, the borrower's ratios are 24.4 / 37.

Mortgage lenders have suggested ratio guidelines. Some mortgage lenders even have restrictions as to how high a borrower's ratios can be and still qualify for a particular mortgage. For example, some lenders can say, "We will not make a loan if the borrower's debt ratios are above 40/50," or "We will not approve a loan if the borrower's front ratio is above 35."

Most conventional and government lenders do not have such specific requirements, which is a major change from just a few years ago. Now, debt ratios are just part of the approval equation and not something that can absolutely stop a deal in its tracks.

But there's an issue with a prequal. It's not verified. It's simply an opinion. A prequal typically means that the client has told you over the phone what his or her current debts and income were as well as other important things, such as how much money the client had for a down payment or closing costs and the quality of the client's credit.

How to Preapprove Your Client

You can issue a prequalification letter to a client, but Realtors want to see a preapproval letter. It means you have verified the important parts of the loan application with regard to credit, income, and having enough money to close the deal. You can issue a preapproval by reviewing documentation that verifies the other elements of the client's financial and credit status.

If the borrower wants to buy a $500,000 home and borrow $400,000, then it's logical that the borrower will need $100,000 for the down payment and another $8,000 for closing costs, or $108,000 in this example.

How do you verify that? You need third-party documentation for all loan verifications. That means if the borrower says she has $108,000, then you just can't take her word for it, you need financial statements showing $108,000. An additional twist to this is that you'll need bank and investment statements that are less than 90 days old. Why?

First, it's obvious that a bank statement from two years ago won't count for much—there's no reason to assume the client still has the money. The underwriter wants to see it now, not then.

Second, three months of statements will also show a pattern of savings. If the borrower had $10,000 two months ago, then last month had $108,000 in the bank, the underwriter is going to want to know something about those sudden funds showing up.

Where did the client get that money? Although at first glance one might say, "Who cares where my client got the money as long as he has it?" But it also could mean that the client borrowed it from someone or somewhere else. If the borrower then has to pay that money back each month, then that in fact will affect his debt ratios. If the maximum allowable debt ratio on a particular loan is 45 and there is a new deposit in the client's bank account that doesn't quite seem to fit (i.e., the clients make $15,000 per month then suddenly $100,000 shows up), then the underwriter will want to determine both the source and nature of the new funds.

The preapproval includes verifying the client's income along with his or her source of funds to close. You verify income by looking at paycheck stubs from the most recent 30-day period, not last year's paycheck stubs.

Finally the preapproval process requires a credit review. We'll look at credit in greater detail in chapter 8, but you'll need to determine whether the clients are creditworthy. Fortunately, today's loans don't always require a credit review from a loan officer. You certainly want to look at your clients' credit reports, but it's not necessary like it once was.

With the advent of credit scoring and the strides made in automated credit evaluation, no longer is a thorough credit review by the individual loan officer as much of a concern. Nowadays, automated underwriting systems, or AUS, do all the work.

Issuing a Commitment Letter

The commitment letter is the final piece of the puzzle. In fact, many Realtors require commitment letters in lieu of preapproval letters. A commitment letter is closer to a legal, binding agreement that says, "Hey, if my clients find a house, we'll provide the money for it and if we don't you can sue us." It is issued after there are absolutely no loose ends. Everything is verified. Loose language, but essentially correct.

Lenders issue most commitment letters to those buying new construction, where the new home won't be completed for several months and the builder wants to make absolutely certain that the client will make good on the deal after months of construction. Lots can change over three to four months.

For existing homes, a typical closing period is within 30 days. A lender may not have the time to clear absolutely everything required for a commitment and still print closing documents, so sometimes it will simply issue a mortgage preapproval that has the client's application, income, assets, and credit reviewed.

Documenting Your Client's Loan

There are two basic considerations when it comes to documenting a loan approval: the borrower and the property.

You must document the borrower's income, credit, and assets, and you must ensure that the property adheres to certain appraisal guidelines and has a clear title.

When documenting a loan file, you can anticipate standard documentation requirements.

Documenting W-2 Employees

These borrowers work for someone else; they have an employer. They get paid typically twice per month, every other week, or once per month. These borrowers are the easiest to document with regard to income.

There is little question regarding W-2 employees. They get paid regularly, can provide you with the most recent 30 days of paycheck stubs verifying their monthly and year-to-date gross income, and they can also provide a definitive W-2, which shows annual earnings.

To verify the income from a client with a W-2, divide the income on the W-2 by 12 months to get a gross monthly income and compare that consistent income with recent pay stubs.

But what about those who are self-employed? What about those who pay themselves? Although many self-employed people pay themselves with paychecks and have pay stubs, underwriters will typically ask for something more than paycheck stubs written by the person qualifying for the loan.

Underwriters require verification from third parties. When you verify the income of an employee with a W-2, you're verifying information provided by the borrower's employer. A third party. A self-employed person, although always completely honest, could in fact be tempted to fudge a paycheck stub or two. That's why underwriters don't accept pay stubs from the self-employed borrower. They want to see tax returns. An underwriter will accept tax returns as third-party verification if the borrower has submitted that same information to the IRS.

Lenders can get fairly serious when it comes to documenting a loan. Or not—at least when it comes to alternative documentation choices.

So why does the degree of documentation vary by borrower? The reasons can be anything from a borrower simply saying, "I don't feel like supplying all of that documentation," to needing to find enough income or assets to meet lender guidelines.

For example, a common requirement for a self-employed applicant for a fully documented loan might be proof that he or she has been in business for more than two years. If the borrower hasn't been in business for that long, he needs to find a loan type that his employment situation allows him to qualify for. In this case, perhaps the borrower needs a "No Doc" loan. (For more on fully documented and "No Doc" loans, see chapter 7.)

Some loan programs require the borrower to keep certain assets in an account for a particular period of time; this is called "seasoning." If a borrower's assets don't meet a particular seasoning requirement but are still available to buy the home, then the borrower would apply for a "Stated Asset" loan.

When it comes to income, lenders also have guidelines they must use when underwriting a fully documented file. They must verify that the borrower not only has a two-year income history, but that the income also has a "likelihood of continuance." It's this likelihood that sometimes borrowers can't provide. A common example might be disability income. Sometimes a lender will ask the borrower's doctor to provide his or her own opinion regarding the borrower's disability and if it will continue for two years or more. Doctors may not know or care to answer. In a fully documented file, that income couldn't be used to qualify the borrower. In this example, a "stated income" or "no income" file could be approved, however.

If your clients have any difficulty qualifying for a mortgage due to their assets, income, or employment history, then perhaps you just haven't found the right loan for them.

Loan Fraud

I've heard on more than one occasion that lenders expect borrowers to lie when applying for a "stated" loan. That's a crock. Lenders do no such thing. That's also a word of caution. If you as the loan officer tell the borrowers to put something untrue on their applications, then you both have committed loan fraud.

Never tell a borrower to leave anything blank so that you can fill it in later. Never ask an underwriter or wholesale account exec how much money your clients need to put on the loan application to get a loan approval. In fact, you may also find that some account execs will call you with a potential loan "decline" yet also say, "You know, if your borrowers made $10,000 per month instead of $8,000 per month, we could approve your loan." Stay away from such wholesale lenders.

Loan fraud is a federal offense. This is not getting a traffic ticket. You will go to prison. Not jail, but prison.

· C H A P T E R · 7

Loan Documentation

Loan documentation is a degree of verification. And verification comes in all shapes and sizes. Some lenders even have their own names for documentation verification status. But most in the industry have accepted a few standard names that mean the same thing to everyone else. Loan documentations come in the following formats:

Full documentation

Alternate documentation

Stated documentation

Stated income documentation

Stated asset documentation

No income documentation

No asset documentation

No income, no asset documentation

No employment documentation

No documentation

Why would lenders offer so many variations on documenting a loan? Lenders are like any other business, they can market a mortgage loan as any other company might market any other product. Lenders can differentiate themselves by doing things differently, or at least appearing to do so. Have you seen television commercials where lenders brag about how little documentation they need? It's a marketing tool. Sometimes less documentation is for borrower convenience and sometimes it's a borrower necessity.

Full Documentation

In this kind of loan, everything about the borrower is verified. This verification comes in written, third-party format. If the borrower states on the application that he makes $5,000 per month, the lender won't simply take the borrower's word for it. Instead, his employer is sent a verification of employment letter, or VOE, which asks the employer to fill out a questionnaire about the applicant's time with the company, employment status, and compensation.

Full Doc for employment also means a couple of paycheck stubs covering the most recent 30-day period and the previous two years of W-2s.

Full Doc for assets means obtaining a verification of deposit form, or VOD, which is mailed and completed by the borrower's financial institution. Alternatively, the bank can submit the most recent three months of bank statements. Borrowers can even provide a printout of an online bank or investment statement as long as the statement shows the borrower's name, part of the borrower's Social Security number, the account number, and the accompanying URL at the top or bottom of the page.

Full Doc for rental or mortgage history can come from the borrower's credit report, if listed, or from 12 months of cancelled checks showing timely payment. Nothing gets by in a Full Doc loan without getting verified by someone who's not the borrower or related to the borrower.

Alternate Documentation

The meaning of Alt Doc has changed over the years, prior to the massive spread of Stated Documentation and No Documentation loans. Alt doc loans primarily accept any type of documentation, but this typically means verbal instead of written verification (as is the case for Full Doc loans). In the case of verbal verification, most often the loan processor makes a phone call to the borrower's employer and asks questions such as, "Does he work there?" and "How much money does he make?" Alt Doc can also mean providing bank statements instead of a VOD.

Stated Documentation

Stated Doc means the underwriter will use what your clients put on the application without any verification whatsoever. If a borrower says she makes $10,000 per month, then that's what the underwriter will use when determining debt ratios. If she makes $100,000 per month, that's the number the underwriter will work with.

A bit of common sense goes with Stated Doc loans. If someone puts down that she makes $100,000 per year but lists her occupation as a store clerk, then the underwriter might ask for some additional documentation or require other information to "make sense" of the income.

One way lenders "verify" a Stated Doc loan is by verifying the borrower's other assets or credit score. Some Stated Doc loans require more down payment or charge a higher interest rate.

Consider a Stated Doc loan that requires three months worth of stated income in a liquid account. If the borrower puts down $100,000 per month as income, the lender would ask to see $300,000 in cash or liquid accounts. Does this make sense? It should. Someone who makes any level of income should also have some assets that relate to that income. If someone makes $3,000 per month, then it is likely that person also has $9,000 in checking, savings, or 401(k)s. Verifying assets is a "backdoor" way of verifying plausible income.

Stated Doc loans can also be used for those who don't wish to verify their assets for whatever reason. I recall a client that made a whole lot of money. I mean, a whole lot. He owned two construction companies and invested in more general partnerships than you could count. His tax returns were at least six inches thick. If he applied on a "Full Doc" basis, then the underwriter would have no choice but to verify each and every item submitted. That meant that because he owned so many different companies he would have to provide that many different sets of tax returns to verify business income. There was no need to "beat him up" with paperwork on all his various businesses, so instead he applied for a Stated Doc loan.

Still another client liked to diversify her assets. Many people have more than one investment or retirement account, but this lady had several—28. For a Full Doc loan, she would have to provide the last three months of investment statements for all 28 accounts. Think for a moment of one 401(k) statement or maybe one from a mutual fund. How many pages are there? Several, right? This client would have to produce over 100 pages of asset documentation simply because that's what she put on her application.

Stated Income Documentation

Lenders of Stated Income loans use the income on the loan application to calculate debt ratios, but they verify everything else on the application including assets, employment, and anything else they want.

Stated Asset Documentation

Lenders of Stated Asset loans use the assets as stated in the loan application, but they verify everything else. Borrowers use assets for down payments and closing costs, so lenders need to see if a borrower has enough money to close a transaction. However, Stated Asset loans don't go through the "provide the last three months of statements" drill.

No Income Documentation

Here's a twist on the Stated Income loan. For this loan type, no income information is put on the application whatsoever. Hence no ratios are calculated, but everything else is. Most No Income loans have fairly steep asset, credit, or down payment requirements.

No Asset Documentation

This loan is essentially the same as a No Income Doc, but no assets are listed on the application. The lender assumes the borrower has enough money to close the transaction without verifying it. The lender does, however, verify income along with other verifiable facets of the loan application.

No Income, No Asset Documentation

This loan is also called a "Nina," for No Income No Asset. No income information is put on the application, and the borrower does not provide any tax returns or pay stubs. The borrower also does not provide any bank or investment statements to prove the borrower's stated assets. The lender verifies everything else, including the borrower's employment and credit history.

No Employment Documentation

In this kind of loan, the borrower discloses nothing with regard to employment on the application, yet the lender verifies everything else.

No Documentation

This term is used too often in the lending industry. As a matter of fact, a true No Doc loan is rare. It means that no proof of employment, income, or assets are used to approve the loan. The borrower's credit history and presence at the closing table with enough money to close are the only requirements.

Hard-to-Prove Income

Okay, so you have a client with "hard to prove" income. How do you qualify him or her for that home loan? The problem is usually that the borrower's income doesn't quite fit the lender's guidelines. That can mean:

The borrower doesn't have a two-year income history.

The income isn't likely to continue for two to three years.

Third-party sources can't document the income.

Note that none of these three requirements mean anyone is trying to fool an underwriter. An underwriter is required to document a loan so it fits the lender's requirements. But that doesn't mean the income doesn't exist. Why would anyone go through all the hassle of buying a home without any means of repaying the note?

Underwriters look for a history of income. If you can't prove the income, it most likely won't be counted. But that's why there are "stated" loans. Here are a few examples of real income that underwriters may or may not accept on a "Full Doc" loan.

The sales of an artist's first paintings

A ballplayer's first paycheck playing baseball

Income from a new businessperson's successful new car wash business

A single parent's income from two or even three jobs to pay for college

A chef's income from a new restaurant

Income from a pension

An author's royalties from a new book that is selling like crazy

Income a general contractor gets on a "job-to-job" basis

Income from a handyman who roves about getting odd jobs

All of these endeavors are worthy, but sometimes in the eyes of lenders the income just isn't dependable. It's not that the income isn't there, it's just that the loans are reserved for those whose paychecks come twice per month or who are paid by the hour. Hourly or monthly wages reported on a W-2 are easy to verify. Other income sources may not be.

So what do you do if your client's income falls outside the standard guidelines? After all, most "stated" loans have a guideline that's nearly impossible to get around: the two-year history of employment. Lenders can apply various credit standards to approve most any type of loan, but the two-year history requirement is usually rock-solid. So how do you verify two years of employment if your client is going "stated?"

If your borrower is self-employed or gets income from different sources, an underwriter will ask for a letter from the borrower's CPA stating how long the borrower has been doing what he's been doing. If your client doesn't have an accountant or any other third party that can verify the most recent two years, then a copy of the borrower's business license with a date on it will work.

Don't have a copy of the business license or don't have one? How about a yellow pages ad that's two years old? Do you have anything at all that can show the client's been working at the same job for at least two years? Lenders can get pretty creative and so can you. But if you can't get past this test, then the choices will be severely limited— probably to No Documentation; No Income; or No Income, No Asset loans.

· C H A P T E R ·

8

Interpreting Credit Reports and Credit Scores

R egardless of the amount of loan programs you have to offer, the bottom line still rests on the client's credit history. Technically speaking, credit is someone's ability and willingness to repay a debt.

Ability means the person has enough money each month to pay her bills, and *willingness* simply means she has the inclination to do so.

If your client has incurred debt and then suddenly finds herself unable to pay her monthly obligations due to the loss of her job, a change of pay scale, or any variety of other reasons, she suddenly can't pay. She no longer has the ability.

On the other side of the coin is the willingness of the consumer to pay. She might have plenty of money in the bank but, well, she's just not always on time with her monthly payments.

With the advent of automated underwriting systems (AUS), having veteran skills at reading credit reports and deciphering their scribble-scrabble is less important than it used to be. Still, it's vital that you know how credit reports are put together and how to read them. This is especially so when working with subprime lenders that may have specific requirements about the maximum number of late payments allowed or about the client's collection-account history.

What's in a Credit Report?

A credit report contains everything reported by participating financial institutions or lending companies about the consumer's payment experience with them. It will be broken down into three areas: who, how, and public records.

"Who" is any identifying information about the consumer including not just his or her name but any other ways that name might have been used when applying for credit. If the client's full name is Billy Bob Smith, Jr., it's also likely that the legal name is in fact William Robert Smith, II. Or Jr. Or Willy Robert. Or Willy Bob. Or Willy Bob, Jr.

Name variations come from the various ways the client originally applied for a credit account. If the borrower applied at Sears under William Smith and later at Target as Bill Smith, Jr., then both names will appear on the credit report. These variations are known as "AKAs" or "also known as."

The report includes the client's Social Security number, his or her date of birth, and a list of previous addresses.

The second batch of information in a credit report relates to how the client has paid his or her debts and who the client borrowed from. The report will list, typically from newest to oldest, the names of the businesses who have extended credit to your client. You will also see other information, such as what type of credit was issued (i.e., a mortgage, an automobile or other installment loan, a lease, or a revolving line of credit such as a standard credit card).

The credit report will show the client's credit limits, the maximum amount of credit each issuer granted, the current balances, and the highest balance the client ever had with that creditor. Next to that is the good part, showing how many times the client has paid late, if ever.

Late payments on a credit report are listed in increments of 30 days and are commonly shown as "30 +," "60 +," "90 +," and "120 +." If a payment is more than 30 days past the due date on the statement but less than 60 days past due, then the number 1 will appear below "30 +" showing that the client was more than 30 days late one time on that account. If there's a "3" below the "90 +," that means the client has been more than 90 days late three times on that particular account. This special section also shows when the client made the last payment on each account.

The final section of the credit report includes any public records that may legally be referenced. Legal entries include those that are financial in nature, such as a bankruptcy filing or wage-earner plan. Are there any foreclosures on the record or financial judgments? If so, they will appear in this third section.

Finally, and these days less significantly, the credit report shows a list of others who have obtained the client's credit report and the corresponding dates of the inquiries.

Each time your clients apply for credit, whatever they put on the credit application is what is stored at the various credit bureaus. If your client suddenly goes by "Gene" instead of "Eugene," then soon "Gene" will begin showing up on the report along with the suddenly expired "Eugene" moniker. Even people who have accidentally misspelled or had their names misspelled on a loan application will ultimately find that mistake in their credit reports.

If a credit card offer arrives with an extra *n* in the client's name (*Donna* instead of *Dona*, for instance), Dona might receive credit card offers or other solicitations with that same misspelling. "Welcome Donna! You're approved!"

There are several things that by law cannot appear in a credit report and still others that you thought might be included but aren't. Ultimately, credit reports can only store information identifying who your clients are and how they pay the bills.

Unless a client applies for credit with a spouse, there won't be anything in there about whether the client is married or not. There's also nothing in there regarding any medical history. You won't find an age listed on a credit report, but you may find that a birth date pops up.

Credit information that is more than seven years old will not be on the credit report. That includes collection accounts. It's important to know that an account with negative credit must not have any "activity" for seven years. So if an old collection account gets transferred from one agency to another, that "activity" can extend the reporting by another seven years. Paying off that collection account can have the same effect.

Credit Scoring

Credit scoring for mortgages is perhaps one of the single most important changes in mortgage lending over the past decade. Credit scoring is a numerical assessment of a person's credit, and it denotes the client's likelihood of defaulting on a loan. The higher the client's score, the less likely he or she is to make late payments on a loan or default.

Credit scores can range from 300 to 850. Is there an average credit score? Maybe, but credit scores are fluid and can change. An "average" consumer credit score is somewhere around 650. But that doesn't mean a score of 649 is terrible credit. Hardly. That's why you need to have a complete understanding of what credit scores are and what they are not.

I believe the lowest score I've ever seen was in the low 500s and the highest I've ever seen was around 810. And I've seen a lot of loans. Frankly, I don't know if anyone can attain a "perfect" credit score, although I'm sure there are people out there who are trying. Sort of like an athlete trying to get a perfect 10 in an Olympic event.

Where do credit scores come from? A company called Fair Isaac Corporation, or FICO for short, developed a system that assigns a three-digit number to a credit report. All three credit bureaus use FICO's credit-scoring engine.

Credit scores evaluate several factors. So many points are issued for no late payments, more points for how long the client has had credit, more points for low balances, and so on. Points can be deducted for things such as being more than 30, 60, 90, or 120 days late on a payment; going over a credit limit; or other such unfortunate events.

Scores are not based on a single event but rather on a snapshot of the previous two-year period. That's why one negative item on a credit report may not, by itself, damage a score. Rather, that one negative item combined with other negative items can kill a score. I've seen excellent credit scores with an open collection account, for example. The collection account was absolutely the only negative item on the report; the client had perfect credit otherwise.

Conventional mortgages and government mortgages do not approve nor deny loans based upon FICO scores. There may be certain "boutique" loans, such as 100-percent programs or certain first-time homebuyer loans that have score requirements, but there is no such thing as a minimum credit score for a conventional or government loan. However, lenders may offer better pricing for a particular loan program or reduce the interest rate by a quarter point for a credit score above 720 for example.

The Role of Credit Scores

Because credit scoring is relatively new, there are also common misunderstandings about what scores can and can't do.

When a loan officer pulls a credit score, the officer is actually pulling three scores, one from each bureau. Some falsely think that these scores are added together and then averaged. Not true. In fact, lenders will throw out the highest score and the lowest score and use the middle one.

There is a reason for doing this. The three credit bureaus are located in three distinct regions of the United States. If an individual has lived all of his or her life in Oregon, for instance, all of the credit data will be limited to businesses and transactions in that section of the country. In this instance, TransUnion would carry most of her credit information, but Equifax in Atlanta wouldn't have as many entries. That's why even though all three bureaus use the same FICO engine, they'll almost always have different scores.

I've seen credit reports where one score was 760, the lowest score was 620, and the middle score was 680. In this case, a lender would use 680. By using the middle number and not the highest and the lowest, lenders feel they can get a better picture of a borrower's credit profile. As the loan officer, you will know the middle score is used for loan underwriting regardless of whether a bank or a wholesale lender is looking at the score.

If the client is using another person as a co-borrower for a mortgage, such as a spouse, friend, relative, or a business partner, then what number do lenders use? Each person on the application also has three numbers. If one person's middle score is 770 and the other person's is 570, what happens then?

Lenders won't average the scores. They have to consider the lower score just as much as they would a higher one. But the irony here is that a high score won't compensate for a low score, but a low score can kill a deal.

In the case of multiple borrowers on one application, lenders will use the score of the borrower who makes the most money. If the person with 770 made $5,000 per month and the person with the 570 number made $10,000 per month, guess what? The score for loan purposes is 570, not 770. Conversely, if the 770 made $10,000 and the 570 made $5,000, the lenders will use the 770 score.

But what if the incomes aren't that much different, or in many cases, almost the same? That's when the bad score can really hurt. There's no way around it for loans that have low scores.

Because a single event doesn't dictate a credit score, paying off any negative credit items won't immediately affect a score. For example, consider what happens if your client's FICO score comes in at 620 but your client needs 630. When you review the credit report, you discover a recent collection account that hasn't been paid. Your client mistakenly rushes to the collection agency, pays the debt, then documents the transaction, and waits for the new score to be calculated. Guess what? Little or no change. In fact, the score could actually drop a little because there was new activity on the collection item.

There is considerable confusion regarding credit scores and rates. There is no one-on-one correlation between a score and a rate for conventional or government products. If your clients are approved for a conventional Fannie Mae loan and their credit score is 600, you shouldn't be getting a much higher rate if under the very same loan program another borrower has a 700 score.

In fact, many websites make this mistake and actually post what rate your clients would likely get if the credit score was such-and-such. A chart on a popular website makes such a claim.

This chart shows that if the FICO score were 620 to 639, the borrower's interest rate could be 7.00%, but a score from 640 to 659 could command 6.45%. That's a drop of more than a half of a percent. On a $200,000 mortgage that difference in rate is about $73 per month, or nearly $9,000 over the next ten years. Still further, the table shows a rate of 5.41% if your borrowers are lucky enough to have a score over 760. That payment goes to about $1,124, or about $206 lower than the 7.00% rate.

But having closed thousands of mortgage loans, I can tell you that's not how it works, and I think too many potential clients simply don't apply for a loan if they see that their scores will cost them $200 more each month.

Although in general it attempts to explain the importance of credit scores, such information makes two false assumptions:

1. A simple one-point change in a credit score can affect an interest rate by half a percent or more.

2. Credit scores are the only determining factor when handing out interest rates.

Some loan programs lend under different guidelines than conventional or government programs. Sometimes private lenders make these unconventional loans because they intend to keep rather than sell them. Other times, subprime lenders make these loans, and the borrower's credit score is in fact the determining factor in rate.

So the method of applying a rate with a particular score works with a smaller part of the available loan choices. Fannie Mae, Freddie Mac, the VA, and the FHA work with nearly 80 percent of the mortgages available in the marketplace today, and such rigid scoring considerations simply don't apply to those loans. Claiming that if the score were 639 instead of 640 means that the payment automatically goes up by $70 on a $200,000 30-year mortgage is nonsense.

Again, although there are specific loan programs that might require a particular score, scoring alone is rarely the single determining factor. I recall a client a couple of years ago that applied for a refinance. His ratios were a little high, around 45 percent for the housing ratio, and he didn't have much money in the bank so his liquid asset count was marginal. His credit score was low: 580.

If the online charts were correct, this person would not even get a rate quote because his score was so low. If he had paid attention to score claims, it's likely he would have never even applied for the refinance and lowered his monthly payments. But he got approved anyway, and he got an interest rate typically reserved for those with 760 or above scores. He got the exact same points and fees as another client who had a 785 score.

This gentleman's loan was $185,000, although his property was worth about $650,000. Thus he had a 28 percent loan-to-value (LTV) ratio. The AUS took his considerable equity into consideration and he got the best rate available. On the other hand, if this borrower's property had an appraised value of only $200,000, it's doubtful he would have gotten the loan—his LTV would have been 92.5 percent. The credit score was extremely low, but other factors played into his approval, and he got the loan he wanted.

Advising Your Client About How to Raise His or Her Score

If many loans don't rely on a score to approve or deny a mortgage applicant, then why try to improve them? Because a credit score isn't a number, it's an indication of credit standing. It's like getting an A on a test. Yes, the A is important, but it's a result of knowing all the answers to the quiz. A credit score is a result of credit patterns. Improve the credit score, and you're really improving the credit profile.

To help your clients improve their scores, you need to know what makes a good score and what makes a bad score. There is no magic formula. Well, maybe there is, but you can bet FICO won't give you its algorithms. Regardless, there are some proven principles that you need to be aware of.

Pay The Bills on Time

The first is the most obvious, but it means paying the accounts on time. Every time. Payment history makes up 35 percent of the credit score. If your clients have late payments on their credit reports, make sure they're not in error. Then put as much time as possible between the late payments and when your clients apply for a mortgage. Because FICO looks primarily at the most recent past, say the previous 24 months, your borrowers need to at least keep the credit report clean for that period.

A 30+ late payment hurts a score, but not as much as a 60+, 90+, or 120+. If the payments hit consistently between 90+ days and 120+ days late, it's likely the creditor will close the account and turn it over to a collection agency.

Having collection accounts hurts a score more than a 30+ late payment. So do charge-offs. Charge-offs are when a lender gets tired of trying to collect and simply wipes the debt off its books.

Rectify Public Records

Public records hurt the score. Do your clients have civil financial judgments against them? Did someone sue your client over an unpaid debt? These kinds of public records can kill a credit score.

So can tax liens, which indicate that the client hasn't paid his or her taxes on time. Tax liens can be for overdue property taxes or local, state, and federal income tax obligations. If tax bills are looming or possible judgments are coming down the pike, attempt to get them settled before they become a public record.

Avoid Bankruptcy If Possible

If there is a foreclosure, the client's credit score will dive. A bankruptcy is worse. But the worst credit mark goes to a borrower who defaults on his or her mortgage by filing Chapter 7 or Chapter 13. Homeowners who get into a financial mess have a choice: keep the home out of the bankruptcy and continue making payments on it, or include the home in the bankruptcy. Certain state bankruptcy laws dictate whether a primary residence can be part of a bankruptcy.

Limit the Available Credit

The next greatest impact on a credit score is what is coined "available credit." Various reports indicate that this single item makes up about 30 percent of the credit scoring model.

Available credit is the amount of credit available to your client compared with the amount actually owed. It is expressed as a percentage. For example, if your client has a $10,000 credit limit on his credit card and owes $8,000 on the same credit card, then the client has 20 percent available credit.

There is a magic number for available credit. That number is 70 percent. Your clients should strive to have 70 percent of their available credit lines ready, willing, and able to charge against.

That means if they have a combined $30,000 credit limit on various credit cards, they should strive to get the balance to 30 percent of the credit limit, leaving them with a 70 percent available-credit number. Thirty percent of $30,000 is $9,000. Likewise, if the credit limit is $100,000, then $30,000 is the target number. They should keep as many trade lines open as possible along with low balances.

Think about the 30 percent balance for a moment in terms of credit responsibility. How will a lender really, really know the borrower is going to pay debt back if the borrower has never charged anything? That's a good question. And in terms of calculating a credit score, that's exactly the question the scoring model wants answered.

By establishing credit lines, using them, and then paying them back on time, a borrower hits three very important bits of score calculation. Not only was the borrower creditworthy enough in the beginning to be granted credit, she was also responsible with that line by not charging up to the limit. Further, the amounts she did in fact charge were paid back on time, every time.

Let's look at that for a moment. If your clients are trying to improve their scores, you need to look at their credit reports, look at their available credit, and then suggest that they begin to methodically pay those balances down to about one-third of the limits. Tell them to concentrate on one account at a time when doing this, particularly by choosing the highest-limit account with the highest interest rate. They should pay that card or credit line down aggressively until they reach the magic percentage, then work on another account.

But whatever they do, don't have them pay off accounts completely and then cancel the accounts altogether. This will actually hurt rather than help their scores.

It used to be that creditors wanted applicants to close unused accounts. In fact, I recall asking borrowers to close out accounts before I could approve their loan. The logic worked this way: If a borrower had high debt ratios or his ratios were reaching acceptable limits and the borrower had an open line of credit, it could then be possible that the borrower would get approved for the loan, charge up the maximum on all his or her cards, then suddenly, wham-o! His ratios would be through the roof and he couldn't pay the mortgage any longer.

It happened all the time, especially where I was in California, where home prices were higher than in most parts of the country and people were forced to stretch ratios more.

People with absolutely sterling credit would be asked to close out an account before we would approve a loan. It sounds silly, but in fact that was good advice back then. We asked people to review their credit reports periodically for the standard stuff such as mistakes or other people's names on their reports, but also for any old credit lines or department store cards they had forgotten about. We wanted them to close those down.

Today, credit scores are much more important than how many lines of credit are open to you. Remember that one of the most important things one can do to improve a credit score is keep one's balances around one-third of available credit lines. If your clients close out an account and still have balances, they're messing with the desired percentage.

Let's say your client has three cards, each with $10,000 credit line, and owes a total of $5,000. The available credit is $30,000 and the balance is $5,000. The client has an 83 percent available-credit number. Not bad for purposes of getting a good credit score.

Now if the client decides to close two of those cards, the credit line falls to $10,000 and the balance stays at $5,000. The available credit zooms to 50 percent. This will hurt the client's score. By closing accounts without making subsequent adjustments in balances, the score is worse than before.

Another event that can affect a credit score is a credit inquiry. A credit inquiry occurs when another creditor obtains the credit report.

Multiple credit inquiries hurt a credit score if those inquiries are for different types of accounts.

Your client getting her own free credit report is an inquiry, but it's a consumer inquiry and doesn't affect her credit score. Going to different automobile dealerships and having each dealer pull her credit report is considered a single inquiry even though five dealerships may have pried into the score. An inquiry is a credit review for a single event. If your clients are buying one car, not five, over a particular period of time, that's only one inquiry.

Likewise, if they're applying for a mortgage to buy a new house and apply with three different mortgage companies, that would be considered only one inquiry, not three, because they're just looking for one mortgage.

If your clients refinanced last year then later decided to sell the home and apply for a new mortgage, that would be considered two inquiries because they applied for two different loans at different times. That can hurt the score as well.

The presence of several inquiries on the report could indicate that a person is getting himself into financial trouble down the road. If your borrowers are opening up a credit line to buy a new boat for the lake house, that might be just fine. But if they are opening up credit lines to pay for stuff they simply don't have the money for, they might be hurting their scores.

Probably the best way to improve a credit score is to continue doing the things that make up a good score. If your client has already gotten a good score, then she should simply do the exact same things that got her that excellent score. Many times, those who first enter the world of credit find themselves surprised that someone will lend them money when they don't have any.

· C H A P T E R ·

Interest Rates: How They're Set, How to Quote Them

S ome of the biggest myths and mysteries center around mortgage interest rates—how they're set, who sets them, and where in the heck they come from in the first place. It's important to be able to address these issues. This knowledge will also help you make more money on each loan.

How Interest Rates Are Set

Mortgage rates are not set by the Federal Reserve Board or any other government entity. The Fed, among other things, controls the cost of money that banks borrow. Banks borrow money from the Fed and various sources at one interest rate, then mark that interest rate up a notch or two when they lend that money out to their individual and business customers.

One of the main challenges the Fed undertakes is controlling inflation. The Fed does so by influencing whether money is more or less expensive to borrow. The more expensive money is, meaning the higher interest rates are, the more the Fed is trying to control inflation.

Inflation is a silent killer of an economy. If a farmer agrees to sell 100 bushels of wheat for $1,000 but after 6 months that $1,000 is now worth only $900 due to inflation, the farmer loses money. Businesses lose money. The government loses money. And when someone loses money, the natural thing to do to make up for it is to raise prices. This stokes the flames of inflation. Inflation is such a difficult phenomenon to stop once it gets started, so the Fed tries to make sure it never gets started in the first place.

The Fed attempts to control inflation by controlling the cost of funds. It does this by influencing the Federal Funds rate and controlling the Federal Discount rate.

The Fed Funds rate is the rate at which banks make short-term loans to each other, usually overnight. For many who don't understand why banks would do that, it's simple if you recall that banks have certain asset-reserve requirements. For every loan it makes, a bank must have a predetermined amount of cash sitting in its vaults. This reserve requirement is a direct result of the infamous bank runs that helped kick start the Great Depression, and sometimes banks need to borrow to have the legally required reserves.

The Fed also regulates the Discount rate, which is the amount set aside for short term lending that is issued by the Federal government directly. Banks can also borrow from the Federal Reserve at discounted rates.

A rise in lending activity is an indication of a strengthening economy. A strong economy increases the demand for money because more businesses are willing to borrow more to expand. When the demand for capital increases, lenders can charge more and often do. But if the economy is not monitored carefully, inflation can kick in.

The Fed looks for signs of an improving economy: lots of new jobs created, lots of new cars being sold, lots of, well, lots of everything good for the economy. If there are too many consecutive signs of a booming economy, the Federal Reserve Board will decide whether to raise the Discount rate at its next meeting.

On the other hand, if the economy seems to be going into a slump, or is currently in one, the Fed will do just the opposite—lower the Discount rate. Lower rates make the cost of money cheaper. In turn, if businesses can borrow more money with less cost, they'll be encouraged to expand, hire more people, and sell more goods.

Your clients may say something such as, "Hey, I saw the Fed lowered rates yesterday, what kind of rate can I get today?" That's not really how it works. Fixed mortgage rates are set by the open markets, specifically mortgage bonds that are bought and sold throughout every trading day. Lenders set their mortgage rates based upon these mortgage bonds, specifically a Fannie Mae or Ginnie Mae bond.

As the price of these bonds goes up or down, so do lenders price their mortgage rates. Mortgage rates are tied to their specific index. Thirty-year rates are tied to a 30-year bond. Fifteen-year rates are tied to a 15-year bond. Conventional loans and government loans both have their indexes. And it's these bonds being bought and sold by traders, public and private investors, that set market rates.

Since bonds are predictable, the return isn't as sexy. Instead, bond owners invest because of that guarantee. They don't want any surprises. But who would invest in a mortgage bond when there are other investment opportunities that could pay much more? When the stock market is going crazy and it seems that everyone is investing something in stocks to get a great return, then investors typically pull their money out of those staid bonds and use that cash to buy high-flying stocks. Remember the dot-com boom? Real estate? Pet rocks? Betamax?

Bonds must compete for those same investment dollars, and when money pulls out of a mortgage bond to chase higher earnings elsewhere, the seller of those bonds must make adjustments to the price of the bond. Less demand means that a lower price will be issued. And a lower price means a higher return, or yield, on that bond.

What causes a price to go up or down? Changes in demand. If the stock market is tanking, then investors might want to sell stocks and put more money in the safe return guaranteed by bonds. But if more people want the same thing, then guess what happens? That's right, the price goes up due to increased demand. A bond holder can get more money for the same bond. When the price goes up, the yield, or return, goes down.

Every single day, all day long, there is a department at a mortgage company that does nothing except watch the prices of various mortgage bonds to determine how they'll set their mortgage rates for the day. This department is called the "secondary" division of the lender, and every mortgage banking operation has one. It's here that rates are set that are distributed to you, the loan officer.

As each business day opens, all of these secondary departments watch the opening trading of the various mortgage bonds. If the price of a 30-year Fannie Mae is selling on the open market at the same price as yesterday, then rates on similar mortgages for that day will probably be the same.

If the price of the bond goes up, the yield then goes down, meaning rates get lower. If there is less demand for a mortgage bond, the yield goes up, raising mortgage rates. This goes on all day long. And mortgage prices change constantly.

Mortgage bonds are priced in basis points. One basis point equals 1/100th of a percent. The secondary department must be wary of any bond-price swings throughout the day. If the price of a particular mortgage bond moves by just a few points, say three or four, the secondary department will usually not change rates.

If, however, there is a move in price of, say, 15 or more basis points, you can expect the lender to make a price adjustment. Different lenders may have different thresholds for price changes, but most will start to get nervous if bond prices move significantly one way or another. You can bet that if bond prices change by 20 or more basis points there will be a midday rate change.

Mostly, the rates themselves won't change as much as the cost to the consumer will change. For example, if a borrower can get a 6.00% loan by paying a one-point fee and mortgage bond prices fall by 50 basis points, lenders will typically adjust the rates to 6.125% or charge an extra half-point fee to get the 6.00%. Don't confuse basis points with discount points. They're different.

Secondary departments watch mortgage bond pricing and the effects of various economic and political events that might trigger a bond selloff or a bond rally. For example, did the latest unemployment numbers show strong job gains? Then one can expect money to move from bonds and into stocks. That means higher interest rates.

Mortgage-Rate Services

How can you find mortgage bond prices throughout the day? One, you could pay thousands of dollars every year to a reporting agency such as Bear Stearns, or you could use a mortgage-rate service. I use a mortgage-rate service.

Mortgage bond pricing isn't available to the general public. But you can get it from companies that provide that information directly to loan officers. There are a few companies that provide that data. The two I like most are MBS Quoteline, at www.mbsquoteline.com and Mortgage Market Guide, at www.mortgagemarketguide.com.

You'll pay for this data, though much less than if you went directly to the source. Check out both. MBS Quoteline is a little less expensive, but Mortgage Market Guide is more thorough and provides you with so many educational tools and marketing ideas that it's worth the extra money.

If you're a mortgage broker, you will get your mortgage rates from your various wholesale lenders by different methods. Some you will go online to get, others will send them to you via e-mail, and a few others might fax them to you.

And they'll all come to you at about the same time each day, usually a couple of hours after the markets have opened. This gives each secondary department time to calculate what its rates will be on any given day.

Because all lenders set their rates on the very same index, you won't find one lender at 7.00% and another at 6.00%. In many cases they'll be exactly the same or extremely close, most likely no more than one-quarter of a point apart. Sometimes you'll see more of a spread, but not very often. The most you'll ever see is a half-point between one wholesale lender and another, but that will be extremely, extremely rare. And as mentioned previously, low, low prices can mean poor service.

Figuring Out What to Charge Using Rate Sheets and Rate Locks

Rate sheets will be confusing to you at first. Each mortgage program will have various rates available for it. A 30-year fixed-rate loan will carry 10–15 different rates or more in 1/8-percent increments.

You will also see "lock" periods for each given rate. A lock period is the time during which the lender will guarantee the availability of a particular interest rate. Borrowers can buy different lock periods, and the prices vary by length. For example, the lock period is one price for 15 days, a slightly higher price for 30 days, 45 days, 60 days, and beyond. The longer your customer wants or needs to lock in a rate, the more expensive it will be. Normally, each additional 30 days costs you or your client another quarter point. Upgrading to a 60-day lock from a 30-day lock on a $400,000 loan could cost another $1,000.

This process is the same for 15-year rates, adjustable rates, hybrids—any and all mortgage programs your lender offers. I worked for a mortgage banker for several years, and our rate sheets were eight pages long and listed over 100 loan programs. No kidding.

The rates you receive are not consumer or retail rates, they're wholesale. You have to mark up the interest rates you get, which is

your profit on the loan. Wholesale rates can be quoted to you two different ways.

Point Increments

The first way is to quote the price as a percentage of the loan amount.
The percentages are in 1/8-point increments. Rates quoted in this manner look like this:

Rate	15 Days	30 Days	60 Days
7.00%	1.00	1.125	1.375
7.125%	.75	.875	1.125
7.25%	.50	.625	.875
7.375%	.25	.375	.625
7.50%	0.00	.125	.375

So if you had a loan that was closing within 15 days, you wanted to
make a one-point profit on the loan, and your client wanted a 7.00%
loan, you would take the 7.00% row, follow across to the 15 Days column, add one point to the point the lender charges for the loan, and
the result is two points charged to the borrower. The lender gets one
point, you get one point.

Mortgage lenders normally price interest rates in 1/8-percent increments. For each 1/8-percent in rate drop, your cost goes up by one-
quarter point, which is $250 on a $100,000 loan. Although lenders
price in 1/8 increments, they use the decimal equivalent when posting
their prices. So 1/8 equals 0.125%; 1/4 equals 0.25%; 3/8 equals
0.375%; and so on.

If your borrower needed 60 days to close but wanted to keep his
points as low as possible, you would first go to 7.50%, then move across
to the 60 Days column. You add your one point to the 0.375% to make
the total fee to the borrower 1.375%.

Notice that as the rates get lower, the cost to you and your client
goes higher. The longer you want to secure an interest rate, the more
it costs you.

In fact, for each 30 days you need, on average it costs you another quarter point. That's the average; there is never a constant trade-off between a rate and a cost, but these figures are the most common and any variance will be minimal.

You control what you quote your borrower. If you want to make a one-percent origination fee on top of the one point you added to the 7.50% 60-day quote, there's nothing stopping you.

The double-edged sword is that pricing mortgages for retail is like any other business—you want to make as much as you can on each unit (mortgage) but not price yourself so high that your client goes elsewhere.

Par-Pricing Method

Another method lenders use is the par-pricing method. Instead of a particular interest rate costing you nothing, or 0.00, the lender prices it similar to how a mortgage bond is priced. A 0.00 equals par, or "even-steven." Anything above or below that is represented as a percentage of "par."

Although 100 equals no points, 99.75 equals one-quarter point (i.e., one hundred minus 25 basis points equals 99.75). That loan costs you, at wholesale, one-quarter point. A loan priced at 99.50 costs half a point, and so on.

When a loan "costs" you one point or half a point, that doesn't mean *you* pay it, it simply means that is the wholesale price. It is your client who will pay all points, you don't pay them. It's simply that is the wholesale price the lender is offering to you, who then marks the price up for the borrower.

Rate	15 Days	30 Days	60 Days
7.00%	99.00	98.875	98.625
7.125%	99.25	99.125	98.875
7.25%	99.50	99.375	99.125

| 7.375% | 99.75 | 99.625 | 99.375 |
| 7.50% | 100 | 98.875 | 96.625 |

These rate sheets are identical, they're simply expressed differently by the lender: 7.25% at 30 days would cost you 99.375, or 0.625 points. Get it? Subtract 99.375 from 100.00. You get 0.625. On a $200,000 loan, 0.625 points is $1,250, or 5/8 of a point.

Figure 9-1 shows another example of a retail rate sheet.

This will be sort of hard to get used to at first, but train yourself to translate 1/8% into decimal equivalents. Don't worry, I know it's confusing but you'll get it.

Figure 9-1. A sample retail rate sheet.

Alethes Wholesale Rates

30 YR FIXED CONVENTIONAL			15 YR FIXED CONVENTIONAL			40 YR FIXED CONVENTIONAL		
Rate	15 day	30 Day	Rate	15 day	30 Day	(95% max ltv for PR & 2nd home;90% NOO)		
7.250	(3.750)	(3.625)	7.125	(3.500)	(3.375)	Rate	15 day	30 Day
7.125	(3.500)	(3.375)	7.000	(3.375)	(3.250)	7.125	n/a	n/a
7.000	(3.250)	(3.125)	6.875	(3.250)	(3.125)	7.000	(2.375)	(2.250)
6.875	(3.000)	(2.875)	6.750	(3.500)	(3.375)	6.875	(2.125)	(2.000)
6.750	(2.750)	(2.625)	6.625	(3.000)	(2.875)	6.750	(1.875)	(1.750)
6.625	(2.375)	(2.250)	6.500	(2.875)	(2.750)	6.625	(1.500)	(1.375)
6.500	(2.125)	(2.000)	6.375	(2.500)	(2.375)	6.500	(1.250)	(1.125)
6.375	(1.625)	(1.500)	6.250	(2.125)	(2.000)	6.375	(0.625)	(0.500)
6.250	(1.250)	(1.125)	6.125	(1.750)	(1.625)	6.250	(0.125)	0.000
6.125	(0.875)	(0.750)	6.000	(1.375)	(1.250)	6.125	0.375	0.500
6.000	(0.375)	(0.250)	5.875	(1.000)	(0.875)	6.000	1.000	1.125
5.875	0.125	0.250	5.750	(0.500)	(0.375)	**Max net price posted**		
5.750	0.625	0.750	5.625	(0.125)	0.000			
5.625	1.125	1.250	5.500	0.250	0.375			
Max net price: -3.375			**Max net price: -2.750**					

Conventional Fixed Adjustments:
(40-10 yr, Alethes Express SISA, My Community)
Ficos < 620 worsen .500
20 yr term improve 30 yr .250
$250K+ improve .125
$75K to $99,999 worsen .250
$50k to $74,999 worsen .750
$49,999 & below worsen 1.750
90.01-95% Duplex worsen .500
NOO 75.01-90% worsen 1.750
NOO < = 75% worsen 1.000
*C/out 70.01-80% worsen .500
*C/out 80.01-90% worsen .750
Escrow waiver worsen .250
CLTV 90.01-95% worsen .250 (n/a for flex & interest 1st)
Interest 1st worsen .750
Interest 1st w/ LTV 90.01-95% worsen .250
Interest 1st > 75% LTV w/ sub.financing worsen .250
Fnma Flex 97 worsen .500 (35% MI)
Fnma Flex 100 worsen 1.000 (35% MI)
Fnma Flex (80/20)- FICO >= 700 w/subordinate financing worsen 1.000
Fnma Flex (80/20)- FICO 680-699 w/subordinate financing worsen 1.250
Fnma Flex (80/20)- FICO < 680 w/subordinate financing worsen 1.500
Manufactured Hsg discontinued
+AK,AR,CO,IN,MO,NM,OK,TN worsen .250
+AL,KY,SC properties worsen .500

*See TX Cash Out Rate Sheet for quotes on primaries in TX

ALETHES EXPRESS - STATED INCOME / STATED ASSET
*Priced off standard conventional pricing & adjustments
*Available products: 30 - 10 yr fixed; 30 yr interest first;
3/1, 5/1, 7/1 arms; 5/1 interest only arm

Purchase & Rate / Term Refi
Occupancy	LTV	CLTV	Fico
PR - 1 unit	90%	90%	680
2nd home- 1 unit	90%	90%	680
NOO - 1 unit	75%	75%	700

Cash Out Refi (not available in Texas)
PR - 1 unit	70%	70%	720
2nd home & NOO - not permitted			

Notes:
1) The "Alethes Express" SISA documentation option is only available with a custom "Alethes Express" automated approval
2) Please put "Alethes Express SISA" in your subject line and email point file to aus@alethes.biz
3) Must have AUS approval before locking
4) Max dti 45%. Income stated must be consistent with line of work
5) 4506 required

---

30 YR My Community			40 YR My Community		
Rate	15 day	30 Day	Rate	15 day	30 Day
7.750	n/a	n/a	7.500	n/a	n/a
7.625	(2.875)	(2.750)	7.375	(2.375)	(2.250)
7.500	(2.750)	(2.625)	7.250	(2.125)	(2.000)
7.375	(2.625)	(2.500)	7.125	(1.875)	(1.750)
7.250	(2.250)	(2.125)	7.000	(1.500)	(1.375)
7.125	(2.125)	(2.000)	6.875	(1.250)	(1.125)
7.000	(1.875)	(1.750)	6.750	(0.625)	(0.500)
6.875	(1.625)	(1.500)	6.625	(0.125)	0.000
6.750	(1.125)	(1.000)	6.500	0.375	0.500
6.625	(0.875)	(0.750)	6.375	1.000	1.125
6.500	(0.625)	(0.500)	**6%**		
6.375	(0.250)	(0.125)	**seller**		
6.250	0.375	0.500	**contribution**		

My Community adjustments
(see conv'l adj. for loan size & geographic)
My Community 97 (1 unit) -.125 to RATE
My Community 3-4 unit +.125 to RATE
Interest 1st (10 yrs): +.125 to RATE on 30 yr; +.250 to RATE on 40 yr

30 YR EXP. APP'L LVL 1			30 YR EXP. APP'L LVL 2			30 YR EXP. APP'L LVL 3		
Rate	15 day	30 Day	Rate	15 day	30 Day	Rate	15 day	30 Day
7.750	(2.500)	(2.375)	8.125	(2.500)	(2.375)	8.500	(2.500)	(2.375)
7.625	(2.250)	(2.125)	8.000	(2.250)	(2.125)	8.375	(2.250)	(2.125)
7.500	(2.000)	(1.875)	7.875	(2.000)	(1.875)	8.250	(2.000)	(1.875)
7.375	(1.750)	(1.625)	7.750	(1.750)	(1.625)	8.125	(1.750)	(1.625)
7.250	(1.625)	(1.500)	7.625	(1.625)	(1.500)	8.000	(1.625)	(1.500)
7.125	(1.250)	(1.125)	7.500	(1.250)	(1.125)	7.875	(1.250)	(1.125)
7.000	(0.875)	(0.750)	7.375	(0.875)	(0.750)	7.750	(0.875)	(0.750)
6.875	(0.625)	(0.500)	7.250	(0.625)	(0.500)	7.625	(0.625)	(0.500)
6.750	(0.250)	(0.125)	7.125	(0.250)	(0.125)	7.500	(0.250)	(0.125)
6.625	0.125	0.250	7.000	0.125	0.250	7.375	0.125	0.250

Levels 2 & 3 may be eligible for timely payment rewards if stated in the DU findings.
Potential rate reductions for levels 2 & 3 are .500 & 1.000, respectively, after 24 months of timely payments. The cost for this option is .125 to the RATE on a level 2 and .250 to the RATE on a level 3.
*Maximum final price on level 3's is -1.500

---

30 / 25 / 20 YR FIXED GOV'T			15 YR FIXED GOV'T		
			Rate	15 Day	30 Day
Rate	15 Day	30 Day	6.750	(3.000)	(2.875)
7.500	(3.250)	(3.125)	6.500	(2.750)	(2.625)
7.375	(2.375)	(2.250)	6.250	(2.000)	(1.875)
7.250	(3.250)	(3.125)	6.000	(1.625)	(1.500)
7.125	(3.000)	(2.875)	5.750	(0.375)	(0.250)
7.000	(3.250)	(3.125)	5.500	0.125	0.250
6.875	(2.375)	(2.250)			
6.750	(2.250)	(2.125)			
6.625	(2.000)	(1.875)			
6.500	(2.250)	(2.125)			
6.375	(1.375)	(1.250)			
6.250	(1.000)	(0.875)			
6.125	(0.375)	(0.250)			
6.000	(0.625)	(0.500)			
5.875	n/a	n/a			
5.750	n/a	n/a			
5.625	n/a	n/a			
5.500	n/a	n/a			

FHA ONE YR ARM (2.50 Margin)			FHA 3/1 ARM (2.25 Margin)*		
caps: 1 / 5; index: 1 yr T bill			*30 year term only		
Rate	15 Day	30 Day	caps: 1 / 1 / 5; index: 1 yr T bill		
6.000	(1.625)	(1.500)	Rate	15 Day	30 Day
5.750	(1.375)	(1.250)	6.250	(0.875)	(0.750)
5.500	(1.250)	(1.125)	6.125	(0.625)	(0.500)
5.250	(0.125)	0.000	6.000	(0.500)	(0.375)
5.000	0.000	0.125	5.875	(0.250)	(0.125)
4.750	1.250	1.375	5.750	0.000	0.125
4.500	1.375	1.500	5.625	0.500	0.625
			5.500	0.625	0.750

GOV'T Notes / Adjustments:
*loan amounts $50k-$70k worsen .500
*loan amounts below $50k worsen 1.25
*VA loans worsen .250
*Manufactured Hsg worsen 1.500
+TN properties worsen .125
+AR,OK properties worsen .250
+AL,KY,SC properties worsen .500
*Buydown quotes for .125,.250 & .375 rates are as posted. Worsen .500 for 5.5, 6.0, 6.5, 7.0 rates. Buydown subsidy to be collected at closing.

Expiration Dates		Extension / relock policy:
15 Day:	11/17/06	Extension**: (before lock expires)-1 day free, 7 days .125,
30 Day:	12/2/06	15 days .250, 30 days .500.
45 Day:	12/17/06	Relock: (after lock expires)- Relock at worse case
60 Day:	1/1/07	**Multiple extensions may be subject to worse case pricing**
45 day price is .125 less than 30 day		
60 day price is .250 less than 30 day		

Texas Cash Out Refi Rates

30 YR FIXED CONVENTIONAL				15 YR FIXED CONVENTIONAL			
Rate	15 Day	30 Day	45 Day	Rate	15 Day	30 Day	45 Day
7.250	(2.750)	(2.625)	(2.500)	7.125	(2.750)	(2.625)	(2.500)
7.125	(2.625)	(2.500)	(2.375)	7.000	(2.625)	(2.500)	(2.375)
7.000	(2.375)	(2.250)	(2.125)	6.875	(2.250)	(2.125)	(2.000)
6.875	(2.125)	(2.000)	(1.875)	6.750	(2.750)	(2.625)	(2.500)
6.750	(1.875)	(1.750)	(1.625)	6.625	(2.375)	(2.250)	(2.125)
6.625	(1.625)	(1.500)	(1.375)	6.500	(1.250)	(1.125)	(1.000)
6.500	(1.250)	(1.125)	(1.000)	6.375	(1.125)	(1.000)	(0.875)
6.375	(1.000)	(0.875)	(0.750)	6.250	(1.125)	(1.000)	(0.875)
6.250	(0.625)	(0.500)	(0.375)	6.125	(1.000)	(0.875)	(0.750)
6.125	(0.125)	0.000	0.125	6.000	(0.625)	(0.500)	(0.375)

Adjustments: (All adjustments to price)
(Lock period must cover 12 day disclosure and three day right of rescission)
*Loan amounts **$75,000 - $417,000**
*Loan amounts greater than $200K improve price by .125
*Loan amounts $75,000 - $99,999 worsen price by .250
*20 Year Term - improve 30 Year price by .250
*10 Year Term - same price as 15 year
*LTV 70.01-80.00 worsen price by .500 (max program LTV is 80.00%)
*FICO less than 620 and LTV 75.01 - 80.00% worsen price by additional 1.000 (30, 25 & 20 yr only)
*Escrow Waiver worsen price by .250 (must have at least 620 ficos to waive escrows)

Program Notes / Highlights:
*30 / 25 / 20 / 15 / 10 Yr loan terms available
*Primary residences only
*Property types: SFR's and warrantable condos; no 2-4 units
*80.00% maximum LTV
*Loan amounts **$75,000 - $417,000**
*DU / DO approve / eligible or LP accept only; **no expanded approval loans**
*Full doc only; **no stated income loans**
*Non-occupant co-borrowers are not eligible
*12 months seasoning required on all Section 50(a)(6) liens (Texas Cash outs / Home equity liens)
*Loan closing documents will not be drawn until 12 days after a signed loan
    application and signed Alethes MBO 12 Day Disclosure (whichever is later.)
*All Closing Costs (exclusive of pre-paids and Yield Spread Premiums) cannot exceed 3% of the loan amount

Expiration Dates
15 Day:	11/17/06
30 Day:	12/2/06
45 Day:	12/17/06

G Series Alt A Rate Sheet

WHOLESALE

*Locks accepted on approved files only.

Effective Date/Time:
11/3/06
10:24 AM

GT

G- Series ALT - A

G Series Alt A 30 Year Fixed Rate					G Series Alt A 15 Year Fixed Rate				
Rate	**15 Day**	**30 Day**	**45 Day**	**60 Day**		**Rate**	**15 Day**	**30 Day**	**45 Day**	**60 Day**
8.750%	103.750	103.625	103.500	103.375		8.750%	104.000	103.875	103.750	103.625
8.625%	103.625	103.500	103.375	103.250	MAX	8.625%	103.750	103.625	103.500	103.375
8.500%	103.500	103.375	103.250	103.125		8.500%	103.500	103.375	103.250	103.125
8.375%	103.375	103.250	103.125	103.000		8.375%	103.250	103.125	103.000	102.875
8.250%	103.250	103.125	103.000	102.875	ALL IN	8.250%	103.000	102.875	102.750	102.625
8.125%	103.250	103.125	103.000	102.875		8.125%	102.750	102.625	102.500	102.375
8.000%	103.125	103.000	102.875	102.750		8.000%	102.625	102.500	102.375	102.250
7.875%	103.000	102.875	102.750	102.625	PRICE	7.875%	102.500	102.375	102.250	102.125
7.750%	102.875	102.750	102.625	102.500		7.750%	102.375	102.250	102.125	102.000
7.625%	102.625	102.500	102.375	102.250		7.625%	102.250	102.125	102.000	101.875
7.500%	102.500	102.375	102.250	102.125		7.500%	102.000	101.875	101.750	101.625
7.375%	102.250	102.125	102.000	101.875	102.500	7.375%	101.875	101.750	101.625	101.500
7.250%	102.000	101.875	101.750	101.625		7.250%	101.625	101.500	101.375	101.250
7.125%	101.625	101.500	101.375	101.250		7.125%	101.375	101.250	101.125	101.000
7.000%	101.375	101.250	101.125	101.000		7.000%	101.125	101.000	100.875	100.750
6.875%	101.125	101.000	100.875	100.750		6.875%	100.875	100.750	100.625	100.500
6.750%	101.000	100.875	100.750	100.625		6.750%	100.500	100.375	100.250	100.125
6.625%	100.750	100.625	100.500	100.375		6.625%	100.375	100.250	100.125	100.000
6.500%	100.500	100.375	100.250	100.125		6.500%	100.125	100.000	99.875	99.750
6.375%	100.125	100.000	99.875	99.750		6.375%	99.875	99.750	99.625	99.500
6.250%	99.750	99.625	99.500	99.375		6.250%				

G Series Alt A 5/1 LIBOR ARM					G Series Alt A 5/1 I/O LIBOR ARM				
Caps - 5/2/5				2.25 Margin		Caps - 5/2/5				2.25 Margin
Rate	**15 Day**	**30 Day**	**45 Day**	**60 Day**		**Rate**	**15 Day**	**30 Day**	**45 Day**	**60 Day**
8.250%	104.500	104.375	104.250	104.125		8.250%	104.375	104.250	104.125	104.000
8.125%	104.375	104.250	104.125	104.000		8.125%	104.125	104.000	103.875	103.750
8.000%	104.250	104.125	104.000	103.875	MAX	8.000%	104.000	103.875	103.750	103.625
7.875%	104.125	104.000	103.875	103.750		7.875%	103.875	103.750	103.625	103.500
7.750%	103.875	103.750	103.625	103.500		7.750%	103.750	103.625	103.500	103.375
7.625%	103.750	103.625	103.500	103.375	ALL IN	7.625%	103.500	103.375	103.250	103.125
7.500%	103.500	103.375	103.250	103.125		7.500%	103.250	103.125	103.000	102.875
7.375%	103.250	103.125	103.000	102.875		7.375%	103.000	102.875	102.750	102.625
7.250%	103.000	102.875	102.750	102.625	PRICE	7.250%	102.750	102.625	102.500	102.375
7.125%	102.750	102.625	102.500	102.375		7.125%	102.500	102.375	102.250	102.125
7.000%	102.500	102.375	102.250	102.125		7.000%	102.250	102.125	102.000	101.875
6.875%	102.250	102.125	102.000	101.875	101.500	6.875%	102.000	101.875	101.750	101.625
6.750%	102.000	101.875	101.750	101.625		6.750%	101.750	101.625	101.500	101.375
6.625%	101.750	101.625	101.500	101.375		6.625%	101.500	101.375	101.250	101.125
6.500%	101.375	101.250	101.125	101.000		6.500%	101.125	101.000	100.875	100.750
6.375%	101.125	101.000	100.875	100.750		6.375%	100.875	100.750	100.625	100.500
6.250%	100.875	100.750	100.625	100.500		6.250%	100.625	100.500	100.375	100.250
6.125%	100.875	100.750	100.625	100.500		6.125%	100.625	100.500	100.375	100.250
6.000%	100.500	100.375	100.250	100.125		6.000%	100.250	100.125	100.000	99.875
5.875%	100.250	100.125	100.000	99.875		5.875%	100.000	99.875	99.750	99.625
5.750%	100.000	99.875	99.750	99.625		5.750%	99.750	99.625	99.500	99.375

G Series Alt A 2/6 Arm

Caps - 3/1/5				2.375 Margin	
	Rate	**15 Day**	**30 Day**	**45 Day**	**60 Day**	
	9.000%	103.375	103.250	103.125	103.000	
	8.875%	103.250	103.125	103.000	102.875	
MAX	8.750%	103.000	102.875	102.750	102.625	MAX
	8.625%	102.875	102.750	102.625	102.500	
	8.500%	102.625	102.500	102.375	102.250	
ALL IN	8.375%	102.500	102.375	102.250	102.125	ALL IN
	8.250%	102.375	102.250	102.125	102.000	
	8.125%	102.250	102.125	102.000	101.875	
PRICE	8.000%	102.000	101.875	101.750	101.625	PRICE
	7.875%	101.875	101.750	101.625	101.500	
	7.750%	101.750	101.625	101.500	101.375	
101.500	7.625%	101.625	101.500	101.375	101.250	101.500
	7.500%	101.500	101.375	101.250	101.125	
	7.375%	101.375	101.250	101.125	101.000	
	7.250%	101.250	101.125	101.000	100.875	
	7.125%	101.250	101.125	101.000	100.875	
	7.000%	101.125	101.000	100.875	100.750	

1 Year Libor Index	0.000
6 Month Libor Index	0.000

Adjustments on following page

G Series Alt A Adjustments

Effective Date/Time:
11/3/06
10:24 AM

G-Series ALT - A Adjustments

	LTV with FICO		LTV Range				
	LTV <=65% & FICO => 660	LTV <=65% & FICO < 660	65.01-75.00	75.01-80.00	80.01-85.00	85.01-90.00	90.01-95.00
Second Home	0.000	-0.500	-0.750	-1.000	-1.250	-1.750	
Second Home	0.000	-0.500	-0.750	-1.000	-1.250	-1.750	
Investment	0.000	-0.750	-0.750	-1.000	-1.500	-2.000	n/a
CashOut	0.000	-0.250	-0.250	-0.500	-0.750	-1.000	-1.250
2 Units	0.000	-0.250	-0.250	-0.250	-0.500	-0.500	-0.500
3-4 Units	0.000	-0.750	-0.750	-0.750	-1.000	-1.250	n/a
Condo <=4	0.000	-0.250	-0.250	-0.500	-0.500	-0.500	-0.500
Condo > 4	-0.250	-1.000	-1.000	-1.250	-1.250	-1.250	-1.500
Non-Warrantable Condo	-0.750	-1.250	-1.250	-1.750	-1.750	-1.750	-1.750
Condotel	-0.750	-1.250	-1.250	-1.750	-1.750	-1.750	n/a
Mixed Use Property	0.000	-0.250	-0.250	-0.250	n/a	n/a	n/a
Rural Property	0.000	-0.250	-0.250	-0.250	-0.500	-0.500	-0.500
Manufactured (Rate Adj)	5.000%	5.000%	5.000%	n/a	n/a	n/a	n/a
DTI > 45% <=50%	-0.500	-0.500	-0.500	-0.500	-0.625	-0.750	-0.750
DTI > 50% (max 55%)	-0.750	-0.750	-0.750	-0.750	-0.750	-0.750	-0.750
	LTV <=65% & FICO => 660	LTV <=65% & FICO < 660	65.01-75.00	75.01-80.00	80.01-85.00	85.01-90.00	90.01-95.00
SIVA	0.000	-0.250	-0.375	-0.500	-0.625	-0.875	-1.500
SISA	0.000	-0.625	-0.750	-1.000	-1.500	-2.000	-2.500
NIVA	0.000	-0.500	-0.625	-0.750	-1.000	-1.250	-2.000
NINANE	0.000	-0.750	-0.875	-1.500	-2.000	-2.375	-3.000
FICO >=780	+0.250	+0.250	+0.250	+0.250	+0.250	+0.250	+0.250
FICO 720 - 779	+0.125	+0.125	+0.125	+0.125	+0.125	+0.125	+0.125
FICO 620 - 679	-0.250	-0.250	-0.250	-0.250	-0.500	-0.500	-0.500
Foreign National	-0.500	-0.500	-0.500	-0.500	n/a	n/a	n/a
$40,000 - $60,000	-1.500	-1.500	-1.500	-1.500	-1.500	-1.500	-1.500
$60,001 - $75,000	-1.000	-1.000	-1.000	-1.000	-1.000	-1.000	-1.000
$100,000 - $417,000	+0.375	+0.375	+0.375	+0.375	+0.375	+0.375	+0.375
$417,001-$650,000	-0.250	-0.500	-0.500	-0.625	-0.875	-1.250	-1.750
$650,001-$1,000,000	-0.500	-1.000	-1.000	-1.250	n/a	n/a	n/a
$1,000,001-$2,000,000	-1.000	-1.250	n/a	n/a	n/a	n/a	n/a
No MI	n/a	n/a	n/a	n/a	-1.500	-2.500	-3.125
CLTV >95% <=100%	-0.250	-0.250	-0.250	-0.250	-0.250	-0.250	-0.250
CLTV >90% <=95%	0.000	0.000	0.000	-0.125	-0.125	n/a	n/a
Escrow Waiver*	-0.125	-0.250	-0.250	-0.250	n/a	n/a	n/a
30 yr fixed Int Only	-0.375	-0.375	-0.375	-0.375	-0.375	-0.375	-0.375

Stacked Enhancements	LTV <=65% & FICO => 660	LTV <=65% & FICO < 660	65.01-75.00	75.01-80.00	80.01-85.00	85.01-90.00	90.01-95.00
Second Home/Condo <= 4 Stories/Standard Doc	0.000	+0.250	+0.250	+0.500	+0.500	+0.500	+0.500
Second Home/Condo > 4 Stories/Standard Doc	0.000	+0.250	+0.250	+0.500	+0.500	+0.500	+0.500
Investment/Condo <= 4 Stories/Standard Doc	0.000	+0.250	+0.250	+0.250	+0.250	+0.250	n/a
Investment/Condo > 4 Stories/Standard Doc	0.000	+0.250	+0.250	+0.250	+0.250	+0.250	n/a
Primary/Condo <= 4 Stories/SIVA	0.000	+0.250	+0.250	+0.250	+0.250	+0.250	+0.250
Primary/Condo > 4 Stories/SIVA	0.000	+0.250	+0.250	+0.250	+0.250	+0.250	+0.250
Second Home/Condo <= 4 Stories/SIVA	0.000	+0.500	+0.500	+0.750	+0.750	+0.750	+0.750
Second Home/Condo > 4 Stories/SIVA	0.000	+0.500	+0.500	+0.750	+0.750	+0.750	+0.750
Investment/Condo <= 4 Stories/SIVA	0.000	+0.375	+0.375	+0.375	+0.375	+0.375	n/a
Investment/Condo > 4 Stories/SIVA	0.000	+0.375	+0.375	+0.375	+0.375	+0.375	n/a

1 Year Libor Index	5.341
6 Month Libor Index	5.388

Notes: Positive number improves price; negative number worsens price
*Escrow waivers require a fico score of at least 700
No geographical price adjustors for other states

A sample retail rate sheet, *continued*.

S Series Alt A Rate Sheet*

Effective Date/Time:
11/3/06
10:24 AM

*In general, use the S Series Alt A Product for higher loan limits and expanded fico score guidelines. See Guidetrac for details. No hits for fico scores and DTI.

S Series ALT - A

	S Series Alt A 30 Year Fixed Rate						S Series Alt A 15 Year Fixed Rate			
Rate	15 Day	30 Day	45 Day	60 Day		Rate	15 day	30 Day	45 Day	60 Day
8.625	n/a	n/a	n/a	n/a	MAX	7.375	n/a	n/a	n/a	n/a
8.500	n/a	n/a	n/a	n/a		7.250	n/a	n/a	n/a	n/a
8.375	103.000	102.875	102.625	102.500		7.125	n/a	n/a	n/a	n/a
8.250	103.000	102.875	102.625	102.500	ALL IN	7.000	n/a	n/a	n/a	n/a
8.125	102.875	102.750	102.500	102.375		6.875	100.750	100.625	100.375	100.250
8.000	102.875	102.750	102.500	102.375		6.750	100.750	100.625	100.375	100.250
7.875	102.750	102.625	102.375	102.250	PRICE	6.625	100.625	100.500	100.250	100.125
7.750	102.625	102.500	102.250	102.125		6.500	100.375	100.250	100.000	99.875
7.625	102.500	102.375	102.125	102.000		6.375	100.125	100.000	99.750	99.625
7.500	102.375	102.250	102.000	101.875		6.250	99.875	99.750	99.500	99.375
7.375	102.250	102.125	101.875	101.750	102.250	6.125	99.625	99.500	99.250	99.125
7.250	102.000	101.875	101.625	101.500		6.000	99.125	99.000	98.750	98.625
7.125	101.750	101.625	101.375	101.250		5.875	n/a	n/a	n/a	n/a
7.000	101.500	101.375	101.125	101.000		5.750	n/a	n/a	n/a	n/a
6.875	101.125	101.000	100.750	100.625		n/a	n/a	n/a	n/a	n/a
6.750	100.875	100.750	100.500	100.375		n/a	n/a	n/a	n/a	n/a
6.625	100.500	100.375	100.125	100.000		n/a	n/a	n/a	n/a	n/a
6.500	100.125	100.000	99.750	99.625						

	S Series Alt A 3/1 Libor Arm						S Series Alt A 5/1 Libor Arm			
Rate	15 Day	30 Day	45 Day	60 Day		Rate	15 Day	30 Day	45 Day	60 Day
7.500	101.750	101.625	101.500	101.375	MAX	7.750	103.000	102.875	102.750	102.625
7.375	101.625	101.500	101.375	101.250		7.625	102.750	102.625	102.500	102.375
7.250	101.500	101.375	101.250	101.125		7.500	102.500	102.375	102.250	102.125
7.125	101.375	101.250	101.125	101.000	ALL IN	7.375	102.375	102.250	102.125	102.000
7.000	101.125	101.000	100.875	100.750		7.250	102.125	102.000	101.875	101.750
6.875	101.000	100.875	100.750	100.625		7.125	101.875	101.750	101.625	101.500
6.750	100.750	100.625	100.500	100.375	PRICE	7.000	101.625	101.500	101.375	101.250
6.625	100.625	100.500	100.375	100.250		6.875	101.375	101.250	101.125	101.000
6.500	100.375	100.250	100.125	100.000		6.750	101.125	101.000	100.875	100.750
6.375	100.250	100.125	100.000	99.875		6.625	100.750	100.625	100.500	100.375
6.250	n/a	n/a	n/a	n/a	102.250	6.500	100.500	100.375	100.250	100.125
6.125	n/a	n/a	n/a	n/a		6.375	100.125	100.000	99.875	99.750
6.000	n/a	n/a	n/a	n/a		6.250	99.875	99.750	99.625	99.500
5.875	n/a	n/a	n/a	n/a		6.125	99.500	99.375	99.250	99.125

* Locks accepted on approved files only

		LTV Range						
	<=65%	65.01-70	70.01-80	80.01-85	85.01-90	90.01-95	95.01-97
Loan Amt: $40,000 - $60,000	-1.500	-1.500	-1.500	-1.500	-1.500	-1.500	-1.500
Loan Amt: $60,000 - $75,000	-1.000	-1.000	-1.000	-1.000	-1.000	-1.000	-1.000
Loan Amt: $417,001 - $650,000	0.000	-0.375	-0.625	-1.000	-1.000	-1.500	-1.500
Loan Amt: $650,001 - $1,000,000	-0.500	-0.750	-0.875	-1.000	-1.000	n/a	n/a
Loan Amt: $1,000,001 - $1,500,000	-0.750	-1.250	-1.750	n/a	n/a	n/a	n/a
Loan Amt: $1,500,001 - $2,000,000	-1.000	-1.500	-2.000	n/a	n/a	n/a	n/a
Low LTV (improvement)	0.000	+.250	n/a	n/a	n/a	n/a	n/a
Cash Out Refi (not available in Tx on PR's)	0.000	-0.250	-0.500	-1.000	-1.500	-2.000	n/a
2 Unit Properties	0.000	-0.250	-0.250	-0.500	-0.500	-0.500	n/a
3 & 4 Unit Properties	0.000	-0.750	-0.750	-1.000	-1.250	-1.500	n/a
Low Rise Condo (< = 4 floors)	0.000	-0.250	-0.500	-0.500	-0.500	-0.500	n/a
High Rise Condo (> 4 floors)	0.000	-0.250	-0.750	-1.000	-1.250	-1.500	n/a
Second Homes	0.000	-0.250	-0.750	-1.000	-1.250	-1.750	n/a
Non Owner Occupied	-0.500	-0.750	-1.500	-1.750	-2.500	n/a	n/a
No MI Option	n/a	n/a	n/a	-1.500	-2.500	-3.125	n/a
Full Documentation	+.750	+.500	n/a	n/a	n/a	n/a	n/a
Stated Income / Verified Assets (SIVA)	0.000	-0.500	-0.500	-0.875	-0.875	-1.500	n/a
No Income / Verified Assets (NIVA)	0.000	-0.750	-0.750	-1.250	-1.250	-2.000	n/a
Stated Income / Stated Assets (SISA)	-0.250	-0.875	-0.875	-1.875	-1.875	-2.500	n/a
No Doc (NINANE)	-0.375	-1.375	-1.375	-2.500	-2.500	-3.000	n/a
Foreign National	-0.500	-0.500	-0.500	n/a	n/a	n/a	n/a
Condotels*	-0.750	-1.250	-1.500	-1.750	-1.750	-1.750	n/a
Interest Only	-0.250	-0.250	-0.250	-0.250	-0.250	-0.250	-0.250
CLTV > 90%	-0.250	-0.250	-0.250	-0.250	-0.250	-0.250	-0.250
40 due in 30	-0.250	-0.250	-0.250	-0.250	-0.250	-0.250	-0.250
Escrow Waiver	-0.250	-0.250	-0.250	n/a	n/a	n/a	n/a

*Condotels must be locked and priced as condotels and non owner occupied.

Notes: Positive number improves price; negative number worsens price
         No geographical price adjustors for other states

IO

How Brokers Make Money

O kay, now hold on to your hat.

Ever heard of a "no point" or "no origination fee" loan? What about a "no point, no origination fee" loan? How can anyone make any money by not charging any points or origination fees? No, it's not by charging a junk fee like "processing" or "administration." Just as your client can pay more points to get a lower rate, he can also pay a higher rate to get no points or even negative points.

When you get your rate sheets, you will also see "premium" pricing. A premium price is how much the lender will pay you if your client takes a particular rate. Premium pricing is designated with parentheses.

Rate	15 Days	30 Days	60 Days
7.00%	1.00	1.125	1.375
7.125%	.75	.875	1.125
7.25%	.50	.625	.875
7.375%	.25	.375	.625
7.50%	0.00	.125	.375
7.625%	(.25)	(.125)	.125

7.75%	(.50)	(.375)	(.125)
7.875%	(.75)	(.625)	(.375)
8.00%	(1.00)	(.875)	(.625)
8.125%	(1.25)	(1.125)	(.875)

Lenders express premium pricing either as a percentage of a point or using the par method. So 101.00 is the same as (1.00). For example, if a $300,000 loan is priced at 101.00, the premium to you would be one percent of $300,000, or $3,000. If a rate shows a price of (1.00), that also means there is one percent, or 1 point, of $300,000 coming to you from the lender. If you wanted to make one point on a $300,000 loan but your borrower didn't want to pay any points, you would resort to premium pricing by increasing the rate so that the borrower doesn't pay any points and you still make your $3,000.

Premium pricing has various names. One of the more common is *yield spread premium*, or YSP. If you are a mortgage broker, current law requires you to disclose any YSP to the borrower up front on the Good Faith Estimate and on the final settlement statement at closing. If you're a mortgage banker, you do not.

So how much do you want to make on every deal? That's entirely up to you. If you want to make a total of two points on a $300,000 loan, go ahead. You can charge two points—one point plus a one-percent origination charge, or a one-percent origination charge plus one point in YSP, or two points in YSP.

YSPs have gotten a bad rap in recent years, primarily from consumer groups that don't understand how rates and points work together (i.e., lower rates equal more points, and higher rates equal no points). A YSP is not a bad thing at all. It's just how loan officers make money when borrowers don't want to pay points or origination charges.

If a borrower wants to pay no closing costs, does the lender pay for them out of charity? No, but the lender does adjust the interest rate high enough so the YSP pays for the closing costs.

Some people have described YSPs as underhanded bribery that wholesale lenders use to get loan officers to steer loans to them. But the fact is that all lenders offer a YSP, yet you never hear that. It's a function of rate and yield to the mortgage lender. Loan officers don't send loans to a particular loan company for a bribe. Instead, a loan officer will review various rate sheets and find a lender that offers a quarter point more in YSP.

When that happens, the loan officer can keep the additional quarter point, or $1,000 on a $400,000 loan, use it to reduce the interest rate, or give it to the borrower in some fashion. Every loan officer who has been in the business for very long has used the YSP as a tool to either make themselves more competitive or make more money.

If the rates aren't competitive that day, a broker can look for a quarter-point of YSP somewhere. She can then take that $1,000 and offer to pay the borrower's appraisal and lender fees to make herself more competitive. YSPs can be a selling tool, and if you're in a hypercompetitive market, you'll want that YSP, all or part of it, to offset your borrower's closing costs and to sweeten your offer.

You're running a business; you need to maximize your profits and be competitive in the marketplace. If you want to make four points on a deal, you could certainly quote that, but it's not likely you'd get the deal, because you're too expensive.

Advising Clients About Rate Locks

How long should you lock in your client's rate? Only for as long as he or she needs it locked. Loans cost more the longer you lock, so don't waste your client's money. Most purchase transactions will take place within a 30-60 day period.

You will be asked a thousand times, "So, what are rates going to do? Should I lock?"

This is a hard question to ignore, but instead of answering it directly, you need to educate your clients on how locks work and let them decide. You don't want to be on the wrong end of rate advice.

Too many loan officers think of themselves as financial gurus who can see into the future. They say things like, "Yeah, well the unemployment numbers will be out this Friday and if nonfarm payrolls lose anything more than 200,000, we'll probably see rates go down, so I would suggest waiting to lock in until after the numbers are released," or some such economic drivel.

Don't misunderstand. It's vital to your business that you understand how economic and political events affect interest rates, but it's immature to try and predict them. No one can predict rates. People a lot smarter than you or me try, and even those who make a living at it every single day get it wrong.

As a loan officer, you're an adviser. A consultant. But you're not a prognosticator. If you advised your client not to lock in a rate for any variety of reasons, you might be stuck watching rates move up while your client is not only swearing at you but pulling her loan from you.

Don't advise clients on what rates are going to do. Instead, counsel them on how rates move and what happens when they do move. For example, here is a better way to answer the question "What are rates going to do?":

"The unemployment numbers will be released this Friday and any news that could show a weakening economy such as low growth numbers or job losses typically affects interest rates and moves them downward. On the other hand, if numbers come out better than expected, rates could move up. It's your call."

Rates can move on one report then be offset by another, or two reports can combine to make for one volatile day. You just need to understand how the rates move and what might move them.

The fact is that it takes forever to get rates to move downward. They're stubborn. It could take an entire year for rates to move down by one percent, and a sneeze from some Fed governor could wipe it all out. Interest rates are nervous. They don't like surprises, and those who trade MBSs don't either. Any hint of inflation that will eat at their yields will cause a sell-off, raising rates.

What if your client insists on guidance? I've always said, "Okay, if you want me to advise you, here's what I always tell my clients: Assume that whatever decision you make will be the wrong one. Now, which way would you rather be wrong—rates move down just a little bit but you got current market rates, or rates shoot through the roof and lose all the rate gains we've made over the past year?"

By answering in this format, you're putting the onus of a rate decision squarely on your clients' shoulders while giving them practical advice. I've used that same quote literally hundreds of times and it always works.

Trouble can happen when rate locks expire. Lenders take a rate lock as seriously, maybe even more so, than a borrower does. If your client locks in for 30 days and your loan, for whatever reason, can't close until the next day or the next week, your client will get whatever she locked in at or current market rates . . . whichever is higher. Not lower.

Delays To Watch For

Locks expire because unanticipated things happen, such as:

Appraisals take longer than anticipated.
There's a problem with the appraisal.
There's a problem with the title report.
The survey is late.
The property is in a flood zone.
The borrowers are slow in getting their documentation.

Perhaps a better reason that locks expire is that things that should have been anticipated weren't. Don't expect a smooth closing every single time. Anticipate problems. Head them off at the pass.

In my experience, and every loan officer out there will back me up on this, the borrower is usually slow in documenting the file. For instance, you might have asked for two paycheck stubs, but the borrower provided only one and couldn't find another. Perhaps you asked for the last three months of bank statements but got three old statements. Or perhaps the underwriter had a question on the file that only the borrower could explain—like why she had two last names.

Whatever the reason for delays, it's your job and your loan processor's job to make certain that whatever is asked for is supplied immediately. More importantly, don't delay in processing the loan. When you get a contract and a loan application, move on it; don't delay in ordering whatever it is you need to order and monitor the document process.

Meet each week with your loan processor and go over each and every file to see what's in, what's still needed, and whether there are any problems on the loan or possible problems.

It took me a while to get used to this concept. I thought my job was just to go out and get loans, bring them in, and dump them on the processor's desk. Big mistake. You, as the loan officer, need to be intimately aware of your loan files and work hand in hand with your processor.

After a few years of working with the same processor, when you've both gained the trust and respect needed to establish a lean, mean, loan machine, you'll be able to let go of the reins and let your support staff run the "back office" while you are out making calls. Until then, know exactly what's going on in your files and help as much as your processor needs your help.

Okay, so you did all that but the lock is still going to expire. What to do? Lenders take your and your client's lock very seriously. Only their commitments run in the millions upon millions of dollars. Once you lock with a lender, it "books" that loan at whatever rate you locked in at and moves on to the next loan. The lender expects you to deliver that loan. If you don't deliver, it has to scramble around and find another commitment at the same rate. This is a function of a lender's secondary department and is too technical to cover here, but just know your lock is a serious deal. Busted locks lose money.

Getting an Extension on a Lock

Lenders offer "extensions" whereby if you need a few more days, your borrower can pay a little extra for a longer lock period, but only if you get the extension before the lock expires.

If your lock expires tomorrow, then you would call the lender today and ask for a lock extension. You will usually only get one extension. There might be lenders that offer multiple extensions, its just that I've never heard of them.

An extension will typically cost you 0.125 point for each day you need to extend. That can be a lot of money. Other extensions can be something to the effect of one-quarter point for one week. This is also expensive, but it's much less expensive than losing a loan. It's also a judgment call you must make from a business standpoint.

If a lock is about to expire and it's not your fault, who pays for the lock extension? Usually it's going to be you, whether the lock expiration was your fault or not. If the appraiser was late or there's a problem with the title, is it your borrower's fault? No.

If there are problems with a loan that will affect your lock, your borrower won't be too pleased with you. It's your responsibility to lock with vision. Know that problems can arise, on any deal, and when they do, let your client know the consequences.

For instance, if your borrower has decided to lock (remember, it's your borrower who decides to lock, not you) you must tell him the date it expires and that there might be bumps in the approval road that you can't foresee. If the approval takes longer than 30 days, understand that rates can go up, so "please Mr. Borrower, be prudent when we ask for documentation."

You need to provide your client with two things relating to locks: A lock confirmation (written) and a lock/float agreement. Usually those two agreements are written into one document. Get the documents signed and keep a copy.

Even though these documents are typically iron-clad, you're still in

A sample lock confirm/lock float agreement.

A LETHES LLC PRICING POLICY

Application Date _____

Loan Originator _____

Application Name(s) _____

Listing Agent _____

_____

Selling Agent _____

Property Address _____

(**X**)   **Float Option:** Loan applications may "float" until the applicant(s) chooses to lock a specific interest rate and discount points (together known as "price"). Because Alethes LLC reserves the right to change the prices it offers more than once each day, it is important that an Alethes LLC representative is contacted immediately once a decision to lock-in is made by the applicant(s). Furthermore, the Alethes LLC representative must confirm all prices with Alethes LLC's marketing department or chosen investor prior to confirmation of a lock-in.

( )   **Lock-In Option:** The interest rate and discount points are guaranteed for a specified number of days, per the term of the LOCK-IN AGREEMENT contained below. Upon notification from the applicant(s), or the listing or selling agent, of an intent to lock a rate and points, Alethes LLC will guarantee the lock-in price despite any subsequent market rate changes, either up or down, until the lock-in expiration date, as provided in a completed LOCK-IN AGREEMENT signed by the applicant(s). Refinance loans are eligible only for a ____ day lock-in. Alethes LLC's policy on expired lock-ins is as follows: The LOCK-IN AGREEMENT establishes the minimum price that Alethes LLC will guarantee to the applicant(s) for a loan. If the lock-in expires, the loan will close at the expired lock-in price or the prevailing market price, **whichever is greater.** Under no condition can the loan close at less than the original lock-in price.

I/We have applied to Alethes LLC for a home mortgage loan. By my/our execution hereof, I/we acknowledge and understand that fees paid for credit reports and appraisals are for expenses incurred to third parties in the process of obtaining this loan and are not refundable; and that any guarantees by Alethes LLC of an interest rate and/or discount points to me/us will expire if this loan does not close prior to the lock-in expiration date for any reason whatsoever, including but not limited to reasons beyond the control of Alethes LLC, such as those related to appraisals, credit reports, mortgage payoffs, and title problems.

_____   _____
Applicant   Date

_____   _____
Applicant   Date

_____   _____
Applicant   Date

_____   _____
Applicant   Date

LOCK-IN AGREEMENT

Lock-in Date _____

Expiration Date _____

Loan Type _____

Mortgage Amount _____

** **Re-Lock Date:** _____

** **Re-Lock Expiration Date** _____

I/We acknowledge and understand that Alethes LLC has agreed and committed to a _____ interest rate, _____ discount point(s), and _____ origination fee on a mortgage loan amount of $ _____ , pursuant to the purchase and financing of _____ (property address), for a period of _____ days from the date hereof. I/We understand that this interest rate and points are guaranteed by Alethes LLC, subject to loan approval, regardless of any change **up or down** in market interest rates. In consideration of this guarantee by Alethes LLC, I/we agree to close at these locked-in terms upon loan approval prior to the lock-in expiration date. I/We further acknowledge and agree that, in the event this LOCK-IN AGREEMENT expires, my/our loan will close at the expired interest rate and points or the prevailing market price, **whichever is greater.**

_____   _____
Applicant   Date

_____   _____
Applicant   Date

_____   _____
Applicant   Date

_____   _____
Loan Representative   Date

business. If you make someone mad at you, they're going to tell their friends, their neighbors, and their Realtor. It's your judgment call, but it's worth the quarter point out of your pocket to make a client happy.

These disclosures make your borrowers aware that locks are serious, that if lock periods expire for whatever reason it's not your fault and so on, and hopefully they'll get off their sofa cushions and help you get their own loan processed in a timely manner.

How Much to Charge Clients

Try charging somewhere around the average. Freddie Mac releases average mortgage-rate data every week; you've probably seen that information in the newspaper or on the Internet. The national survey reports the average interest rate on a 30-year fixed-rate mortgage and how much consumers are paying for that rate.

Although rates will change, the survey indicates consumers on average paid about a half point or more. More points were in fashion during years of higher rates, and fewer points are usually found when rates are at relative lows.

If you can make a couple of points in any combination of point, origination fee, or YSP, you're doing well. In a competitive environment, however, it's likely you won't make that much and get closer to one point in total compensation.

Don't forget that points are a percentage of the loan amount. If you're quoting an $800,000 loan, don't feel shy about quoting three-quarters of a point, giving you a $6,000 profit. On smaller deals, you'll need to charge more or you'll have trouble covering your overhead.

If you're closing a $45,000 FHA loan and only making one point, $450 is not much. Take into consideration how much you'd like to make on a per-loan basis and adjust accordingly.

There is typically just as much work in a smaller loan as there is with a big one. In fact, often you'll find that the smaller deals take more work than the bigger ones. Smaller government loans may face more documentation, unstable income, or a variety of issues.

Big loans where your borrower has lots of money, great credit, and stable employment might mean an easier go of it. Take your personal time in each deal as a consideration in what to price. There have been times where I've reviewed a loan application, the credit report, and the AUS decision, and saw that I had a "golden" borrower that would take little or no effort. On such deals, I'd quote less knowing it would be a no-brainer, low-maintenance application.

On harder deals, I would hold firm on my pricing, knowing that if I went any lower on my quote I'd in effect be losing money by spending time on a difficult loan instead of being out in the field making sales calls.

Predatory Lending: Don't Do It

On another note, you should price subprime loans the same way you price any other loan. In fact, various predatory-lending laws exist because loan officers were screwing their clients with onerous charges.

I personally have witnessed loan officers making 10 points on deals. And bragging about it. These borrowers had bad credit and were being taken advantage of by the loan officer. Granted, this was before predatory-lending laws began to take hold, but still. Loan officers who prey on people when they've fallen on hard times are scum.

Predatory-lending laws vary from state to state, typically limiting closing costs and lender profit to a particular interest rate or a percentage of the loan amount. The original predatory-lending law was the Home Ownership and Equity Protection Act, or HOEPA, passed in 1994. It gives specific guidelines as to what could be considered predatory.

In HOEPA's case, predatory is also called "high cost." There is a specific section (Section 32) within HOEPA that contains the calculation for high cost. For example, if the APR is eight percentage points above a comparable Treasury note, bill, or bond then the loan would be considered high cost. Thus, if a 10-year note had a yield of 5.75 percent, then any 10-year loan that was 8 percentage points above that (i.e., anything beyond 13.75%), would be considered high cost or predatory.

The problem with HOEPA was that it didn't make the loan illegal per se, just that the borrowers would have to sign additional forms and disclosures letting the borrower know the loan triggered "Section 32" and is considered high cost.

There is no national predatory standard, but several state laws attempt to define predatory. Texas, for example, limits interest rates on second mortgages to 10.00% APR.

State laws limiting predatory lending do in fact have the authority to say whether a loan is legal in a state. Most states take the HOEPA statute and make their own, enforceable, antipredatory lending law.

An APR that is 3 percent higher than the loan's interest rate might be considered predatory. In some states, only points and lender fees are used to calculate high-cost loans. In others, it could be a total of all closing costs, regardless of whether those fees are from the lender or not. A complete list of state-by-state predatory-lending laws and links to those laws are available at the HUD website (www.hud.gov).

Mortgage loans are supposed to help people. Yeah, you can make a lot of money along the way but if you get into the business solely for the money and don't care about the welfare of your clients, you'll fail.

Making Yourself Successful

11

Marketing Yourself

I've always had a simple approach to originating loans. At first glance, it's an intimidating process. You've got your office, your computer, your license, your business cards, and even a website. But you don't have any clients. Scary? It can be.

But there's no need to reinvent the wheel. Why not copy proven concepts? In mortgage origination, there is no "one" way. There are multitudes of ways to find mortgage loans and generate new business.

I'm going to introduce you to several successful loan officers who all do things their own ways. In many ways, they're pioneers. They've taken basic ideas and made them their own. They work, and work well.

If you follow this advice and do the things they do, you will soon be in the top 5 percent of all income earners in the United States. That's six figures, folks. Big ones.

My success in origination comes from a basic formula that I may have picked up several years ago from someone else or maybe I just thought it up myself, I can't remember. But it's how I trained myself and my loan officers, and it works.

First, don't be intimidated. It's a daunting task to start a new market. But remember this simple formula: 5 X 2.

Easy enough, right? 5 X 2. Don't think of anything else. There, not so intimidating is it?

Find five sources of business that will send you two loans per month. Ten loans. That's about $2 million in monthly production and somewhere around $30,000 in gross monthly income. Can you live on that?

Is that impossible? Heck no. Far from it. In fact, the people you will meet in this chapter earn more than that. Much more.

"Okay, David. Big deal. 5 X 2. But that doesn't tell me where to get the five in the first place," you say. Fair enough. But by implanting that in your mind, you've overcome the biggest obstacle: intimidation.

Without a road map on where you want to go and with no way to get there you're lost. But by concentrating on 5 X 2 it becomes easier. Just find five. That's all. Then find two.

Where did I find 5 X 2? Realtors and tax accountants. Your 5 X 2 doesn't have to come from the same source, such as from just one Realtor giving you five deals each month. It can come from three different sources. Or five. Three Realtors and two accountants each giving you two deals each month. Just as long as you get to that magic number 10.

Realtors

How do you get Realtor business? You begin making sales calls to them. You stop by their offices, introduce yourself, and begin establishing a regular sales route.

1. Ask the office manager or sales manager when the Realtors have their sales meetings. Usually they're in the morning on a regular day of the week and month. This is the time you show up, before their meetings. All the Realtors will be there, and it's a nice time to be seen.

Simply being seen on a regular basis breeds familiarity, and once Realtors see that you're serious about your job and what you do, soon they'll be asking about loan programs you offer, perhaps showing you some deals that have been difficult for them.

2. Identify the top producers in the office. In real estate, there are "listing" agents and there are "selling" agents. Listing agents are the ones who find homes to sell. Selling agents are agents who work with buyers to find homes to buy.

You want both. Listing agents are usually the top producers in the office. They're active and they have a lot of clients. They may also tell you something like, "I'm not a buyer's agent, I only list homes," meaning they don't use loan officers.

Nothing could be further from the truth. When you hear this from a Realtor, take note. This is someone you want to be one of your 5 X 2 sources. Listing agents always have buyers, in fact, the houses they're listing are full of them.

You can also identify the top producers by finding the office "tote" board. Usually this big whiteboard is a chart located in the kitchen or meeting room, probably where the coffee is served. This board is a monthly tally of who has the most listings and who has the most sales.

Remember the top agents and begin calling on them. These people will be on your regular list.

Tax Accountants

Tax accountants have always been one of my best sources of income, probably because they're rarely called on by mortgage-loan officers. You'll need to be comfortable with numbers and be professional, but tax accountants usually handle income taxes for self-employed borrowers. They also handle taxes for people who might be having tax problems.

If you can make a presentation that emphasizes your expertise on the self-employed borrower, then that's your ticket to referrals. Accountants take care of their client's taxes and finances, so it's a natural for a client to ask his accountant, "Whom do you suggest I get a mortgage from?"

The beauty of getting a referral from an accountant is that people put a great deal of trust in their accountants. If an accountant tells a client to contact you for a mortgage loan, then you can bet that person is going to take that referral seriously.

You won't have any competition. Accountant referrals rarely "shop" you and are a loyal bunch. Those clients are yours and come from a trusted source.

Tax accountants are also "numbers" people. Get used to preparing spreadsheets that show various amortization tables, monthly payments, and the effects of different interest rates. You can get as elaborate as you want, perhaps the more the merrier, but only as long as you understand what you're providing.

The Mortgage Coach, located at www.themortgagecoach.com, is one of the most thorough number crunchers; it provides most anything imaginable with regard to number presentation. This product is the most comprehensive mortgage-analysis program there is. It's a little pricey, but one new loan as a result of The Mortgage Coach will pay for it.

Tax accountants are not the only group that will appreciate this type of marketing. CPAs and financial planners are also good markets for you to call on. But whichever market you choose to solicit, be it just one or all of them, you'll find no better referral source.

Client Database

Remember that one of the most important things to do when you get referrals and close loans is to create a database.

Every single lead you get and every single loan you close should be recorded and stored for future regular marketing materials. You could send out a newsletter every month or you could send out a regular e-zine or a postcard. Whatever it is you send out, you need to keep in touch with them. Or else they'll forget about you. They'll also forget about your competitors if your competition doesn't also market to them.

By creating a database, you're expanding your market exponentially. You're no longer just relying on outside sources for business, you're getting business from previous clients and referrals. This type of database is what separates successful, seasoned loan officers from those who merely scrape by.

It's much easier to market to your previous clients than it is to find new ones. So by building your database of old clients and continuously keeping in touch with them, you'll find your job much easier and be more successful.

How to Advertise Your Interest Rates

When refinancing activity begins to swell, or you just want to keep your name in your market on a continual basis, you may want to consider advertising your interest rates. Advertising your rates can help make the phone ring and get new leads. Advertising your interest rates is also a delicate matter, and unless you do it properly it will be more trouble than it's worth.

There are two basic ways to advertise your rates: In print or online. But however you do it, you must adhere to some strict laws governing interest-rate ads, specifically in accordance with Federal Truth in Lending Act, which is Regulation Z ("Reg. Z") of the Consumer Protection Act.

Reg. Z requires than any time you advertise a mortgage rate you must also show, in plain and obvious lettering, the APR, the amount financed, and the term of the loan. For example, if you want to advertise a 30-year fixed-rate mortgage at 7.00%, you just can't put 7.00% all by itself.

It's too easy to mislead a consumer. Instead, you must also disclose the fact that the principal is $300,000, the term is 30 years, and the APR is 7.125%, or whatever your terms end up being. You may see an occasional ad that blatantly violates Reg. Z, but don't you do it. It can get you in a lot of trouble.

When you advertise in print publications such as a newspaper or magazine, remember that by the time the newspaper goes to print your rates may be way out of date. Even just a couple of days can pass and rates can move negatively. If you quote a low rate to a newspaper on a Thursday for a Sunday-edition print and rates move up, the phone calls you get will be from people asking for the lower rate you had available on Thursday.

You won't have it, and then you must explain to the consumer that rates have indeed moved up because you turned them in several days ago. Here is another example of why it's critical to understand when and how rates move. If you don't, you'll look like you're just trying to bait and switch your potential customer. If they think that, you won't get their business. And they might tell their buddies about your so-called "tactics."

However, if you say, "Thank you for your call, unfortunately there was a rate move on Friday after the rate-posting deadline. You see, the unemployment numbers came in much higher than expected, causing the prices of mortgage bonds to fall. Everyone's rates moved up."

In this fashion, not only have you explained "why" rates moved up but your statement is verifiable. They can check back and see that yes, the unemployment numbers were higher than anticipated, and they can also see related stories on how bonds took a hit. You'll look like a pro.

When you advertise rates, you're looking to initiate a phone call. If a consumer is shopping for rates, is he shopping for the highest mortgage rate he can find? Of course not. He's looking for the lowest.

It's nearly impossible to quote the lowest rate all the time. In fact, you'll start to notice other rate advertisements from other lenders and you'll say to yourself, "Hey, wait a minute . . . that rate is too low to be found anywhere." That lender is baiting and switching.

You know from experience and from looking at practically every rate sheet imaginable that one lender can't be a half-point lower than everyone else, but you'll still see ads with such claims. Don't be tempted to do the same. It will sully your reputation and you'll lose more business than you'll earn.

So what do you quote? My experience is to try and make about one point, but get it from the YSP. That way you're giving a competitive rate quote, but you're keeping the consumer's up-front costs down. I would always try and quote a rate with zero points and zero origination. It's much easier to compete with someone who's charging a point but offering a lower rate.

For example, pretend that you have quoted 7.00% with no points and no origination charges on a 30-year fixed-rate loan of $200,000. The monthly payment is about $1,331. However, your competitor is advertising a lower rate of 6.75% but charges a point. At 6.75%, the payment is about $1,297.

Now you tell your prospect, "Yes, I understand my competitor is 6.75% and I'm 7.00%. But the difference in monthly payment is only $34.00. The point is $2,000. You wouldn't make up that point until after the fifth year! I can match that rate, but I think it might be in your better interest to pay no points."

Points or origination charges typically have such long payoffs that not only does a no-point rate often work out better, but you're also showing your customer that you have more choices and you have his or her financial interests in mind.

You will also encounter people who aren't looking for the lowest rate but want to get a competitive rate at a lower cost. When you advertise your rates with a newspaper, usually one option is to list your rates alongside other lenders' quoted rates.

If you want the phone to ring, you're going to want to offer as low a rate as you can without any points or origination fees. This may also depend on how other lenders are quoting. In fact, different markets may dictate how you quote.

In some parts of the country it is standard practice to quote loans with origination fees. In other parts of the country, origination fees are almost unheard of. You may want to experiment on how you quote your rates to see which method gets you the most leads.

Just remember, rate shoppers are a very disloyal bunch. If someone quickly finds you just because of a rate, he'll leave you just as quickly if rates go up.

Although it's perfectly fine to advertise your rates, don't base your business on low rates. Rates are just a part of the package. You need to treat your mortgage operation as a full-service enterprise. Providing superior customer service while still being competitive is your ultimate goal.

12

Marketing Secrets from the Pros

You're about to read secrets from successful loan officers who have spent years developing their loan success. The neat thing is that you don't have to spend 20 years figuring it out—all you need to do is do what they do.

Every article in this final chapter was written by real loan officers. Not "advisors" or people who have never originated a loan in their lives, but bona fide megaproducers.

This stuff works. Take a bit here, take a bit there. Or take it all. Hopefully this last chapter will get your brain going . . . and soon you'll be on your way to making a whole lot of money! Ain't life great?

Employee Benefits System: Marketing to Businesses
By Karen Deis

Many streams make a river. Most loan originators feel that they only have two streams—purchases and refinances. However, these categories are too broad to market to effectively. In fact, using the river-stream analogy, you also need tributaries to feed into your income river.

There is a wealth of information contained in your closed files.

Most of your past clients fall into two categories—employed or self-employed. Your files contain the names of their employers. It's one of the best sources of data you have to create and implement a marketing system called an employee benefits program.

So, what's an employee benefits program? It's a program where you offer a discounted closing-costs package (of over $1,000 in savings) only to employees of certain companies, labor unions, or groups. It's a systematic, targeted list created from your closed loans or groups that you are personally associated with.

Over a six-year time period, I personally worked with 42 companies that distributed my mortgage brochures to over 36,000 employees on an annual basis. Here are some tips on how you can create your own employee benefits program.

Step #1—Develop a Package of Benefits with Your Vendors

Ask your title company for $50 off the closing fee. Ask appraisers to discount the appraisal $50. Reduce your junk fees by $50. Get discounts from the surveyor, home inspector, etc. Your vendor discounts should be around $200.

Step #2—Develop Affinity Partner Discounts

Most real estate attorneys will provide a free, one-hour consultation to review purchase agreements, closing docs, etc. Financial planners—ditto. By *placing a value* on their services, you are providing additional benefits valued around $350. Find an independent insurance agent to work with and provide an additional benefit of three homeowners' insurance quotes.

Step #3—Develop Relationships with Three or Four Real Estate Agents

Most real estate agents will pay another agent a 25 percent commission for a client referral. Because you are the *referring source,* you don't want a referral fee—but you want them to pay $350 of your client's closing costs. The additional benefit is that your client will usually stay with the agent you referred because of the incentive.

Step #4—Develop Discounts with Local Retail Companies

Support your local companies by offering to promote their services to your clients. Call and ask for coupons from companies like truck rentals, home-improvement stores, carpet-cleaning services, painters, electricians, plumbers, etc. Develop your list based on what your clients will need IMMEDIATELY after they move into their homes.

The magic number here is $1,000 in employee savings. Although not every client will use EVERY benefit, the entire package of savings is worth over $1,000. Any dollar amount less than that will not have the same impact.

Identifying the companies and groups is both an art and a science. Start with groups you belong to, because these are people who know you, trust you, and want you to succeed. Review your database or 1003s and target midsized companies (because the big-name mortgage companies usually have developed programs for the big-name corporations).

Identify your raving fans—the clients who think you are the best thing since sliced bread—and give them a call. Tell them that you have created an employee benefits program and ask if you can refer to them in the letters you are going to send to their companies' presidents.

Don't make the mistake of sending a letter to the human resource director. They are not the decision makers, so start at the top and send a letter to the president. The first paragraph begins with a question:

"How would you like to offer your employees the benefit of saving over $1,000 when they purchase or refinance their mortgages—without costing you a dime?" (For a free copy of the entire letter, e-mail Karen@LoanOfficerTraining.com and mention David Reed's book.)

Target only companies and groups of people that you are personally acquainted with. It's the referral factor at work here. You'll waste your time and money if you take the shotgun approach and send letters to people who know nothing about you.

Although you might use the phrase "employee benefits program" for company programs, don't limit this offer to corporations only. Think about other niche markets that would benefit from the reduced closing costs and services.

When you create a savings program for groups other than corporations, I suggest that you rename the program to be consistent with the group. For example:

Labor Unions	Union Advantage Mortgage Benefits
Teachers, Firefighters, Police	Community Heroes Mortgage Benefits
Church Groups	Christian (Denomination Name) Mortgage Benefits
Hospitals	Health-Providers Mortgage Benefits

Once they have given you the okay, create a brochure listing each and every benefit along with the dollar value of the savings. If a company's representatives tell you that they want to participate but will not agree to distribute your brochures, DO NOT do business with them. Your goal here is to get your information into their employees' hot little hands with the implied endorsement from their employer. Your campaign is worthless if you can't distribute your info.

Just one last thought! When creating your savings program and distributing your brochures, be sure to include an expiration date of one year after the implementation date. This gives you a chance to update your closing costs and add or delete benefits. It also gives you a chance to remind employees of these benefits again in a year and get your info into the hands of new employees at the same time.

The employee benefits program is your tributary!

Purchases and refinances are your streams!

Your river of income is fed by these niche resources!

About Karen Deis

With 28 years worth of experience in the mortgage business, Karen has created systems that she personally used in her own mortgage practice. They're easy to implement, and employers, groups, and clubs will endorse you as their "lender of choice."

Networking with Your Peers
By Sue Woodard

Working WITH the competition—sounds like it may be a contradiction in terms, right? Believe it or not, there are a multitude of advantages in having strong relationships with the people we would normally consider to be our competition.

Let's take a closer look at who is *really* our competition, identify the rewards of having strong relationships with other originators, and gain ideas to position ourselves to initiate and develop these beneficial relationships.

Whom Do We Consider to Be Our Competition?

We might be tempted to answer that we compete with two different parties: the originators within our own company (with whom our numbers and units are compared on a monthly or weekly basis), and the originators outside our company whom we may feel we are working against to get the same deals.

In reality, our only competition is ourselves.

Each and every originator has very different goals and ideas in terms of financial levels, lifestyle, profit margins, and the methods and practice of doing business. Although having a competitive nature is usually a part of being in sales, in reality we are only competing against ourselves. Rather than making blanket comparisons of how our business appears in relation to someone else's, it is wiser to look at our own goals and visions for life and business, and set our own bars.

Remember that the fastest runners in a race are not spending much time with their heads turned to the side watching the people next to them. They are paying attention to their own form and speed and have their eyes on the finish line. Looking at it this way, it is easier to take the next step and begin to see more clearly all of the advantages of forming great relationships with the family of originators who surround us every day.

Surrounding Yourself with a Network of Professionals That You Can Call Upon for Advice and Information Is Invaluable

Have you ever had clients tell you that they heard ABC Mortgage is offering a jumbo loan with zero down, at 5%, for 30 years fixed, with no closing costs? It just sounds too good to be true, doesn't it? But given how quickly our business can change, it can be hard to keep up with every new product and program being offered. We want to know if there is truly something out there that maybe we just have not heard about yet or whether those things are really as they sound—too good to be true.

In these situations, if we have a great network both in and outside the company to run a quick check, we can generally confirm the validity of the information. It does not necessarily mean that the program is not out there somewhere, but it probably means there is more to the story than the client is aware of.

Have you ever had a deal come up that throws you a curveball and you're not sure how to structure it properly for your client? Having great relationships with other originators inside and outside the company means that you have professionals you can turn to. Sometimes simply talking it through makes the solution clear.

Do you ever wonder if your programs, rates, and fees are competitive? It can be helpful to periodically check with your network outside of the company to ensure that your offerings are commensurate with your area, and it will help your company determine whether to add any new products.

Referrals!

Many originators have certain types of loans that they either specialize in as a niche or know that they want to avoid like the plague. First-time homebuyers, new-construction loans, government loans, and challenged-credit clients are all examples of transactions that one originator might highly desire but that another might not want to touch with a 10-foot pole.

This is another great opportunity if we have formed strong relationships and partnerships with a trusted network of originators. You can trade referrals or arrange other methods of compensation. If your business is generated by referrals, you obviously want to be respectful of the referral sources; generally their largest concern is that the client and the transaction be handled with the same care that they would provide themselves.

Trust is of the utmost importance in these partnerships, and it is crucial that the originators that we refer loans to know and uphold the standard of service we expect. Over time, we may even meet originators in other parts of the country and form a network of individuals that we can trade relocation referrals with as well.

A Good Reputation Is Invaluable

Let's face it—people talk. You want your name to come up when new opportunities become available in the industry. You want to know who is moving where and why. If you currently manage your own employees, or see it in your future, having these relationships across the local industry is not an option, it's a must for recruiting and retention. You need the knowledge and connection with the local players so that you know the factors that will help you recruit and retain a great team.

This is a challenging industry. It is necessary to have others with whom we can celebrate, commiserate, trade ideas, and share the ups and downs of everyday business. No one understands like someone who is in the business.

The Connectivity and Support Gained by Building Strong Relationships Is Priceless

By having a small group of trusted colleagues with whom you share ideas, you can gain great synergies. We often feel "proprietary" about our own new ideas. However, being able to trade ideas and participate in give-and-take with your network is powerful. We share some of the ideas that are our own stock and trade, but we also gain new ideas in return. Realistically, is it really going to cost anyone business to share a few ideas and gain a few in return? Of course not, plus it feels good to be of assistance to others and hear their feedback on what you are doing.

Like many other industries, there is a natural "grapevine" in the mortgage world, and it pays to stay on top of who is doing what, who is moving where, what company is offering what in terms of compensation or new programs, who is up-and-coming, and what hot topics are coming down the pipe. Many new regulatory changes are looming on the horizon, and it is vital to stay aware of what may be ahead. As an industry, it is a time to band together. Benjamin Franklin wisely once said, "We must all hang together, or assuredly we shall all hang separately." Individually, it is difficult to influence legislation, but as a group, we have a very strong voice.

In a day-to-day sense, sometimes connectivity is just the ability to have another originator within your company back you up, and to do the same for them. If you do not have a team to hold down the fort while you are on vacation, chances are good that you might feel uncomfortable leaving for longer than just a day or two. If you have someone you can trust to watch your business, you can offer the same service in return.

Now That You See All the Advantages, How Do You Do It?

The good news is that it is amazingly simple. Build your local peer network first. Within your company, take an extra moment to extend courtesy and build ties with the other originators. You never know when you might need a favor, and it helps to have laid the groundwork in advance. This is also the group most readily available to discuss difficult deals, and it is likely that someone else has had a situation similar to yours and can point you in the correct direction.

Again, it often helps just to have someone with whom to talk it through. Go to lunch together and talk about plans and goals. These are the people who will be around when you get discouraged or the going gets tough.

Next, build your top-level support network. Look up the top producers or managers in your company, and ask if you can have just a few moments of their time on the phone or in person. Ask for only 15 or 20 minutes, as this should be ample and you are more likely to get a positive response because their time is quite valuable. Start with only a few simple questions, such as how they got started, their biggest challenges, their number-one piece of advice for someone wanting to grow their business, or whatever seems appropriate for you.

You will probably find that top producers are passionate about the business and are generally willing to share information. It is also in your best interest to associate with the best—it has been said, "If you want to soar with the eagles, don't flock with the turkeys." Top producers associate with other top producers. As a side note, do not go in and ask if you can have copies of their most successful flyers or marketing ideas. That can be somewhat offensive and you may have not earned the right to ask for that quite yet.

Build a peer network outside the company next. First and foremost, it is wise on a number of levels to be active in your local industry. Local mortgage banker and broker associations usually hold a number of events, seminars, and meetings throughout the year.

It pays to be involved in terms of education, new ideas, and awareness of local and national changes affecting our industry. Generally, individuals who are serious about the mortgage profession attend these events, and they are great places to network and meet other originators.

Finally, develop the top-level network outside of your company. Try approaching these producers in the same way you would approach a new realtor or business partner. Find out a bit about the people you want to get to know, perhaps by using your peer networks, and make a phone call. Mention that you know a bit about them, know that they are at the top of the profession, and that you wonder if you could have just 15 minutes of their time to meet them. It is a flattering request and you will generally not be turned down. This can grow into a powerful relationship, as you want the best of the best to know you. You will now come to mind when they are asked who could be looked at for new opportunities that might come up in the industry.

A last suggestion would be to add these new connections to your database, and send a note or holiday card just like you would any other friend, family member, or valued business partner. It is amazing how far simple respect and courtesy can take you in this business, even when you extend it to those that you might have normally viewed as your competition.

Compete only with yourself, and work with, not against the competition. Don't let the opportunities to initiate and grow these beneficial relationships pass you by! Challenge yourself. Take the few simple steps needed to add this powerful network to your arsenal and shift your business to a new level!

About Sue Woodard
Sue Woodard is an originator and sales trainer for CTX Mortgage in Minneapolis, MN. She is also vice president of the Mortgage Market Guide, the industry's leading advisory service for mortgage originators. Sue can be reached at sue@mortgagemarketguide.com.

Choosing Between Two Roads: Transactional Loan Officer vs. Mortgage Planner
By Dave Savage
As interest rates change, so does your market. In strong economic times, everybody's buying, everybody's taking what they can. But when

rates move down, people refinance, looking for nothing except the lowest rate available . . . regardless of the competency of their loan officers.

To make matters more challenging, Realtors now have more loan officers knocking on their doors than ever before, many real estate companies have an in-house lender, and most home builders have an in-house mortgage division. Add to that the fact that more and more borrowers are shopping only for the best rate, and it means you're not making as much commission on each transaction as you would like. Plus, you're not generating enough referrals and new purchases to replace what you're losing.

Bottom line: You need to generate more business. But how?

Answer: By changing the game and becoming a Certified Mortgage Planner.

Mortgage planning will help you generate new leads and referrals, reduce rate shopping, and get Realtors and other financial planners to bring new business right to your door. In fact, becoming a mortgage planner is as close as you can get to being paid residual commission on each loan you close.

In this article, you'll discover how mortgage professionals are becoming mortgage planners, generating new incremental business and referrals, and simultaneously reducing rate shopping. You'll hear from **Stacey Harding**, Senior Vice President and National Production Manager of Cherry Creek Mortgage in Greenwood Village, CO; **Mark Klein**, Mortgage Planner and President of Pacific Coast Lending in Agoura Hills, CA; **Dylan Kramer**, Mortgage Planner and Agency Director of Starpointe Mortgage, Chicago, IL; and **Randy Luebke**, Mortgage Planner and Principal of First Reliance Mortgage in Newport Beach, CA;

But first, a little history on Mortgage Planning:

What Is Mortgage Planning?

Mortgage planning is a relationship-focused service that enables homeowners to make intelligent decisions that have obvious tangible value.

Traditional Loan Officer Defined:

A traditional loan is a transaction-focused process, so a traditional loan officer is someone who delivers an efficient and compliant mortgage transaction.

MP vs. TLO

Traditional loan officers (TLOs) and mortgage planners (MPs) have obvious similarities. Although both processes result in a mortgage transaction, MPs focus on the long-term relationship and financial well-being of the homeowner. TLOs focus on the transaction—getting the loan closed and moving on.

TLO Objectives:

- Transaction speed
- Taking applications
- Measuring units and outcomes

MP Objectives:

- Relationship value
- Delivering valued advice to earn a trusted relationship
- Measuring margin and key performance indicators

In today's highly competitive environment, mortgage professionals can't risk a single transaction, and they need to optimize every lead and client relationship. Mortgage planning is today's ultimate competitive weapon to optimize your client relationships in a marketplace with intense price shopping.

The key to making the transition from average loan officer to mortgage planner is by doing more than quoting interest rates. Mortgage planners offer a wide range of services, including **mortgage plans** that help homeowners integrate their mortgages into their financial plans. Mortgage planners also offer **monthly mortgage reviews**, which help homeowners compare their current interest rates with the current marketplace, and a**nnual equity reviews**, which help homeowners optimize debt and equity.

Here's a quote from Stacey Harding, Senior Vice President and National Production Manager at Cherry Creek Mortgage: "Some of my customers would probably rather get a root canal than a mortgage loan. There are so many different options. What's the best thing to do with the down payment money? Am I getting the best deal, or just the lowest payment for the moment?"

"Competition in the Chicago market is ferocious," says Dylan Kramer, mortgage planner and agency director of Starpointe Mortgage. "In addition to a shrinking market, the Internet is complicating matters by equalizing the mortgage industry and making all loan officers look the same. In fact, nothing could be further from the truth.

While some are content to offer the lowest price, complete the transaction, and move on, there are others who take the time to evaluate a mortgage strategy that best meets a homeowner's unique financial goals and integrates the mortgage into their personal financial plan."

"In the past, originators simply provided a loan transaction," says Stacey Harding. "Today, our mortgage originators have to be more financially savvy than that. They must be better financial advisors as to what the right mortgage is and the lowest-cost mortgage, not just the lowest payment at the moment."

Loan officers who want to stand out in the crowd must capture home buyers' attention quickly or lose the sale and the residual commission of a valued relationship.

The difference is the way you position your business and the experience you deliver to your clients. As a TLO, you are continually seeking new business. With mortgage planning, your business is continually seeking you. The bottom line is that loan officers focus on finding new loan applications and mortgage planners focus on winning and optimizing relationships and referrals.

By transitioning from a loan officer to a mortgage planner, you will be able to:

- Reduce rate shopping
- Increase credibility and trust
- Obtain more leads
- Get more referrals
- Close more sales

I used to struggle with producing $1 million monthly. Becoming a mortgage planner has helped me become a consistent $30 million producer. Additionally, I closed over $60 million in 2003 with Mortgage Coach as the cornerstone of my client retention program.

About Dave Savage

Dave has more than 20 years of experience as an entrepreneur and business leader. As CEO of The Mortgage Coach and author of the "Savage Insights" blog, he integrates his passion for leveraging technology to increase the success of mortgage professionals. As a mortgage industry leader, Dave consults and speaks to thousands of mortgage professionals each year on topics relating to sales, marketing, and leadership.

During the creation of the Mortgage Coach, Dave was one of the nation's top 100 originators, working exclusively with CPAs and financial planners.

How to Become a Mortgage Planner
By Dylan Kramer

To become a mortgage planner, you must constantly conduct research, educate yourself, learn as you go, properly position yourself at the point of sales, ask the right questions, and use mortgage-planning solutions like Mortgage Coach and Mortgage Market Guide to name a few. Below are a few quotes from loan officers who became mortgage planners. They illustrate the best practices and definitions of the services that mortgage planners deliver.

Steven Marshall—To Help You Manage Your Home Equity

"We are certified mortgage planners. We help our clients successfully manage their home equity to increase liquidity, safety, rate of return, and tax deductions. Unlike a traditional loan officer, our role is to help our clients integrate the loan that they select into their overall long- and short-term financial and investment plan to help minimize taxes, improve cash flow, and minimize interest expense."

Jim McMahan—To Build Wealth for Your Family

"Today, I see a mortgage, more than ever, not as a mortgage loan once was, but instead as a financial planning instrument that must be integrated into your long- and short-term personal financial plan. My goal is to help you create a mortgage strategy that builds wealth for your family."

Eric Union—To Eliminate Financial Stress

"Financial stress is one of the leading causes of divorce and family breakdown in America today. My goal is to become your trusted advisor to help you make informed decisions regarding your real-estate debt and equity structure, which will allow you to become financially bullet-proof and on a wealth-building track to financial independence."

Dave Savage—To Help You Make the Most Informed Decision Possible

"As a mortgage planner, I am dedicated to helping you make the most informed mortgage decision possible—one that integrates with your personal financial plan and major life goals like retirement and wealth accumulation. A mortgage isn't just a loan; it's one of your most important financial-planning tools."

Questions You Should Ask Your Borrowers

If you are a mortgage planner, there are a few things these contributors felt you should be certain to learn about your clients.

FIRST QUESTION

- "Help me understand, what's important about this loan to you?" By Steven Marshall.
- "What one or two things have been or were weighing on your mind in advance of speaking with me that you would like me to address and clarify for you?" By John Bell.
- "What are your expectations for our time together?" By Eric Union.

MY ULTIMATE QUESTION

- How old do you want to be when your home is paid off or when paying off your home is a strategic decision? Based on your current situation, how old are you actually going to be when that happens? This creates a GAP.

MORTGAGE PLANNING QUESTIONS

- How long do you plan to live in your home? (a) Less than 3 years, (b) 3 to 7 years, or (c) more than 7 years. I want to help you determine how long you are going to use this real estate asset.
- During this period, do you anticipate your income to (a) increase, (b) remain stable, or (c) decrease?
- How would you rate your financial mindset? (a) conservative, (b) moderate, or (c) aggressive.
- What percentage of your monthly income are you currently paying toward your mortgage?
- Are you better prepared financially now after having met with me than you were before?

- What percentage of your monthly income are you currently saving per month?
- How old do you want to be when you retire?
- Based on your current savings plan, are you on track?
- What is holding you back from saving more?
- Based on your current savings, when will you reach a "freedom point" when your liquid assets exceed your mortgage?

ANNUAL EQUITY REVIEW QUESTIONS

- Where are you feeling financial stress?
- How is your team of advisors performing?
- Do you plan to purchase a new car in the next 12 months? If yes, how do you plan to pay for it?
- Do you have any goals to purchase a bigger home in the next few years? *If yes, define those goals and make sure they understand the value of their current equity.*
- How long do you intend to use this asset? (This pertains to the client's primary residence.)
- Do you want to see how your credit rating has changed since last year?
- Are you familiar with the concept of using your home equity to increase your net worth and/or plan for your retirement?

Descriptions of the Services That Mortgage Planners Deliver

- A **mortgage plan** is a professional report designed to help homeowners make informed decisions that integrate with their personal financial plans and dollarize the total mortgage cost over time.
- A **monthly mortgage review** is a monthly service that helps homeowners track their current interest rates and mortgage programs and compare them with the current market conditions.

- An **annual equity review** is an annual service that helps home-owners make informed decisions about whether to restructure their debt and/or equity to achieve their personal financial goals.

Positioning Yourself as a Mortgage Market Expert
By Barry Habib

Your competition is other loan officers, right? What are they touting each and every day to your Realtors? Great rates? Great service? How about a "one-time close" loan?

Doesn't everyone have that? They'd better, or they won't be in the mortgage business for very long. How do you position yourself to be not only different from your competitors but also *smarter*?

If there's one thing you should do in this industry it's to position yourself as the "market guru." How is this done? Put together a Power-Point presentation and some marketing flyers entitled "How Mortgage Rates are Set: The Untold Truth."

But you must first understand the intricate details of mortgage pricing. It's not just enough to say "non-farm payroll numbers are up/down." You need to know it all.

From the first day an originator enters the mortgage business, he is often asked to comment on the direction of mortgage rates. Additionally, he is often asked what factors will determine the interest rate or price. Surprisingly, even originators with many years of experience have difficulty getting their arms around this subject. Let's take a closer look at some of the facts, myths, and keys to the mortgage-rate puzzle—you might just be surprised.

First, let's discuss what does not affect mortgage pricing. Many individuals in the mortgage industry look at the 10-year U.S. Treasury note as a guide to the direction of mortgage rates and pricing. The fact is, the 10-year U.S. Treasury note has nothing to do with daily mortgage pricing. It does however, have a lot to do with price hedging after a loan closes.

It is important to know the difference between "bonds" and

"notes." Maturities that are greater than one year but less than or equal to 10 years are known as "notes." Maturities greater than 10 years are called "bonds," and maturities less than one year are called "bills." Once again, U.S. Treasury bonds, notes, or bills do not have any direct relationship to mortgage pricing. Treasuries are backed by the full faith and credit of the U.S. government, but mortgages are secured by the underlying real estate value.

Is the 10-Year Note Really a Mortgage Benchmark?

Why all the confusion? I have heard it over and over; people in the financial media presenting information on the bond markets and continually making erroneous assumptions about the relationship between mortgage interest rates and U.S. Treasury bond and note prices. This happens because these financial reporters may understand the bond markets in general but they are not mortgage experts and do not fully understand how mortgage interest rates are determined. Bond market reporters mistakenly tie mortgage rates to the performance of the 10-year U.S. Treasury note on a routine basis. You see this happen on CNBC all the time. In reality, mortgage interest rates and the intraday repricing that occur are determined by the performance of mortgage-backed securities (MBSs) or mortgage bonds, not 10-year U.S. Treasury notes.

So why do so many mortgage originators look at the wrong security? The information on MBSs is not easily available. Moreover, in order to get live, real-time pricing of MBSs you must subscribe to a quote service like www.mortgagemarketguide.com. Following actual MBS prices will allow you to make much better decisions on locking because you will know what your daily price sheets will look like *before* you get them.

Living in Two Separate Worlds

Clients and loan originators live in the "lock the rate" world. Customers want the best rate and we want to help them while getting a fair profit.

Once a mortgage is closed, it must be sold. Quite often, loans are sold to Fannie Mae or Freddie Mac, who then turn them into MBS to be sold to the public through the securities markets. As the daily pricing is bid higher or lower in the open securities markets, your rate sheet reflects the exact price changes that occur. Therefore, we are concerned with the prices of MBSs, which directly affects our rate sheet.

After the loan closes, the wholesale lender or servicing entity must sell it to Fannie Mae, Freddie Mac, etc., so it can be securitized for sale to the public. But many times, that loan will need post closing documentation before it can be moved off the wholesale lender's books. This adds some large risks because the market is moving during this period. Lenders live in the "after the closing" world.

Sure if the market improves, the lender will make a lot of extra money. But what if the market significantly worsens? The lender can be exposed to huge losses. A great way to protect themselves from losses would be to find a way to make money when the MBS market significantly worsens. Additionally, they would need to do this at an affordable cost. Unfortunately, there is no such way to do this with MBSs, but you can do this with *10-year U.S. Treasury notes*. A lender can buy a security that trades like a stock and emulate the yield of the 10-year U.S. Treasury note. Affordable call options can be purchased to generate profits when yields rise. Although this strategy will not exactly follow the movement of the MBS market, it gives lenders a way to affordably protect their pipeline from significant price worsening in the market.

This type of insurance is called "hedging" and is why you may often hear comments that mortgage rates are pegged to the 10-year U.S. Treasury note. In their "after the closing" world, the 10-year note does play a major role, but in our "lock the rate" world, the 10-year U.S. Treasury note has no bearing on our pricing—we must only follow the pricing of mortgage bonds.

Everything that is printed on your business cards and any promotional material should showcase your market savvy. Instead of being just another "mortgage person," be the financial whiz who Realtors call up right out of the blue and say, "Gee, Barry . . . what are rates going to do?"

If you market your industry acumen, you're light years ahead of your competition. You're not just another loan officer, you're THE loan officer.

About Barry Habib

Barry Habib is the CEO of the Mortgage Market Guide service, which helps over 14,000 of America's best originators monitor market conditions, improve their production, better manage their pipeline, and strengthen their position as trusted advisors.

Mr. Habib has over 20 years of experience in the mortgage industry. Barry has consistently been recognized as one of America's top loan originators. He has averaged nearly $100 million per year in individual production during his 20 years in the industry and is one of very few originators who have produced almost $2 billion in individual production over his career. Barry has achieved these levels with only one assistant and is still an active loan originator.

Barry is regularly featured on the CNBC television network. Additionally, Barry is often featured on NBC, CNN, and FOX. Barry has been the keynote speaker for 50 different state mortgage banking associations.

Appendix A: The 1003 and Disclosure Forms

All forms in Appendix A are reprinted with permission from Calyx Software, creators of POINT.

Figure A-1.

Uniform Residential Loan Application

This application is designed to be completed by the applicant(s) with the Lender's assistance. Applicants should complete this form as "Borrower" or "Co-Borrower", as applicable. Co-Borrower information must also be provided (and the appropriate box checked) when ☐ the income or assets of a person other than the "Borrower" (including the Borrower's spouse) will be used as a basis for loan qualification or ☐ the income or assets of the Borrower's spouse or other person who has community property rights pursuant to state law will not be used as a basis for loan qualification, but his or her liabilities must be considered because the spouse or other person has community property rights pursuant to applicable law and Borrower resides in a community property state, the security property is located in a community property state, or the Borrower is relying on other property located in a community property state as a basis for repayment of the loan.

If this is an application for joint credit, Borrower and Co-Borrower each agree that we intend to apply for joint credit (sign below):

Borrower _____   Co-Borrower _____

I. TYPE OF MORTGAGE AND TERMS OF LOAN

Mortgage Applied for:	☐ VA ☐ FHA	☑ Conventional ☐ USDA/Rural Housing Service	☐ Other (explain):	Agency Case Number	Lender Case Number

Amount $	Interest Rate %	No. of Months	Amortization Type:	☑ Fixed Rate ☐ GPM	☐ Other (explain): ☐ ARM (type):

II. PROPERTY INFORMATION AND PURPOSE OF LOAN

Subject Property Address (street, city, state, & ZIP)	No. of Units

Legal Description of Subject Property (attach description if necessary)	Year Built

Purpose of Loan ☑ Purchase ☐ Construction ☐ Other (explain): ☐ Refinance ☐ Construction-Permanent

Property will be: ☑ Primary Residence ☐ Secondary Residence ☐ Investment

Complete this line if construction or construction-permanent loan.

Year Lot Acquired	Original Cost $	Amount Existing Liens $	(a) Present Value of Lot $	(b) Cost of Improvements $	Total (a+b) $

Complete this line if this is a refinance loan.

Year Acquired	Original Cost $	Amount Existing Liens $	Purpose of Refinance	Describe Improvements ☐ made ☐ to be made
				Cost: $

Title will be held in what Name(s)	Manner in which Title will be held	Estate will be held in: ☑ Fee Simple ☐ Leasehold (show expiration date)

Source of Down Payment, Settlement Charges and/or Subordinate Financing (explain)

III. BORROWER INFORMATION

Borrower	Co-Borrower
Borrower's Name (include Jr. or Sr. if applicable)	Co-Borrower's Name (include Jr. or Sr. if applicable)

Social Security Number	Home Phone (incl. area code)	DOB (mm/dd/yyyy)	Yrs. School	Social Security Number	Home Phone (incl. area code)	DOB (mm/dd/yyyy)	Yrs. School

☐ Married ☐ Separated	☐ Unmarried (include single, divorced, widowed)	Dependents (not listed by Co-Borrower) no. ages	☐ Married ☐ Separated	☐ Unmarried (include single, divorced, widowed)	Dependents (not listed by Borrower) no. ages

Present Address (street, city, state, ZIP) ☐ Own ☐ Rent _____ No. Yrs.	Present Address (street, city, state, ZIP) ☐ Own ☐ Rent _____ No. Yrs.

Mailing Address, if different from Present Address	Mailing Address, if different from Present Address

If residing at present address for less than two years, complete the following:

Former Address (street, city, state, ZIP) ☐ Own ☐ Rent _____ No. Yrs.	Former Address (street, city, state, ZIP) ☐ Own ☐ Rent _____ No. Yrs.

Former Address (street, city, state, ZIP) ☐ Own ☐ Rent _____ No. Yrs.	Former Address (street, city, state, ZIP) ☐ Own ☐ Rent _____ No. Yrs.

IV. EMPLOYMENT INFORMATION

Borrower			Co-Borrower		
Name & Address of Employer	☐ Self Employed	Yrs. on this job	Name & Address of Employer	☐ Self Employed	Yrs. on this job
		Yrs. employed in this line of work/profession			Yrs. employed in this line of work/profession
Position/Title/Type of Business	Business Phone (incl. area code)		Position/Title/Type of Business	Business Phone (incl. area code)	

If employed in current position for less than two years or if currently employed in more than one position, complete the following:

Name & Address of Employer	☐ Self Employed	Dates (from-to)	Name & Address of Employer	☐ Self Employed	Dates (from-to)
		Monthly Income $			Monthly Income $
Position/Title/Type of Business	Business Phone (incl. area code)		Position/Title/Type of Business	Business Phone (incl. area code)	

Name & Address of Employer	☐ Self Employed	Dates (from-to)	Name & Address of Employer	☐ Self Employed	Dates (from-to)
		Monthly Income $			Monthly Income $
Position/Title/Type of Business	Business Phone (incl. area code)		Position/Title/Type of Business	Business Phone (incl. area code)	

Name & Address of Employer	☐ Self Employed	Dates (from-to)	Name & Address of Employer	☐ Self Employed	Dates (from-to)
		Monthly Income $			Monthly Income $
Position/Title/Type of Business	Business Phone (incl. area code)		Position/Title/Type of Business	Business Phone (incl. area code)	

Name & Address of Employer	☐ Self Employed	Dates (from-to)	Name & Address of Employer	☐ Self Employed	Dates (from-to)
		Monthly Income $			Monthly Income $
Position/Title/Type of Business	Business Phone (incl. area code)		Position/Title/Type of Business	Business Phone (incl. area code)	

V. MONTHLY INCOME AND COMBINED HOUSING EXPENSE INFORMATION

Gross Monthly Income	Borrower	Co-Borrower	Total	Combined Monthly Housing Expense	Present	Proposed
Base Empl. Income*	$	$	$	Rent	$	
Overtime				First Mortgage (P&I)		$
Bonuses				Other Financing (P&I)		
Commissions				Hazard Insurance		
Dividends/Interest				Real Estate Taxes		
Net Rental Income				Mortgage Insurance		
Other (before completing. see the notice in "describe other income," below)				Homeowner Assn. Dues		
				Other:		
Total	$	$	$	Total	$	$

* Self Employed Borrower(s) may be required to provide additional documentation such as tax returns and financial statements.

Describe Other Income   Notice: Alimony, child support, or separate maintenance income need not be revealed if the Borrower (B) or Co-Borrower (C) does not choose to have it considered for repaying this loan.

B/C		Monthly Amount
		$

Fannie Mae Form 1003   07/05
CALYX Form Loanapp2.frm 09/05

Page 2 of 5

Borrower _____
Co-Borrower _____

Freddie Mac Form 65   07/05

VI. ASSETS AND LIABILITIES

This Statement and any applicable supporting schedules may be completed jointly by both married and unmarried Co-borrowers if their assets and liabilities are sufficiently joined so that the Statement can be meaningfully and fairly presented on a combined basis; otherwise, separate Statements and Schedules are required. If the Co-Borrower section was completed about a non-applicant spouse or other person, this Statement and supporting schedules must be completed by that spouse or other person also.

Completed ☑ Jointly ☐ Not Jointly

ASSETS Description	Cash or Market Value	Liabilities and Pledged Assets. List the creditor's name, address and account number for all outstanding debts, including automobile loans, revolving charge accounts, real estate loans, alimony, child support, stock pledges, etc. Use continuation sheet, if necessary. Indicate by (*) those liabilities which will be satisfied upon sale of real estate owned or upon refinancing of the subject property.		
Cash deposit toward purchase held by:	$			
		LIABILITIES	Monthly Payment & Months Left to Pay	Unpaid Balance
List checking and savings accounts below		Name and address of Company	$ Payment/Months	$
Name and address of Bank, S&L, or Credit Union				
		Acct. no.		
Acct. no.	$	Name and address of Company	$ Payment/Months	$
Name and address of Bank, S&L, or Credit Union				
		Acct. no.		
Acct. no.	$	Name and address of Company	$ Payment/Months	$
Name and address of Bank, S&L, or Credit Union				
		Acct. no.		
Acct. no.	$	Name and address of Company	$ Payment/Months	$
Stocks & Bonds (Company name/number description)	$			
		Acct. no.		
		Name and address of Company	$ Payment/Months	$
Life insurance net cash value	$			
Face amount: $				
Subtotal Liquid Assets	$	Acct. no.		
Real estate owned (enter market value from schedule of real estate owned)	$	Name and address of Company	$ Payment/Months	$
Vested interest in retirement fund	$			
Net worth of business(es) owned (attach financial statement)	$	Acct. no.		
Automobiles owned (make and year)	$	Alimony/Child Support/Separate Maintenance Payments Owed to:	$	
Other Assets (itemize)	$	Job-Related Expense (child care, union dues, etc.)	$	
		Total Monthly Payments	$	
Total Assets a.	$	Net Worth (a minus b) => $	Total Liabilities b.	$

Schedule of Real Estate Owned (if additional properties are owned, use continuation sheet)

Property Address (enter S if sold, PS if pending sale or R if rental being held for income)	Type of Property	Present Market Value	Amount of Mortgages & Liens	Gross Rental Income	Mortgage Payments	Insurance, Maintenance, Taxes & Misc.	Net Rental Income
		$	$	$	$	$	$
Totals		$	$	$	$	$	$

List any additional names under which credit has previously been received and indicate appropriate creditor name(s) and account number(s):

Alternate Name	Creditor Name	Account Number

Fannie Mae Form 1003   07/05
CALYX Form Loanapp3.frm 09/05

Page 3 of 5

Borrower _____
Co-Borrower _____

Freddie Mac Form 65   07/05

VII. DETAILS OF TRANSACTION		VIII. DECLARATIONS					
		If you answer "Yes" to any questions a through i, please use continuation sheet for explanation.		Borrower		Co-Borrower	
				Yes No		Yes No	
a. Purchase price	$	a. Are there any outstanding judgments against you?		☐ ☐		☐ ☐	
b. Alterations, improvements, repairs		b. Have you been declared bankrupt within the past 7 years?		☐ ☐		☐ ☐	
c. Land (if acquired separately)		c. Have you had property foreclosed upon or given title or deed in lieu thereof in the last 7 years?		☐ ☐		☐ ☐	
d. Refinance (incl. debts to be paid off)							
e. Estimated prepaid items		d. Are you a party to a lawsuit?		☐ ☐		☐ ☐	
f. Estimated closing costs		e. Have you directly or indirectly been obligated on any loan which resulted in foreclosure, transfer of title in lieu of foreclosure, or judgment?		☐ ☐		☐ ☐	
g. PMI, MIP, Funding Fee							
h. Discount (if Borrower will pay)		(This would include such loans as home mortgage loans, SBA loans, home improvement loans, educational loans, manufactured (mobile) home loans, any mortgage, financial obligation, bond, or loan guarantee. If "Yes," provide details, including date, name and address of Lender, FHA or VA case number, if any, and reasons for the action.)					
i. Total costs (add items a through h)							
j. Subordinate financing		f. Are you presently delinquent or in default on any Federal debt or any other loan, mortgage, financial obligation, bond, or loan guarantee? If "Yes," give details as described in the preceding question.		☐ ☐		☐ ☐	
k. Borrower's closing costs paid by Seller							
l. Other Credits (explain)							
		g. Are you obligated to pay alimony, child support, or separate maintenance?		☐ ☐		☐ ☐	
		h. Is any part of the down payment borrowed?		☐ ☐		☐ ☐	
		i. Are you a co-maker or endorser on a note?		☐ ☐		☐ ☐	
		j. Are you a U. S. citizen?		☐ ☐		☐ ☐	
m. Loan amount (exclude PMI, MIP, Funding Fee financed)		k. Are you a permanent resident alien?		☐ ☐		☐ ☐	
		l. Do you intend to occupy the property as your primary residence? If "Yes," complete question m below.		☐ ☐		☐ ☐	
n. PMI, MIP, Funding Fee financed							
		m. Have you had an ownership interest in a property in the last three years?		☐ ☐		☐ ☐	
o. Loan amount (add m & n)		(1) What type of property did you own-principal residence (PR), second home (SH), or investment property (IP)?					
p. Cash from/to Borrower (subtract j, k, l & o from i)		(2) How did you hold title to the home-solely by yourself (S), jointly with your spouse (SP), or jointly with another person (O)?					

IX. ACKNOWLEDGEMENT AND AGREEMENT

Each of the undersigned specifically represents to Lender and to Lender's actual or potential agents, brokers, processors, attorneys, insurers, servicers, successors and assigns and agrees and acknowledges that: (1) the information provided in this application is true and correct as of the date set forth opposite my signature and that any intentional or negligent misrepresentation of this information contained in this application may result in civil liability, including monetary damages, to any person who may suffer any loss due to reliance upon any misrepresentation that I have made on this application, and/or in criminal penalties including, but not limited to, fine or imprisonment or both under the provisions of Title 18, United States Code, Sec. 1001, et seq.; (2) the loan requested pursuant to this application (the "Loan") will be secured by a mortgage or deed of trust on the property described in this application; (3) the property will not be used for any illegal or prohibited purpose or use; (4) all statements made in this application are made for the purpose of obtaining a residential mortgage loan; (5) the property will be occupied as indicated in this application; (6) the Lender, its servicers, successors or assigns may retain the original and/or an electronic record of this application, whether or not the Loan is approved; (7) the Lender and its agents, brokers, insurers, servicers, successors and assigns may continuously rely on the information contained in the application, and I am obligated to amend and/or supplement the information provided in this application if any of the material facts that I have represented herein should change prior to closing of the Loan; (8) in the event that my payments on the Loan become delinquent, the Lender, its servicers, successors or assigns may, in addition to any other rights and remedies that it may have relating to such delinquency, report my name and account information to one or more consumer reporting agencies; (9) ownership of the Loan and/or administration of the Loan account may be transferred with such notice as may be required by law; (10) neither Lender nor its agents, brokers, insurers, servicers, successors or assigns has made any representation or warranty, express or implied, to me regarding the property or the condition or value of the property; and (11) my transmission of this application as an "electronic record" containing my "electronic signature," as those terms are defined in applicable federal and/or state laws (excluding audio and video recordings), or my facsimile transmission of this application containing a facsimile of my signature, shall be as effective, enforceable and valid as if a paper version of this application were delivered containing my original written signature.

Acknowledgement. Each of the undersigned hereby acknowledges that any owner of the Loan, its servicers, successors and assigns, may verify or reverify any information contained in this application or obtain any information or data relating to the Loan, for any legitimate purpose through any source, including a source named in this application or a consumer reporting agency.

Borrower's Signature	Date	Co-Borrower's Signature	Date
X		X	

X. INFORMATION FOR GOVERNMENT MONITORING PURPOSES

The following information is requested by the Federal Government for certain types of loans related to a dwelling in order to monitor the lender's compliance with equal credit opportunity, fair housing and home mortgage disclosure laws. You are not required to furnish this information, but are encouraged to do so. The law provides that a Lender may not discriminate either on the basis of this information, or on whether you choose to furnish it. If you furnish the information, please provide both ethnicity and race. For race, you may check more than one designation. If you do not furnish ethnicity, race, or sex, under Federal regulations, this lender is required to note the information on the basis of visual observation and surname if you have made this application in person. If you do not wish to furnish the information, please check the box below. (Lender must review the above material to assure that the disclosures satisfy all requirements to which the lender is subject under applicable state law for the particular type of loan applied for.)

BORROWER	☐ I do not wish to furnish this information	CO-BORROWER	☐ I do not wish to furnish this information
Ethnicity:	☐ Hispanic or Latino ☐ Not Hispanic or Latino	Ethnicity:	☐ Hispanic or Latino ☐ Not Hispanic or Latino
Race:	☐ American Indian or Alaska Native ☐ Asian ☐ Black or African American	Race:	☐ American Indian or Alaska Native ☐ Asian ☐ Black or African American
	☐ Native Hawaiian or Other Pacific Islander ☐ White		☐ Native Hawaiian or Other Pacific Islander ☐ White
Sex:	☐ Female ☐ Male	Sex:	☐ Female ☐ Male

To be Completed by Interviewer This application was taken by:	Interviewer's Name (print or type)		Name and Address of Interviewer's Employer
☐ Face-to-face interview	Interviewer's Signature	Date	CD Reed
☐ Mail			2000 Mortgage Street
☐ Telephone	Interviewer's Phone Number (incl. area code)		Austin, TX 78730
☐ Internet			(P) 512-555-5555
			(F) 866-555-5555

Continuation Sheet/Residential Loan Application

Use this continuation sheet if you need more space to complete the Residential Loan Application. Mark B for Borrower or C for Co-Borrower.	Borrower:	Agency Case Number:
	Co-Borrower:	Lender Case Number:

VI. ASSETS AND LIABILITIES

ASSETS	Cash or Market Value	LIABILITIES	Monthly Payment & Months Left to Pay	Unpaid Balance
Name and address of Bank, S&L, or Credit Union		Name and address of Company	$ Payt./Mos.	$
Acct. no.	$	Acct. No.		
Name and address of Bank, S&L, or Credit Union		Name and address of Company	$ Payt./Mos.	$
Acct. no.	$	Acct. No.		
Name and address of Bank, S&L, or Credit Union		Name and address of Company	$ Payt./Mos.	$
Acct. no.	$	Acct. No.		
Name and address of Bank, S&L, or Credit Union		Name and address of Company	$ Payt./Mos.	$
Acct. no.	$	Acct. No.		
Name and address of Bank, S&L, or Credit Union		Name and address of Company	$ Payt./Mos.	$
Acct. no.	$	Acct. No.		
Name and address of Bank, S&L, or Credit Union		Name and address of Company	$ Payt./Mos.	$
Acct. no.	$	Acct. No.		
Name and address of Bank, S&L, or Credit Union		Name and address of Company	$ Payt./Mos.	$
Acct. no.	$	Acct. No.		

I/We fully understand that it is a Federal crime punishable by fine or imprisonment, or both, to knowingly make any false statements concerning any of the above facts as applicable under the provisions of Title 18, United States Code, Section 1001, et seq.

Borrower's Signature:	Date	Co-Borrower's Signature:	Date
X		X	

Figure A-2.

GOOD FAITH ESTIMATE

Applicants:	Application No:
Property Addr:	Date Prepared: 01/01/2008
Prepared By: CD Reed Ph. 512-555-5555	Loan Program: 30 year fixed
2000 Mortgage Street, Austin, TX 78730	

The information provided below reflects estimates of the charges which you are likely to incur at the settlement of your loan. The fees listed are estimates-actual charges may be more or less. Your transaction may not involve a fee for every item listed. The numbers listed beside the estimates generally correspond to the numbered lines contained in the HUD-1 settlement statement which you will be receiving at settlement. The HUD-1 settlement statement will show you the actual cost for items paid at settlement.

Total Loan Amount $ 200,000   Interest Rate: 7.000 %   Term: mths

800	ITEMS PAYABLE IN CONNECTION WITH LOAN:		PFC S F POC
801	Loan Origination Fee	$	
802	Loan Discount	1.000%	2,000.00
803	Appraisal Fee		350.00
804	Credit Report		15.00
805	Lender's Inspection Fee		100.00
808	Mortgage Broker Fee		
809	Tax Related Service Fee		67.00
810	Processing Fee		400.00
811	Underwriting Fee		350.00
812	Wire Transfer Fee		50.00

1100	TITLE CHARGES:		PFC S F POC
1101	Closing or Escrow Fee:	$	350.00
1105	Document Preparation Fee		200.00
1106	Notary Fees		
1107	Attorney Fees		200.00
1108	Title Insurance:		175.00

1200	GOVERNMENT RECORDING & TRANSFER CHARGES:		PFC S F POC
1201	Recording Fees:	$	85.00
1202	City/County Tax/Stamps:		
1203	State Tax/Stamps:		2,000.00

1300	ADDITIONAL SETTLEMENT CHARGES:		PFC S F POC
1302	Pest Inspection	$	200.00

		Estimated Closing Costs	6,542.00

900	ITEMS REQUIRED BY LENDER TO BE PAID IN ADVANCE:			PFC S F POC
901	Interest for 1 days @ $	38.8889 per day	$	38.89
902	Mortgage Insurance Premium			
903	Hazard Insurance Premium			
904				
905	VA Funding Fee			

1000	RESERVES DEPOSITED WITH LENDER:				PFC S F POC
1001	Hazard Insurance Premium	12 months @ $	100.00 per month	$	1,200.00
1002	Mortgage Ins. Premium Reserves	months @ $	per month		
1003	School Tax	months @ $	per month		
1004	Taxes and Assessment Reserves	months @ $	per month		
1005	Flood Insurance Reserves	months @ $	per month		
		months @ $	per month		
		months @ $	per month		

	Estimated Prepaid Items/Reserves	1,238.89
TOTAL ESTIMATED SETTLEMENT CHARGES		7,780.89

COMPENSATION TO BROKER (Not Paid Out of Loan Proceeds):		
1%	$	$2,000.00

TOTAL ESTIMATED FUNDS NEEDED TO CLOSE:			TOTAL ESTIMATED MONTHLY PAYMENT:	
Purchase Price/Payoff (+)	300,000.00	New First Mortgage(-)	Principal & Interest	
Loan Amount (-)	200,000.00	Sub Financing(-)	Other Financing (P & I)	
Est. Closing Costs (+)	6,542.00	New 2nd Mtg Closing Costs(+)	Hazard Insurance	100.00
Est. Prepaid Items/Reserves (+)	1,238.89		Real Estate Taxes	
Amount Paid by Seller (-)			Mortgage Insurance	
			Homeowner Assn. Dues	
			Other	

Total Est. Funds needed to close		107,780.89	Total Monthly Payment	100.00

[✓] This Good Faith Estimate is being provided by   CD Reed , a mortgage broker, and no lender has been obtained. These estimates are provided pursuant to the Real Estate Settlement Procedures Act of 1974, as amended (RESPA). Additional information can be found in the HUD Special Information Booklet, which is to be provided to you by your mortgage broker or lender, if your application is to purchase residential real property and the lender will take a first lien on the property. The undersigned acknowledges receipt of the booklet "Settlement Costs," and if applicable the Consumer Handbook on ARM Mortgages.

Applicant	Date	Applicant	Date

Figure A-3.

TRUTH-IN-LENDING DISCLOSURE STATEMENT
(THIS IS NEITHER A CONTRACT NOR A COMMITMENT TO LEND)

Applicants:

Property Address: 123 Main Street
Bivins, TX 75555

Application No: 061025003

Prepared By: CD Reed
2000 Mortgage Street
Austin , TX 78730
512-555-5555

Date Prepared: 01/01/2008

ANNUAL PERCENTAGE RATE	FINANCE CHARGE	AMOUNT FINANCED	TOTAL OF PAYMENTS
The cost of your credit as a yearly rate	The dollar amount the credit will cost you	The amount of credit provided to you or on your behalf	The amount you will have paid after making all payments as scheduled
7.000 %	$ 279,021.94	$ 200,000.00	$ 479,021.94

☐ REQUIRED DEPOSIT: The annual percentage rate does not take into account your required deposit
PAYMENTS: Your payment schedule will be:

Number of Payments	Amount of Payments **	When Payments Are Due	Number of Payments	Amount of Payments **	When Payments Are Due	Number of Payments	Amount of Payments **	When Payments Are Due
		Monthly Beginning:			Monthly Beginning:			Monthly Beginning:
359	1,330.60	03/01/2008						
1	1,336.54	02/01/2038						

☐ DEMAND FEATURE: This obligation has a demand feature.
☐ VARIABLE RATE FEATURE: This loan contains a variable rate feature. A variable rate disclosure has been provided earlier.

CREDIT LIFE/CREDIT DISABILITY: Credit life insurance and credit disability insurance are not required to obtain credit, and will not be provided unless you sign and agree to pay the additional cost.

Type	Premium	Signature	
Credit Life		I want credit life insurance.	Signature:
Credit Disability		I want credit disability insurance.	Signature:
Credit Life and Disability		I want credit life and disability insurance.	Signature:

INSURANCE: The following insurance is required to obtain credit:
☐ Credit life insurance ☐ Credit disability ☑ Property insurance ☐ Flood insurance
You may obtain the insurance from anyone you want that is acceptable to creditor
☐ If you purchase ☐ property ☐ flood insurance from creditor you will pay $ for a one year term.
SECURITY: You are giving a security interest in:
☐ The goods or property being purchased   ☐ Real property you already own.
FILING FEES: $
LATE CHARGE: If a payment is more than   15 days late, you will be charged   5.000 % of the payment
PREPAYMENT: If you pay off early, you
☐ may   ☑ will not   have to pay a penalty.
☐ may   ☑ will not   be entitled to a refund of part of the finance charge.
ASSUMPTION: Someone buying your property
☐ may   ☐ may, subject to conditions   ☑ may not   assume the remainder of your loan on the original terms.
See your contract documents for any additional information about nonpayment, default, any required repayment in full before the scheduled date and prepayment refunds and penalties
☐ * means an estimate   ☐ all dates and numerical disclosures except the late payment disclosures are estimates.

* * NOTE: The Payments shown above include reserve deposits for Mortgage Insurance (if applicable), but exclude Property Taxes and Insurance.

THE UNDERSIGNED ACKNOWLEDGES RECEIVING A COMPLETED COPY OF THIS DISCLOSURE.

(Applicant)	(Date)		(Applicant)	(Date)
(Applicant)	(Date)		(Applicant)	(Date)
(Lender)	(Date)			

Figure A-4.

Borrowers' Certification and Authorization

CERTIFICATION

The Undersigned certify the following:

1. I/We have applied for a mortgage loan through CD Reed_____. In applying for the loan, I/We completed a loan application containing various information on the purpose of the loan, the amount and source of the down payment, employment and income information, and the assets and liabilities. I/We certify that all of the information is true and complete. I/We made no misrepresentations in the loan application or other documents, nor did I/We omit any pertinent information.

2. I/We understand and agree that CD Reed_____reserves the right to change the mortgage loan review processes to a full documentation program. This may include verifying the information provided on the application with the employer and/or the financial institution.

3. I/We fully understand that it is a Federal crime punishable by fine or imprisonment, or both, to knowingly make any false statements when applying for this mortgage, as applicable under the provisions of Title 18, United States Code, Section 1014.

AUTHORIZATION TO RELEASE INFORMATION

To Whom It May Concern:

1. I/We have applied for a mortgage loan through CD Reed_____. As part of the application process, CD Reed_____ and the mortgage guaranty insurer (if any), may verify information contained in my/our loan application and in other documents required in connection with the loan, either before the loan is closed or as part of its quality control program.

2. I/We authorize you to provide to CD Reed_____ and to any investor to whom CD Reed_____ may sell my mortgage, any and all information and documentation that they request. Such information includes, but is not limited to, employment history and income; bank, money market and similar account balances; credit history; and copies of income tax returns.

3. CD Reed_____ or any investor that purchases the mortgage may address this authorization to any party named in the loan application.

4. A copy of this authorization may be accepted as an original.

Borrower Signature _____   Co-Borrower Signature _____

SSN: _____ Date: _____   SSN: _____ Date: _____

Figure A-5.

EQUAL CREDIT OPPORTUNITY ACT

APPLICATION NO: 061025003   Date: 01/01/2008

PROPERTY ADDRESS: 123 Main Street
                     Bivins, TX 75555

The Federal Equal Credit Opportunity Act prohibits creditors from discriminating against credit applicants on the basis of race, color, religion, national origin, sex, marital status, age (provided the applicant has the capacity to enter into a binding contract); because all or part of the applicant's income derives from any public assistance program; or because the applicant has in good faith exercised any right under the Consumer Credit Protection Act. The Federal Agency that administers compliance with this law concerning this company is the Office of the Comptroller of the Currency, Customer Assistance Group, 1301 McKinney Street, Suite 3710, Houston, Texas 77010

We are required to disclose to you that you need not disclose income from alimony, child support or separate maintenance payment if you choose not to do so.

Having made this disclosure to you, we are permitted to inquire if any of the income shown on your application is derived from such a source and to consider the likelihood of consistent payment as we do with any income on which you are relying to qualify for the loan for which you are applying.

(Applicant)   (Date)   (Applicant)   (Date)

(Applicant)   (Date)   (Applicant)   (Date)

Figure A-6.

FLOOD HAZARD NOTICE
(Notice Of Special Flood Hazards and Availability Of Federal Disaster Relief Assistance)

Applicant(s): 123 Main Street Bivins, TX 75555	Lender:

You have applied to us for a loan secured by real estate or a mobile home in the amount of $200,000   located or to be located at: 123 Main Street. Bivins, TX 75555

NOTICE 1:   Notice to Borrower of Special Flood Hazard Area

We are giving you this notice to inform you that:

☐   The building securing the loan for which you have applied is or will be located in an area with special flood hazards.
☐   The mobile home securing the loan for which you have applied is or will be located in an area with special flood hazards.

The area has been identified by the Director of the Federal Emergency Management Agency (FEMA) as a special flood hazard area using FEMA's Flood Insurance Rate Map or the Flood Hazard Boundary Map for the following community: _____. This area has at least a one percent (1%) chance of a flood equal to or exceeding the base flood elevation (a 100-year flood) in any given year. During the life of a 30-year mortgage loan, the risk of a 100-year flood in a special flood hazard area is 26 percent (26%).

Federal law allows a lender and borrower jointly to request the Director of FEMA to review the determination of whether the property securing the loan is located in a special flood hazard area. If you would like to make such a request, please contact us for further information.

NOTICE 2:   Notice to Borrower about Federal Disaster Relief Assistance
(The ONE section indicated below applies to your application. Please read carefully.)

☐   The community in which the property securing the loan is located participates in the National Flood Insurance Program (NFIP). Federal law will not allow us to make you the loan that you have applied for if you do not purchase flood insurance. The flood insurance must be maintained for the life of the loan. If you fail to purchase or renew flood insurance on the property, federal law authorizes and requires us to purchase the flood insurance for you at your expense.

- Flood Insurance coverage under the NFIP may be purchased through an insurance agent who will obtain the policy either directly through the NFIP or through an insurance company that participates in the NFIP. Flood insurance also may be available from private insurers that participate in the NFIP.

- At a minimum, flood insurance purchased must cover the lesser of:
    1. The outstanding principal balance of the loan; or
    2. The maximum amount of coverage allowed for the type of property under the NFIP.
  Flood insurance coverage under the NFIP is limited to the overall value of the property securing the loan minus the value of the land on which the property is located.

- Federal disaster relief assistance (usually in the form of a low-interest loan) may be available for damages incurred in excess of your flood insurance if your community's participation in the NFIP is in accordance with NFIP requirements.

☐   Flood insurance coverage under the NFIP is not available for the property securing the loan because the community in which the property is located does not participate in the NFIP. In addition, if the non-participating community has been identified for at least one year as containing a special flood hazard area, properties located in the community will not be eligible for federal disaster relief assistance in the event of a Federally-declared flood disaster.

I/we have received a copy of this disclosure.

_____   _____   _____   _____
                                    Date   Date

Figure A-7.

Customer Identification Documentation
Patriot Act

The USA Patriot Act requires all financial institutions to obtain, verify and record information that identifies every customer. Completion of this documentation is required in order to comply with the USA Patriot Act. A completed copy of this information must be retained with the loan file.

Application Number ___061025003_____   Date _____

Name of Applicant _____

Social Security # _____   Date of Birth _____

Present Address _____

Mailing Address _____

Primary Identification Documentation

Document Type _____   Other Document Type _____

Document Number _____

Issue Date _____   Expiration Date _____

Issued by _____

Secondary Identification Documentation

Document Type _____   Other Document Type _____

Document Number _____

Issue Date _____   Expiration Date _____

Issued by _____

Discrepancies and Resolution

Completed by _____

Calyx Form (4/04)
BRWIDDoc.frm

PRIVACY POLICY DISCLOSURE
(Protection of the Privacy of Personal Non-Public Information)

Respecting and protecting customer privacy is vital to our business. By explaining our Privacy Policy to you, we trust that you will better understand how we keep our customer information private and secure while using it to serve you better. Keeping customer information secure is a top priority, and we are disclosing our policies to help you understand how we handle the personal information about you that we collect and disclose. This notice explains how you can limit our disclosing of personal information about you. The provisions of this notice will apply to former customers as well as current customers unless we state otherwise.

The Privacy Policy explains the Following:

- Protecting the confidentiality of our customer information.
- Who is covered by the Privacy Policy.
- How we gather information.
- The types of information we share, why, and with whom.
- Opting Out - how to instruct us not to share certain information about you or not to contact you.

Protecting the Confidentiality of Customer Information:

We take our responsibility to protect the privacy and confidentiality of customer information very seriously. We maintain physical, electronic, and procedural safeguards that comply with federal standards to store and secure information about you from unauthorized access, alteration, and destruction. Our control policies, for example, authorize access to customer information only by individuals who need access to do their work.

From time to time, we enter into agreements with other companies to provide services to us or make products and services available to you. Under these agreements, the companies may receive information about you but they must safeguard this information, and they may not use it for any other purposes.

Who is Covered by the Privacy Policy:

We provide our Privacy Policy to customers when they conduct business with our company. If we change our privacy policies to permit us to share additional information we have about you, as described below, or to permit disclosures to additional types of parties, you will be notified in advance. This Privacy Policy applies to consumers who are current customers or former customers.

How We Gather Information:

As part of providing you with financial products or services, we may obtain information about you from the following sources:

- Applications, forms, and other information that you provide to us, whether in writing, in person, by telephone, electronically, or by any other means. This information may include your name, address, employment information, income, and credit references;

- Your transaction with us, our affiliates, or others. This information may include your account balances, payment history, and account usage;

- Consumer reporting agencies. This information may include account information and information about your credit worthiness;

- Public sources. This information may include real estate records, employment records, telephone numbers, etc.

Information We Share:

We may disclose information we have about you as permitted by law. We are required to or we may provide information about you to third-parties without your consent, as permitted by law, such as:

- To regulatory authorities and law enforcement officials.

- To protect against or prevent actual or potential fraud, unauthorized transactions, claims, or other liability.

- To report account activity to credit bureaus.

- To consumer reporting agencies.

- To respond to a subpoena or court order, judicial process or regulatory authorities.
- In connection with a proposed or actual sale, merger, or transfer of all or a portion of a business or an operating unit, etc.

In addition, we may provide information about you to our service providers to help us process your applications or service your accounts. Our service providers may include billing service providers, mail and telephone service companies, lenders, investors, title and escrow companies, appraisal companies, etc.

We may also provide information about you to our service providers to help us perform marketing services. This information provided to these service providers may include the categories of information described above under "How We Gather Information" limited to only that which we deem appropriate for these service providers to carry out their functions.

We do not provide non-public information about you to any company whose products and services are being marketed unless you authorize us to do so. These companies are not allowed to use this information for purposes beyond your specific authorization.

Opting Out

We also may share information about you within our corporate family of office(s). We may share all of the categories of information we gather about you, including identification information (such as your name and address), credit reports (such as your credit history), application information (such as your income or credit references), your account transactions and experiences with us (such as your payment history), and information from other third parties (such as your employment history).

By sharing this information we can better understand your financial needs. We can then send you notification of new products and special promotional offers that you may not otherwise know about. For example, if you originally obtained a mortgage loan with us, we would know that you are a homeowner and may be interested in hearing how a home equity loan may be a better option than an auto loan to finance the purchase of a new car.

You may prohibit the sharing of application and third-party credit-related information within our company or any third-party company at any time. If you would like to limit disclosures of personal information about you as described in this notice, just check the appropriate box or boxes to indicate your privacy choices.

☐ Please do not share personal information about me with non-affilliated third-parties.

☐ Please do not share personal information about me with any of your affiliates except as necessary to effect, administer, process, service or enforce a transaction requested or authorized by myself.

☐ Please do not contact me with offers of products or services by mail.

☐ Please do not contact me with offers of products or services by telephone.

Note for Joint Accounts: Your Opt Out choices will also apply to other individuals who are joint account holders. If these individuals have separate accounts, your Opt Out will not apply to those separate accounts.

	CD Reed
Name	Company Name
	2000 Mortgage Street
Address	Address
	Austin TX, 78730
City, State, Zip	City, State, Zip
	512-555-5555
Phone#	Phone #
061025003	
Loan #	

_____   _____   _____   _____
Borrower's Signature   Date   Co-Borrower's Signature   Date

Calyx Form - privacy2.frm (06/05)

Figure A-9.

NOTICE TO APPLICANT OF RIGHT
TO RECEIVE COPY OF APPRAISAL REPORT

APPLICATION NO: 061025003 Date: 01/01/2008

PROPERTY ADDRESS: 123 Main Street
Bivins, TX 75555 County:Cass

You have the right to receive a copy of the appraisal report to be obtained in connection with the loan for which you are applying, provided that you have paid for the appraisal. We must receive your written request no later than 90 days after we notify you about the action taken on your application or you withdraw your application. If you would like a copy of the appraisal report, contact :

CD Reed
2000 Mortgage Street
Austin, TX 78730

(Applicant) (Date)	(Applicant) (Date)
(Applicant) (Date)	(Applicant) (Date)

Calyx Form rra.frm 12/96

Figure A-10.

SERVICING DISCLOSURE STATEMENT

Lender: CD Reed   Date: 01/01/2008
        2000 Mortgage Street
        Austin , TX 78730

NOTICE TO FIRST LIEN   MORTGAGE LOAN APPLICANTS: THE RIGHT TO COLLECT YOUR
MORTGAGE LOAN PAYMENTS MAY BE TRANSFERRED. FEDERAL LAW GIVES YOU CERTAIN
RELATED RIGHTS.   IF YOUR LOAN IS MADE,   SAVE THIS STATEMENT WITH YOUR LOAN
DOCUMENTS. SIGN THE ACKNOWLEDGMENT AT THE END OF THIS STATEMENT ONLY IF YOU
UNDERSTAND ITS CONTENTS.

Because you are applying for a mortgage loan covered by the Real Estate Settlement Procedures Act (RESPA)
(12 U.S.C. Section 2601 et seq.) you have certain rights under that Federal law.

This statement tells you about those rights. It also tells you what the chances are that the servicing for this loan
may be transferred to a different loan servicer.   "Servicing" refers to collecting your principal, interest and
escrow account payments, if any.   If your loan servicer changes, there are certain procedures that must be
followed. This statement generally explains those procedures.

Transfer practices and requirements

If the servicing of your loan is assigned, sold, or transferred to a new servicer, you must be given written
notice of that transfer.   The present loan servicer must send you notice in writing of the assignment, sale
or transfer of the servicing not less than 15 days before the effective date of the transfer.   The new loan
servicer must also send you notice within 15 days after the effective date of the transfer.   The present servicer
and the new servicer may combine this information in one notice, so long as the notice is sent to you 15 days
before the effective date of transfer.   The 15 day period is not applicable if a notice of prospective transfer
is provided to you at settlement.   The law allows a delay in the time (not more than 30 days after a transfer)
for servicers to notify you, upon the occurrence of certain business emergencies.

Notices must contain certain information.   They must contain the effective date of the transfer of the servicing
of your loan to the new servicer, and the name, address, and toll-free or collect call telephone number of the
new servicer, and toll-free or collect call telephone numbers of a person or department for both your present servicer
and your new servicer to answer your questions.   During the 60 day period following the effective date of the
transfer of the loan servicing, a loan payment received by your old servicer before its due date may not be treated
by the new loan servicer as late, and a late fee may not be imposed on you.

Complaint Resolution

Section 6 of RESPA (12 U.S.C. Section 2605) gives you certain consumer rights, whether or not your loan
servicing is transferred.   If you send a "qualified written request" to your servicer, then your servicer must
provide you with a written acknowledgment within 20 Business Days of receipt of your request.   A "qualified
written request" is a written correspondence, other than notice on a payment coupon or other payment medium
supplied by the servicer, which includes your name and account number, and the information regarding your
request.   Not later than 60 Business Days after receiving your request, your servicer must make any appropriate
corrections to your account, or must provide you with a written clarification regarding any dispute.   During this
60 Business Day period, your servicer may not provide information to a consumer reporting agency concerning any
overdue payment related to such period or qualified written request.

A Business Day is any day in which the offices of the business entity are open to the public for carrying on
substantially all of its business functions.

Damages and Costs

Section 6 of RESPA also provides for damages and costs for individuals or classes of individuals in circumstances
where servicers are shown to have violated the requirements of that Section.

CALYX Form Sds.hp 6/96   Page 1 of 2

Servicing Transfer Estimates

1. The following is the best estimate of what will happen to the servicing of your mortgage loan:

   A. ☐ We may assign, sell or transfer the servicing of your loan while the loan is outstanding.

   We are able to service your loan, and we
   ☐ will service your loan.
   ☐ will not service your loan.
   ☐ haven't decided whether to service your loan.

   B. ☐ We do not service mortgage loans ☐ and we have not serviced mortgage loans in the past three years.
   We presently intend to assign, sell or transfer the servicing of your mortgage loan. You will be informed about your servicer.

2. For all mortgage loans that we make in the 12 month period after your mortgage loan is funded, we estimate that the percentage of such loans for which we will transfer servicing is between:

   _____ 0 to 25%   _____ 26 to 50%   _____ 51 to 75%   _____ 76 to 100%

   This estimate ☐ does ☐ does not   include assignments, sales or transfers to affiliates or subsidiaries.

   This is only our best estimate and it is not binding. Business conditions or other circumstances may affect our future transferring decisions.

3. A. ☐ We have previously assigned, sold, or transferred the servicing of mortgage loans.

   B. ☐ This is our record of transferring the servicing of mortgage loans we have made in:

Year	Percentage of Loans Transferred
	%
	%
	%

   This information ☐ does ☐ does not   include assignments, sales or transfers to affiliates or subsidiaries.

Acknowledgment of Mortgage Loan Applicant(s)

I/We have read and understood the disclosure; and understand that the disclosure is a required part of the mortgage application as evidenced by my/our signature(s) below;

Applicant	Date	Applicant	Date

Applicant	Date	Applicant	Date

Appendix B: Ten Steps to Becoming a Successful Mortgage Loan Officer

1. Understand how mortgage rates move and how rates are set. This will make you more money per loan and keep more clients from going to other mortgage companies.

2. Subscribe to trade publications and join local associations. Educate yourself and network as often as possible.

3. Start out processing your own loans so you know the intricacies of loan submission and approvals.

4. Establish a database of clients as soon as possible and begin a regular marketing campaign to them.

5. Be best friends with your loan processor. He or she will save you when you least expect it and will promote you when you don't know it.

6. Don't try to learn every loan at once; concentrate on one loan program until you get it down pat.

7. Take a loan application to get to know your client, not just to close a deal.

8. Be loyal. Don't shop your clients' loans around for another quarter point in income.

9. Establish affiliate relationships with appraisers, title agencies, attorneys—anyone whom you'll be working with while closing loans. You refer business to them, they'll refer business to you.

10. Don't forget that although a mortgage loan makes you money, what you're really doing is helping people buy their own homes.

Appendix C: Ten Steps to Becoming a Megaproducer ($250,000 + per year)

1. Become intimately aware of the financial impact of a mortgage on a client's portfolio, and establish relationships with certified financial planners, stock brokers, and certified public accountants.

2. Become a certified mortgage planner.

3. Hire a marketing assistant and a loan assistant to help promote you and to take loan applications while you work your relationships. Loan officers who close over 100 loans per year need help. Those who close over 500 per year need top-shelf assistants.

4. Establish yourself as "the authority." Concentrate on a niche segment of the marketplace instead of trying to be all things to all consumers.

5. Write a book, become a columnist, or speak in public about mortgage loans to establish your authority.

6. Learn to say no to loans that will take up too much of your time.

7. Subscribe to as many proven wealth-building programs as you can, such as Mortgage Market Guide, The Mortgage Coach, and read, read, read material from proven sources such as *Loan Officer* magazine and *Mortgage Originator* magazine.

8. Form your own "club" with other professionals outside the mortgage business.

9. Set goals with your financial planner and work to achieve them.

10. Always remember that you're not in the business to make money, but to help people achieve their own goals. Do that, and the money takes care of itself. I'm not kidding.

Appendix D:
Sample Marketing Pieces

Figure D-1. Greeting card.

Figure D-2. Calendar.

Agent Name
Company Name
Office: (555) 123-4567
Cell: (555) 000-1234
info@sharperagent.com
www.website.com

Autumn
2006

SEPTEMBER

SUN	MON	TUES	WED	THU	FRI	SAT
					1	2
3	4	5	6	7	8	9
10	11	12	13	14	15	16
17	18	19	20	21	22	23
24	25	26	27	28	29	30

OCTOBER

SUN	MON	TUES	WED	THU	FRI	SAT
1	2	3	4	5	6	7
8	9	10	11	12	13	14
15	16	17	18	19	20	21
22	23	24	25	26	27	28
29	30	31				

NOVEMBER

SUN	MON	TUES	WED	THU	FRI	SAT
			1	2	3	4
5	6	7	8	9	10	11
12	13	14	15	16	17	18
19	20	21	22	23	24	25
26	27	28	29	30		

9/4 - Labor Day | 9/23 - Rosh Hashana | 9/24 - Ramadan Begins | 10/2 - Yom Kippur
10/9 - Columbus Day | 10/31 - Halloween | 11/11 - Veteran's Day | 11/23 - Thanksgiving Day

Figure D-3. Debt-to-income.

Appendix E: Industry Resources

Here are some more ways to learn about and stay current on the mortgage industry.

Print

Mortgage Originator **Magazine.** A monthly publication geared solely toward the mortgage-origination business. Covers all aspects of a mortgage loan officer's world, from technology questions to management styles to loan-origination techniques. If you get one magazine, get this one: www.mortgageoriginator.com.

National Mortgage Broker **Magazine.** The official magazine of the National Association of Mortgage Brokers. Geared for the mortgage broker and broker-related issues regarding sales, management, and regulatory issues: www.nationalmortgagebroker.com.

Broker **Magazine.** Published by National Mortgage News, this magazine concentrates on loan officer production, technology, and management issues: www.brokermagazine.com.

Lender in Touch. This is not a magazine or newspaper but a company that mails predesigned postcards, notes, and e-zines to your past clients, friends, and anyone else in your database. The service provides professionally written and produced glossy cards that keep you in front of your marketing database. You pay Lender in Touch an annual fee and it keeps in touch with your past clients on a regular basis. I like these pieces; they are very nicely done, very inexpensive, and they do what they're supposed to do by keeping your name in front of every person you know and wish to keep in touch with: www.lenderintouch .com.

Organizations

National Association of Mortgage Brokers. Official website for this organization with links to various state organizations as well: www .namb.org.

Mortgage Bankers Association of America. Official website for the Mortgage Bankers Association: www.mbaa.org.

National Association of Professional Mortgage Women. The group's slogan is, "Serving all mortgage professionals who want to excel and employers who want excellence." This is a dynamic organization that provides training, resources, and networking for mortgage professionals. Don't let the name fool you, NAPMW was founded by women but everyone is invited to join: www.napmw.org.

Training and Schools

Loan Officer School. The site www.loanofficerschool.com provides a wealth of educational materials for the novice loan officer and the experienced. You can take courses online, but the school also "tours" the country all year long holding different training events. Topics range from how to read a rate sheet to understanding compliance issues to how to analyze tax returns and profit-and-loss statements.

Loan Officer School is perhaps one of the most thorough online training tools for loan officers there is.

Mortgage Training Institute. The site www.mortgageknowledge.com is another worthwhile educational site that provides both introductory and advanced mortgage and mortgage-related courses.

This company offers live training in cities across the country on a regular basis. For certain states that require continuing education credits, this site is a good resource because it offers online training, live online classes, and self-study courses.

CMPS Institute. The www.cmpsinstitute.org site is where you obtain your Certified Mortgage Planner (CMP) accreditation. A CMP can integrate a client's mortgage, debt, and home-equity strategy into an overall financial plan. This site is very high-level, not for the novice loan officer, but after an originator establishes a solid client base, becoming a CMP should be a strong consideration for anyone wanting to get into the mid-to-high six figures.

Taught by industry veterans Barry Habib, Jim McMahan, and Gibran Nicholas, CMP training takes a loan officer to the next level of professionalism.

Production Skills

Loan Officer Magazine. Its slogan is "Guerilla Sales & Marketing Concepts for the Mortgage Loan Originator." This is a bimonthly e-zine that has never failed to pack a punch. The articles are written by other successful loan officers and managers, and they provide solid, everyday advice and ideas you can put to use immediately. Very "street smart." I can't recommend this site enough: www.loanofficermagazine.com.

The Mortgage Coach. Its slogan is "Stop selling loans . . . Start building wealth." To take your production to the next level, this is your first stop. I've always been a fan of providing solid, evaluative numbers a client can review, but nobody does it better than The Mortgage Coach. This makes you stand head and shoulders above your competition and is especially effective with the higher-income client. In fact, it's not only effective, it's essential.

The site also offers marketing tips, top-producer newsletters, and industry conference calls. When you get close to making six figures in this business, you'll soon be using The Mortgage Coach: www.the mortgagecoach.com.

LoanToolbox. Its slogan is "Building Better Loan Officers." This company offers a full suite of Web-based mortgage materials, training, and education. Designed, written, and compiled by some of the most successful loan officers in the country, this is a great place for the new loan officer to learn the basics, then gradually move up the ladder to a pro. It's not called "Loan Toolbox" for nothing: www.loantoolbox.com.

MBS Quoteline. For a monthly fee, you can get live mortgage-backed securities (MBS) prices sent to your computer, your e-mail, cell phone, or PDA. As MBS prices move throughout the day, interest rates can change. MBS Quoteline can alert you to bond moves in advance of lenders' rate increases during the day.

If you're in the mortgage business, it's essential that you have access to live MBS pricing: www.mbsquoteline.com.

Mortgage Market Guide. This is also a live MBS pricing service, but it offers much, much more. In fact, there may not be a more universal, practical website for the serious loan officer.

If you want to truly understand mortgage rates, how they're set, and also get that information to your computer, your cell phone, PDA, and e-mail, there is no better website on the market. MMG takes complex financial subjects and puts them in everyday, understandable language that not only trains you, but helps you explain those same sometimes-complex subjects to your clients.

There are less expensive sites that offer bond pricing, but there is definitely none more thorough. MMG also partners with other industry peers to offer discounts on other products and services geared toward loan officer production.

MMG might be the most "bang for the buck" of any online service or publication I've seen. It's a wealth of solid information that I can't recommend enough: www.mortgagemarketguide.com.

Loan Origination Software (LOS)

Calyx Point. This end-to-end loan origination software starts with the loan application, goes through processing, and all the way to loan submission and approval. Everything you need to process loans is in Point.

Point claims to own over two-thirds of the LOS market, and I believe it. Calyx is a solid company with an easy-to-use product that is recognized by all wholesale lenders and affiliate service providers: www.calyxsoftware.com.

Ellie Mae. Ellie Mae actually offers three LOS systems: Genesis; Contour; and its flagship product, Encompass. Fewer and fewer Genesis and Contour systems are being put in place—they're being replaced by Encompass. Encompass is not only a powerful LOS, it's also a marketing and loan-pipeline-management tool. It's definitely worth a look: www.elliemae.com.

BYTE. BYTE has been around for maybe 20 years. It's a solid, proven application that provides all a loan officer needs to run a loan-origination business. It also contains sales and marketing tools loan officers can use to market to new and previous clients: www.byte-cbc .com.

Website Design

Myers Internet. This is the oldest mortgage-website design firm in the industry. It's geared to the mortgage operation and offers a suite of Web design choices, from the least-expensive "template" to custom-designed sites. Myers is reliable and inexpensive: www.myers.com.

ETrafficers.com. This company is not as established as Myers, but it has been around for a long time. It provides full-service website design for mortgage companies and offers a full selection of mortgage-website templates and add-ons, which lets you choose how much money you want to spend. This is who I use.

ETrafficers.com also offers a search engine optimization (SEO) package that helps search engines such as Google and Yahoo! find and log your site: www.etrafficers.com.

Appendix F: State Licensing Chart

Mortgage Licensing Agencies

State	State Agency	License Regulated
Alabama	State Banking Department Center for Commerce 401 Adams Avenue, Suite 680 Montgomery, Alabama 36130 Telephone: 334-242-3452 Main fax: 334-242-3500 Bureau of Loans fax: 334-353-5961 Internet: http://www.bank.state.al.us/	Mortgage Broker, Mortgage Lender entitled Consumer Credit
Alaska	Department of Commerce, Community, and Economic Development Division of Banking, Securities & Corporations Mailing Address: P.O. Box 110807 Juneau, AK 99811-0807 Physical Address: 150 Third Street, Ste. 217 Juneau, AK 99801 Telephone: 907-465-2521 Fax: 907-465-2549 Internet: http://www.dced.state.ak.us/bsc/home.htm	1st and 2nd Mortgage brokering and lending is not regulated
Arizona	State Banking Department 2910 N. 44th Street, Suite 310 Phoenix, AZ 85018 Telephone: 602-255-4421 Fax: 602-381-1225 Internet: http://www.azbanking.com	Mortgage Broker, Mortgage Banker
Arkansas	Securities Department Heritage West Building, Suite 300 201 E. Markham Little Rock, AR 72201 Telephone: 501-324-9260 Fax: 501-324-9268 Internet: http://www.state.ar.us/arsec/	Mortgage Broker, Mortgage Banker
California	California Department of Corporations 320 West 4th Street, Suite 750 Los Angeles, CA 90013 Telephone: (213) 576-7500 Facsimile: (213) 576-7181 Internet: http://www.corp.ca.gov	Consumer Finance Lender [Broker/Lender], Residential Mortgage Lending (Banker)
California	Department of Real Estate 320 West 4th Street, Suite 350 Los Angeles CA 90013-1105 Telephone: 213-620-2072 Facsimile: 213-576-6903 (Enforcement) 213- 576-6917 (Legal) Internet: http://www.dre.ca.gov	Real Estate Broker permitting mortgage brokering
Colorado	Division of Real Estate 1560 Broadway, Suite 925 Denver, CO 80202	Mortgage Broker

State	State Agency	License Regulated
	Telephone: 303-894-5953 (broker) or 303-894-2166 (main) Fax: 303-894-7885 (broker) or 303-894-2683 (main) Internet: http://www.dora.state.co.us/real-estate/	
Colorado	Department of Law Uniform Consumer Credit Code Unit 1525 Sherman Street, Fifth Floor Denver, CO 80203 Telephone: 303-866-4494 Fax: 303-866-5691 Internet: http://www.ago.state.co.us/uccchome.htm	1st mortgage lending is not regulated, 2nd mortgage lender entitled Supervised Lender
Connecticut	Connecticut Department of Banking Consumer Credit Division 260 Constitution Plaza Hartford, Connecticut 06103 Telephone: 860-240-8200 Facsimile: 860-240-8178 Internet: http://www.state.ct.us/dob/pages/ccdiv.htm	1st and 2nd Mortgage Broker, 1st and 2nd Mortgage Lender
Delaware	Delaware Office of the State Bank Commissioner 555 E. Loockerman Street, Suite 210 Dover, DE 19901 Telephone: 302-739-4235 Facsimile: 302-739-3609 or 302-739-2356 (licensing/consumer complaints) Internet: http://www.state.de.us/bank	Mortgage Broker, Mortgage Lender entitled Licensed Lender
District of Columbia	Department of Insurance, Securities and Banking Banking Bureau 810 First Street, NE, Suite 701 Washington, DC 20005 Phone: 202-727-8000 Fax: 202-535-1197 E-mail: BankingBureau@dc.gov Internet: http://www.disb.dc.gov	Mortgage Broker, Mortgage Lender
Florida	Department of Financial Services Division of Securities and Finance 200 E. Gaines Street Tallahassee, FL 32399 Telephone: 850-410-9895 (licensing) or 850-410-9805 (enforcement) Facsimile: 850-410-9882 (licensing) or 850-410-9748 (enforcement) Internet:http://www.flofr.com/licensing/index.htm	Mortgage Lender and Correspondent Lender, Individual Mortgage Broker, Mortgage Broker Business
Georgia	Department of Banking and Finance 2990 Brandywine Road, Suite 200 Atlanta, GA 30341 Telephone: 770-986-1633 or 888-986-1633 Facsimile: 770-986-1654 Internet: http://www.ganet.org/dbf/dbf.html	Mortgage Broker, Mortgage Lender
Hawaii	Professional and Vocational Licensing Division Department of Commerce and Consumer Affairs Mailing address: P.O. Box 3469 Honolulu, HI 96801 Physical address: 335 Merchant Street, Room 301 Honolulu, HI 96813 Telephone: 808-586-3000 Internet: http://www.hawaii.gov/dcca/areas/pvl	Mortgage Broker
Hawaii	Division of Financial Institutions Department of Commerce and Consumer Affairs	Mortgage Lender, Nondepository Financial Services Loan Company

State	State Agency	License Regulated
	Mailing Address: P.O. Box 2054 Honolulu, HI 96805 Physical Address: King Kalakaua Building 335 Merchant Street, Room 221 Honolulu, HI 96813 Telephone: 808-586-2820 Facsimile: 808-586-2818 Internet: http://www.hawaii.gov/dcca/areas/dfi	
Idaho	Department of Finance 700 West State Street, 2nd Floor P.O. Box 83720 Boise, ID 83702 Telephone: 208-332-8002 Facsimile: 208-332-8096 or 208-332-8097 Internet: http://finance.idaho.gov	Mortgage Broker, Mortgage Lender
Illinois	Bureau of Residential Finance Department of Financial and Professional Regulation Illinois Division of Banks & Real Estate 310 South Michigan Avenue, Suite 2130 Chicago, IL 60604 Telephone: 312-793-3000 Facsimile: 312-793-7097 Internet: http://www.obre.state.il.us	Mortgage Broker, Mortgage Lender
Indiana	Indiana Secretary of State Securities Division 302 W. Washington Street, Room E-111 Indianapolis, IN 46204 Telephone: 317-232-6681 Facsimile: 317-233-3675 Internet: http://www.sos.in.gov/	Mortgage Broker
Indiana	Indiana Department of Financial Institutions 30 South Meridian Street, Suite 300 Indianapolis, IN 46204 Telephone: 317-232-3955 Facsimile: 317-232-7655 Internet: http://www.in.gov/dfi/	1st Mortgage Lending is not regulated, 2nd Mortgage Lending entitled Licensed Lender
Iowa	Iowa Division of Banking 200 East Grand Avenue, Suite 300 Des Moines, IA 50309 Telephone: 515-281-4014 Facsimile: 515-281-4862 Internet: http://www.idob.state.ia.us	Mortgage Broker, Mortgage Banker
Kansas	Office of the State Bank Commissioner Division of Consumer and Mortgage Lending 700 SW Jackson St., Suite 300 Topeka, KS 66603 Telephone: 785-296-2266 Facsimile: 785-296-6037 Internet: http://www.osbckansas.org	1st Mortgage Lending and Brokering entitled Mortgage Company, 2nd Mortgage Lending and Brokering entitled Supervised Loan
Kentucky	Department of Financial Institutions Division of Financial Institutions 1025 Capital Center Drive, Suite 200 Frankfort, KY 40601 Telephone: 502-573-3390 Facsimile: 502-573-8787 Internet: http://www.dfi.state.ky.us	Mortgage Broker, Mortgage Lender entitled Mortgage Loan Company

State	State Agency	License Regulated
Louisiana	Office of the Financial Institutions Mailing Address: P.O. Box 94095 Baton Rouge, LA 70804Physical address: 8660 United Plaza Boulevard, 2nd Floor Baton Rouge, LA 70809 Telephone: 225-925-4660 Facsimile: 225-925-4548 Internet: http://www.ofi.state.la.us	Mortgage Broker, Mortgage Lender
Maine	Department of Professional & Financial Regulation Office of Consumer Credit Regulation Mailing address: 35 State House Station Augusta, Maine 04333 Physical address: Department of Professional & Financial Regulation Office of Consumer Credit Regulation 122 Northern Avenue Gardiner, Maine 04345 Telephone: 207-624-8527 Facsimile: 207-582-7699 Internet: http://www.MaineCreditReg.org	Mortgage Broker entitled Loan Broker, Mortgage Lender entitled Supervised Lender
Maryland	Division of Labor, Licensing and Regulation Commissioner of Financial Regulation 500 North Calvert Street, Suite 402 Baltimore, Maryland 21202 Telephone: 410-230-6100 Facsimile: 410-333-3866 or 410-333-0475 Internet: http://www.dllr.state.md.us/finance/	Mortgage Broker, Mortgage Lender
Massachusetts	Division of Banks Consumer Compliance Unit One South Station Boston, Massachusetts 02110 Telephone: 617-956-1500 Facsimile: 617-956-1599 Internet: http://www.mass.gov/dob	Mortgage Broker, Mortgage Lender
Michigan	Office of Financial and Insurance Services Physical Address: 611 West Ottawa Street, 3rd Floor Lansing, MI 48909 Mailing Address: P.O. Box 30220 Lansing, MI 48909 Telephone: 517-373-0220 or 877-999-6442 Facsimile: 517-335-4978 Internet: http://www.michigan.gov/cis/0,1607,7-154- 10555---,00.html	1st and 2nd Mortgage Broker, 1st and 2nd Mortgage Lender
Minnesota	Department of Commerce Division of Financial Examinations 85 7th Place East, Suite 500 Saint Paul, MN 55101 Telephone: 651-296-2135 Facsimile: 651-282-9855 Internet: http://www.commerce.state.mn.us	Mortgage Broker and Mortgage Lender entitled Residential Mortgage Originator/Servicer
Mississippi	Department of Banking and Consumer Finance Mailing address: P.O. Box 23729 Jackson, MS 39225 Physical Address: 501 North West Street 901 Woolfolk Building, Suite A Jackson, MS 39201 Telephone: 601-359-1031 Facsimile: 601-359-3557 Internet: http://www.dbcf.state.ms.us	Mortgage Broker, Correspondent Lender, Mortgage Lender

State	State Agency	License Regulated
Missouri	Division of Finance Mailing Address: P.O. Box 716 Jefferson City, MO 65102 Physical Address: 301 W. High Street Harry S. Truman State Office Building, Room 630 Jefferson City, MO 65102 Telephone: 573-751-3242 (main), 573-751-4243 (section) Facsimile: (573) 751-9192 Internet: http://www.missouri-finance.org	Mortgage Broker and Mortgage Lender entitled Mortgage Broker
Montana	Division of Banking and Financial Institutions 301 South Park, Suite 316 Helena, MT 59620 Telephone: 406-841-2920 Facsimile: 406-841-2930 Internet: http://www.discoveringmontana.com/doa/ banking	Mortgage Broker and 1st Mortgage Lender entitled Mortgage Broker, 2nd Mortgage Lender entitled Consumer Loan
Nebraska	Department of Banking & Finance Mailing address: P.O. Box 95006 Lincoln, NE 68509 Physical address: Commerce Court 1230 'O' Street, Suite 400 P.O. Box 95006 Lincoln, NE 68508 Telephone: 402-471-2171 Facsimile: 402-471-3062 Internet: http://www.ndbf.org	Mortgage Broker and Mortgage Lender entitled Mortgage Banker
Nevada	Department of Business and Industry Mortgage Lending Division Carson City Office: 400 West King Street, Suite 406 Carson City, NV 89703 Telephone: 775-684-7060 Facsimile: 775-684-7061 Las Vegas Office: 3075 East Flamingo, #104A Las Vegas, NV 89121 Telephone: 702-486-0780 Facsimile: 702-486-0785 Internet: http://mld.nv.gov	Mortgage Broker, Mortgage Lender
New Hampshire	Banking Department 64B Old Suncook Road Concord, New Hampshire 03301 Telephone: 603-271-3561 Facsimile: 603-271-1090 (licensing), 603-271-7050 (consumer credit) Internet: http://www.state.nh.us/banking	Mortgage Broker, Mortgage Lender
New Jersey	Department of Banking and Insurance Division of Banking, Consumer Finance 20 West State Street P.O. Box 473 Trenton, NJ 08625 Also: Department of Banking and Insurance Licensing Services Bureau 20 West State Street, 8th Floor Trenton, NJ 08608 Telephone: 609-292-5340 Facsimile: 609-633-0822 E-mail: blic@dob.state.nj.us Internet: http://www.state.nj.us./dobi/ banklicensing/licensedlender.html	Mortgage Broker, Mortgage Banker, Correspondent Mortgage Banker, secondary Mortgage Lender entitled Licensed Lender

State	State Agency	License Regulated
New Mexico	Regulation and Licensing Department Financial Institutions Division Mailing Address: P.O. Box 25101 Santa Fe, NM 87504 Physical address: 2550 Cerrillos Road, 3rd Floor Santa Fe, NM 87505 Telephone: 505-476-4885 Facsimile: 505-476-4670 Internet: http://www.rld.state.nm.us/FID/index.htm	Mortgage Broker entitled Loan Broker, Mortgage Lender entitled Mortgage Loan Company
New York	Banking Department Mortgage Banking Division One State Street New York, NY 10004 Telephone: 212-709-5579 (broker questions), 212-709-3847 (banker questions) Facsimile: 212-709-5555 Internet: http://www.banking.state.ny.us	Mortgage Broker, Mortgage Banker
North Carolina	Office of the Commissioner of Banks Mailing Address: 4309 Mail Service Center Raleigh, NC 27699 Physical address: 316 West Edenton Street Raleigh, NC 27603 Telephone: 919-733-3016 Facsimile: 919-733-6918 Internet: http://www.nccob.org/NCCOB	Mortgage Broker, Mortgage Lender
North Dakota	Department of Financial Institutions 2000 Schafer Street, Suite G Bismarck, ND 58501 Telephone: 701-328-9933 Facsimile: 701-328-9955 Internet: http://www.discovernd.com/dfi	Mortgage Broker and Mortgage Lender entitled Money Broker
Ohio	Department of Commerce Division of Financial Institutions 77 South High Street, 21st Floor Columbus, OH 43215 Telephone: 614-728-8400 Facsimile: 614-644-1631 Internet: http://www.com.state.oh.us	Mortgage Broker and 1st Mortgage Lender entitled Mortgage Broker, 2nd Mortgage Lender entitled Mortgage Loan Act License
Oklahoma	Department of Consumer Credit 4545 North Lincoln Boulevard, Suite 104 Oklahoma City, OK 73105 Telephone: 405-521-3653 Facsimile: 405-521-6740 Internet: http://www.okdocc.state.ok.us	1st Mortgage Broker and Lender entitled Mortgage Broker, 2nd Mortgage Broker and Lender entitled Supervised Lender
Oregon	Department of Consumer and Business Services Division of Finance & Corporate Securities Mailing Address: P.O. Box 14480 Salem, OR 97309 Physical address: 350 Winter Street, NE, Room 410 Salem, OR 97301 Telephone: 503-378-4140 or 503-378-4387 Facsimile: 503-947-7862 Internet: http://www.oregondfcs.org	Mortgage Broker, Mortgage Lender
Pennsylvania	Department of Banking 333 Market Street, 16th Floor Harrisburg, PA 17101 Telephone: 800-722-2657 or 717-214-8343 Facsimile: 717-787-8773 Internet: http://www.banking.state.pa.us	1st Mortgage Broker, 1st Correspondent Lender, 1st Mortgage Banker, 1st Wholesale Lender, 2nd Mortgage Broker, 2nd Correspondent Lender, 2nd Mortgage Banker

State	State Agency	License Regulated
Rhode Island	Department of Business Regulation Division of Banking 233 Richmond Street, Suite 231 Providence, RI 02903 Telephone: 401-222-2405 Facsimile: 401-222-5628 Internet: http://www.dbr.state.ri.us	Mortgage Broker, Mortgage Lender
South Carolina	Consumer Finance Division State Board of Financial Institutions 1015 Sumter Street, 3rd floor Columbia, SC 29201 Telephone: 803-734-2020 Facsimile: 803-734-2025 Internet: http://www.scconsumer.gov	Mortgage Broker, 1st Mortgage Lending is not regulated, 2nd Mortgage Lending entitled Supervised Lender
South Dakota	Division of Banking 217 1/2 W. Missouri Avenue Pierre, South Dakota 57501 Telephone: 605-773-3421 Facsimile: 605-773-5367 Internet: http://www.state.sd.us/banking	Mortgage Broker, Mortgage Lender
Tennessee	Department of Financial Institutions 511 Union Street, Suite 400 Nashville, TN 37219 Telephone: 615-741-2236 Facsimile: 615-741-2883 Internet: http://www.state.tn.us/financialinst	Mortgage Broker, Mortgage Lender
Texas	Department of Savings and Mortgage Lending 2601 North Lamar, Suite 201 Austin, TX 78705 Telephone: 512-475-1350 Facsimile: 512-475-1360 Internet: http://www.tsld.state.tx.us	1st Mortgage Broker and Lender entitled Mortgage Broker
Texas	Office of Consumer Credit Commissioner 2601 North Lamar Boulevard Austin, TX 78705 Telephone: 512-936-7600 Facsimile: 512-936-7610 Internet: http://www.occc.state.tx.us	2nd Mortgage Lender and Broker entitled Regulated Lender
Utah	Division of Real Estate Department of Commerce Mailing Address: P.O. Box 146711 Salt Lake City, UT 84114 Physical Address: Heber M. Wells Building 160 East, 300 South, 2nd Floor Salt Lake City, UT 84111 Telephone: 801-530-6747 Facsimile: 801-530-6749 Internet: http://www.commerce.utah.gov/dre/index.html	Residential First Mortgage Lenders and Brokers
Utah	Department of Financial Institutions Mailing Address: P.O. Box 146800 Salt Lake City, UT 84114 Physical Address: 324 South State, Suite 201 Salt Lake City, UT 84111 Telephone: 801-538-8830 Facsimile: 801-538-8894 Internet: http://www.dfi.utah.gov	Second Mortgage Lender (Consumer Credit Notification)
Vermont	Department of Banking, Insurance, Securities & Health Care Administration	Mortgage Lender, Mortgage Broker,

State	State Agency	License Regulated
	Division of Banking 89 Main Street, Drawer 20 Montpelier, VT 05620 Telephone: 802-828-3301 or 802-828-3307 Facsimile: 802-828-3306 Internet: http://www.bishca.state.vt.us/	
Virginia	State Corporation Commission Bureau of Financial Institutions 1300 East Main Street, Suite 800 P.O. Box 640 Richmond, VA 23218 Telephone 804-371-9657 Facsimile: 804-371-9416 Internet: http://www.state.va.us/scc/division/ banking/index.htm	Mortgage Lender, Mortgage Broker
Washington	Department of Financial Institutions Division of Consumer Services Mailing Address: P.O. Box 41200 Olympia, WA 98504 Physical Address: 150 Israel Road SW Tumwater, WA 98501 Telephone: 360-902-8703 Facsimile: 360-664-2258 Internet: http://www.dfi.wa.gov	Mortgage Broker, Mortgage Banker entitled Consumer Loan
West Virginia	Division of Banking State Capitol Complex Building #3, Room 311 Charleston, West Virginia 25305-0240 Telephone: 304-558-2294 Facsimile: 304-558-0442 Internet: http://www.wvdob.org	Mortgage Broker, Mortgage Lender
Wisconsin	Department of Financial Institutions Division of Banking 345 West Washington Avenue, 4th Floor Madison, WI 53707 Telephone: 608-261-7578 Facsimile: 608-267-6889 Internet: http://www.wdfi.org	Mortgage Broker, Mortgage Banker
Wyoming	Department of Audit Division of Banking-UCCC Herschler Building, 3rd Floor East 122 West 25th Street Cheyenne, WY 82002 Telephone: 307-777-7797 Facsimile: 307-777-3555 Internet: http://audit.state.wy.us/banking	Mortgage Broker and 1st Mortgage Lender, 2nd Mortgage Lender entitled Consumer Credit

Mortgage Licensing Chart courtesy of Thomas Law Firm, www.thomas-law.com. Thomas Law Firm provides counseling and licensing assistance in all fifty states, and is helpful if you want to become licensed in other parts of the country where you don't yet have a physical presence, or would like to begin originating loans in other states.

Appendix G: Payments Per Thousand Dollars Financed

These tables give you a quick way to calculate the monthly payment on a mortgage if you know the term of the mortgage and the interest rate. To use the tables, first find your interest rate, move across to the column matching the term of your loan, and multiply that number by the number of thousand dollars financed.

For example, if you want to calculate the monthly payment on a $150,000 loan that carries a 6.50% interest rate and a 30-year term, simply find 6.50% on the left side of the table, and then move over to the 30-Year column. Then multiply that number by the principal (in thousands). In this example, the monthly payment is $6.32 x $150, or $948.00. Note that the payment includes interest and principal.

Rate	40 yr	30 yr	25 yr
2.500	$3.30	$3.95	$4.49
2.625	$3.37	$4.02	$4.55
2.750	$3.44	$4.08	$4.61
2.875	$3.51	$4.15	$4.68
3.000	$3.58	$4.22	$4.74
3.125	$3.65	$4.28	$4.81
3.250	$3.73	$4.35	$4.87
3.375	$3.80	$4.42	$4.94
3.500	$3.87	$4.49	$5.01
3.625	$3.95	$4.56	$5.07
3.750	$4.03	$4.63	$5.14
3.875	$4.10	$4.70	$5.21
4.000	$4.18	$4.77	$5.28
4.125	$4.26	$4.85	$5.35

Rate	40 yr	30 yr	25 yr
4.250	$4.34	$4.92	$5.42
4.375	$4.42	$4.99	$5.49
4.500	$4.50	$5.07	$5.56
4.625	$4.58	$5.14	$5.63
4.750	$4.66	$5.22	$5.70
4.875	$4.74	$5.29	$5.77
5.000	$4.82	$5.37	$5.85
5.125	$4.91	$5.44	$5.92
5.250	$4.99	$5.52	$5.99
5.375	$5.07	$5.60	$6.07
5.500	$5.16	$5.68	$6.14
5.625	$5.24	$5.76	$6.22
5.750	$5.33	$5.84	$6.29
5.875	$5.42	$5.92	$6.37
6.000	$5.50	$6.00	$6.44
6.125	$5.59	$6.08	$6.52
6.250	$5.68	$6.16	$6.60
6.375	$5.77	$6.24	$6.67
6.500	$5.85	$6.32	$6.75
6.625	$5.94	$6.40	$6.83
6.750	$6.03	$6.49	$6.91
6.875	$6.12	$6.57	$6.99
7.000	$6.21	$6.65	$7.07
7.125	$6.31	$6.74	$7.15
7.250	$6.40	$6.82	$7.23
7.375	$6.49	$6.91	$7.31
7.500	$6.58	$6.99	$7.39
7.625	$6.67	$7.08	$7.47
7.750	$6.77	$7.16	$7.55
7.875	$6.86	$7.25	$7.64
8.000	$6.95	$7.34	$7.72
8.125	$7.05	$7.42	$7.80
8.250	$7.14	$7.51	$7.88
8.375	$7.24	$7.60	$7.97
8.500	$7.33	$7.69	$8.05

Rate	40 yr	30 yr	25 yr
8.625	$7.43	$7.78	$8.14
8.750	$7.52	$7.87	$8.22
8.875	$7.62	$7.96	$8.31
9.000	$7.71	$8.05	$8.39
9.125	$7.81	$8.14	$8.48
9.250	$7.91	$8.23	$8.56
9.375	$8.00	$8.32	$8.65
9.500	$8.10	$8.41	$8.74
9.625	$8.20	$8.50	$8.82
9.750	$8.30	$8.59	$8.91
9.875	$8.39	$8.68	$9.00
10.000	$8.49	$8.78	$9.09
10.125	$8.59	$8.87	$9.18
10.250	$8.69	$8.96	$9.26
10.375	$8.79	$9.05	$9.35
10.500	$8.89	$9.15	$9.44
10.625	$8.98	$9.24	$9.53
10.750	$9.08	$9.33	$9.62
10.875	$9.18	$9.43	$9.71
11.000	$9.28	$9.52	$9.80
11.125	$9.38	$9.62	$9.89
11.250	$9.48	$9.71	$9.98
11.375	$9.58	$9.81	$10.07
11.500	$9.68	$9.90	$10.16
11.625	$9.78	$10.00	$10.26
11.750	$9.88	$10.09	$10.35
11.875	$9.98	$10.19	$10.44
12.000	$10.08	$10.29	$10.53
12.125	$10.19	$10.38	$10.62
12.250	$10.29	$10.48	$10.72
12.375	$10.39	$10.58	$10.81
12.500	$10.49	$10.67	$10.90
12.625	$10.59	$10.77	$11.00
12.750	$10.69	$10.87	$11.09
12.875	$10.79	$10.96	$11.18

Rate	40 yr	30 yr	25 yr
13.000	$10.90	$11.06	$11.28
13.125	$11.00	$11.16	$11.37
13.250	$11.10	$11.26	$11.47
13.375	$11.20	$11.36	$11.56
13.500	$11.30	$11.45	$11.66
13.625	$11.40	$11.55	$11.75
13.750	$11.51	$11.65	$11.85
13.875	$11.61	$11.75	$11.94
14.000	$11.71	$11.85	$12.04
14.125	$11.81	$11.95	$12.13
14.250	$11.92	$12.05	$12.23
14.375	$12.02	$12.15	$12.33
14.500	$12.12	$12.25	$12.42
14.625	$12.22	$12.35	$12.52
14.750	$12.33	$12.44	$12.61
14.875	$12.43	$12.54	$12.71
15.000	$12.53	$12.64	$12.81
15.125	$12.64	$12.74	$12.91
15.250	$12.74	$12.84	$13.00
15.375	$12.84	$12.94	$13.10
15.500	$12.94	$13.05	$13.20
15.625	$13.05	$13.15	$13.30
15.750	$13.15	$13.25	$13.39
15.875	$13.25	$13.35	$13.49
16.000	$13.36	$13.45	$13.59
16.125	$13.46	$13.55	$13.69
16.250	$13.56	$13.65	$13.79
16.375	$13.67	$13.75	$13.88
16.500	$13.77	$13.85	$13.98
16.625	$13.87	$13.95	$14.08
16.750	$13.98	$14.05	$14.18
16.875	$14.08	$14.16	$14.28
17.000	$14.18	$14.26	$14.38
17.125	$14.29	$14.36	$14.48
17.250	$14.39	$14.46	$14.58

Rate	40 yr	30 yr	25 yr
17.375	$14.49	$14.56	$14.68
17.500	$14.60	$14.66	$14.78
17.625	$14.70	$14.77	$14.87
17.750	$14.80	$14.87	$14.97
17.875	$14.91	$14.97	$15.07
18.000	$15.01	$15.07	$15.17

Payments Per Thousand Dollars Financed

Here is the same information for 20-year, 15-year, and 10-year loans.

Rate	20 yr	15 yr	10 yr
2.500	$5.30	$6.67	$9.43
2.625	$5.36	$6.73	$9.48
2.750	$5.42	$6.79	$9.54
2.875	$5.48	$6.85	$9.60
3.000	$5.55	$6.91	$9.66
3.125	$5.61	$6.97	$9.71
3.250	$5.67	$7.03	$9.77
3.375	$5.74	$7.09	$9.83
3.500	$5.80	$7.15	$9.89
3.625	$5.86	$7.21	$9.95
3.750	$5.93	$7.27	$10.01
3.875	$5.99	$7.33	$10.07
4.000	$6.06	$7.40	$10.12
4.125	$6.13	$7.46	$10.18
4.250	$6.19	$7.52	$10.24
4.375	$6.26	$7.59	$10.30
4.500	$6.33	$7.65	$10.36
4.625	$6.39	$7.71	$10.42
4.750	$6.46	$7.78	$10.48
4.875	$6.53	$7.84	$10.55
5.000	$6.60	$7.91	$10.61
5.125	$6.67	$7.97	$10.67
5.250	$6.74	$8.04	$10.73
5.375	$6.81	$8.10	$10.79
5.500	$6.88	$8.17	$10.85

Rate	20 yr	15 yr	10 yr
5.625	$6.95	$8.24	$10.91
5.750	$7.02	$8.30	$10.98
5.875	$7.09	$8.37	$11.04
6.000	$7.16	$8.44	$11.10
6.125	$7.24	$8.51	$11.16
6.250	$7.31	$8.57	$11.23
6.375	$7.38	$8.64	$11.29
6.500	$7.46	$8.71	$11.35
6.625	$7.53	$8.78	$11.42
6.750	$7.60	$8.85	$11.48
6.875	$7.68	$8.92	$11.55
7.000	$7.75	$8.99	$11.61
7.125	$7.83	$9.06	$11.68
7.250	$7.90	$9.13	$11.74
7.375	$7.98	$9.20	$11.81
7.500	$8.06	$9.27	$11.87
7.625	$8.13	$9.34	$11.94
7.750	$8.21	$9.41	$12.00
7.875	$8.29	$9.48	$12.07
8.000	$8.36	$9.56	$12.13
8.125	$8.44	$9.63	$12.20
8.250	$8.52	$9.70	$12.27
8.375	$8.60	$9.77	$12.33
8.500	$8.68	$9.85	$12.40
8.625	$8.76	$9.92	$12.47
8.750	$8.84	$9.99	$12.53
8.875	$8.92	$10.07	$12.60
9.000	$9.00	$10.14	$12.67
9.125	$9.08	$10.22	$12.74
9.250	$9.16	$10.29	$12.80
9.375	$9.24	$10.37	$12.87
9.500	$9.32	$10.44	$12.94
9.625	$9.40	$10.52	$13.01
9.750	$9.49	$10.59	$13.08
9.875	$9.57	$10.67	$13.15

Rate	20 yr	15 yr	10 yr
10.000	$9.65	$10.75	$13.22
10.125	$9.73	$10.82	$13.28
10.250	$9.82	$10.90	$13.35
10.375	$9.90	$10.98	$13.42
10.500	$9.98	$11.05	$13.49
10.625	$10.07	$11.13	$13.56
10.750	$10.15	$11.21	$13.63
10.875	$10.24	$11.29	$13.70
11.000	$10.32	$11.37	$13.78
11.125	$10.41	$11.44	$13.85
11.250	$10.49	$11.52	$13.92
11.375	$10.58	$11.60	$13.99
11.500	$10.66	$11.68	$14.06
11.625	$10.75	$11.76	$14.13
11.750	$10.84	$11.84	$14.20
11.875	$10.92	$11.92	$14.27
12.000	$11.01	$12.00	$14.35
12.125	$11.10	$12.08	$14.42
12.250	$11.19	$12.16	$14.49
12.375	$11.27	$12.24	$14.56
12.500	$11.36	$12.33	$14.64
12.625	$11.45	$12.41	$14.71
12.750	$11.54	$12.49	$14.78
12.875	$11.63	$12.57	$14.86
13.000	$11.72	$12.65	$14.93
13.125	$11.80	$12.73	$15.00
13.250	$11.89	$12.82	$15.08
13.375	$11.98	$12.90	$15.15
13.500	$12.07	$12.98	$15.23
13.625	$12.16	$13.07	$15.30
13.750	$12.25	$13.15	$15.38
13.875	$12.34	$13.23	$15.45
14.000	$12.44	$13.32	$15.53
14.125	$12.53	$13.40	$15.60
14.250	$12.62	$13.49	$15.68

Rate	20 yr	15 yr	10 yr
14.375	$12.71	$13.57	$15.75
14.500	$12.80	$13.66	$15.83
14.625	$12.89	$13.74	$15.90
14.750	$12.98	$13.83	$15.98
14.875	$13.08	$13.91	$16.06
15.000	$13.17	$14.00	$16.13
15.125	$13.26	$14.08	$16.21
15.250	$13.35	$14.17	$16.29
15.375	$13.45	$14.25	$16.36
15.500	$13.54	$14.34	$16.44
15.625	$13.63	$14.43	$16.52
15.750	$13.73	$14.51	$16.60
15.875	$13.82	$14.60	$16.67
16.000	$13.91	$14.69	$16.75
16.125	$14.01	$14.77	$16.83
16.250	$14.10	$14.86	$16.91
16.375	$14.19	$14.95	$16.99
16.500	$14.29	$15.04	$17.06
16.625	$14.38	$15.13	$17.14
16.750	$14.48	$15.21	$17.22
16.875	$14.57	$15.30	$17.30
17.000	$14.67	$15.39	$17.38
17.125	$14.76	$15.48	$17.46
17.250	$14.86	$15.57	$17.54
17.375	$14.95	$15.66	$17.62
17.500	$15.05	$15.75	$17.70
17.625	$15.15	$15.84	$17.78
17.750	$15.24	$15.92	$17.86
17.875	$15.34	$16.01	$17.94
18.000	$15.43	$16.10	$18.02

Abstract of Title. A written record of the historical ownership of the property. It helps determine whether the seller can in fact transfer the property to another party without the risk of any previous claims. Lenders use an abstract of title in certain parts of the country.

Acceleration: A loan accelerates when it's paid off early, usually at the request or demand of the lender. This is usually associated with an acceleration clause within a loan document. The clause states what must happen when a loan is repaid immediately, but most acceleration clauses apply in the event of late payments, nonpayment, or transfer of the property without the lender's permission.

Adjustable-Rate Mortgage. Obviously, this is a loan program where the interest rate may change throughout the life of the loan. The rate adjusts based upon agreed-upon terms between the lender and the borrower, but typically may only change once or twice a year.

Amortization: The time during which the principal balance of a loan is being repaid. These payments are at regular intervals and are made according to a predetermined schedule. With a *fully amortized loan,* the borrower's principal balance is zero at the end of the loan term. Amortization terms can vary, but generally accepted terms for mortgage loans run in five-year increments from 10 years to 40.

Appraisal: A report that helps determine the market value of a property. This report can be done in various degrees as required by a lender, from simply driving by the property in a car to a full-blown inspection complete with color pictures of the real estate. Appraisers

227

compare the property in question with similar properties in the area to substantiate the value of the property in question.

APR: Annual Percentage Rate. The APR is the cost of money borrowed expressed as an annual rate. The APR is a useful consumer tool to compare different lenders, but unfortunately it is not used correctly. The APR is useful only when comparing the same exact loan type from one lender to another. It doesn't work as well when comparing different types of mortgage programs with different down payments, terms, and so on.

Assumable mortgage: Homes sold with assumable mortgages let buyers take over the terms of the loan associated with the house being sold. Assumable loans may be *fully assumable* or *nonqualifying assumable*. Nonqualifying assumable loans let buyers take over the mortgage without being qualified or otherwise evaluated by the original lender. Qualifying assumable loans let buyers assume the terms of the existing mortgage if they qualify with the original lender as if they were applying for a brand-new loan.

Automated Valuation Model. This is an electronic method of evaluating a property's appraised value. It focuses on scanning public records for recent home sales and other data in the subject property's neighborhood. This is not yet widely accepted as a replacement for full-blown appraisals, but many expect AVMs to replace traditional appraisals altogether.

Balloon mortgage: A type of mortgage whereby the remaining balance must be paid in full at the end of a preset term. For example, a five-year balloon mortgage might amortize as if it were over a 30-year period, but any remaining balance is due in full at the end of five years.

Bankers: Lenders who use their own funds to lend money. Historically these funds would have come from their deposits from other bank customers. But with the evolution of mortgage banking, that's the old way of doing business. Even though bankers use their own money, it may come from other sources such as lines of credit or through selling loans to other institutions.

Basis Point: 1/100th of a percent. Twenty-five basis points is one-fourth of a discount point. One hundred basis points is one discount point.

Bridge Loan: A short-term loan primarily used to pull equity out of one property for a down payment on another. This loan is paid off when the original property sells. Because these are short-term loans, sometimes for just a few weeks, usually only retail banks will offer them. Usually the borrower doesn't make any monthly payments and only pays off the loan when the property sells.

Brokers: Brokers are mortgage companies that set up home loans between bankers and borrowers. Brokers don't have money to lend directly but have experience in finding various loan programs that can suit borrowers. The concept is similar to how independent insurance agents operate. Brokers don't work for the borrower but instead provide mortgage loan choices from other mortgage lenders.

Bundling: The act of putting together several real estate or mortgage services in one package. Instead of paying for an appraisal here or an inspection there, some or all of the buyer's services are packaged together. Usually this is to offer discounts on all services, although when they're bundled it's hard to parse all the services out to see whether you're getting a good deal or not.

Buy Down: Paying more money to get a lower interest rate. A *permanent buy down* is a reduction in the interest rate for the life of the loan in exchange for a fee (discount points). The more points the borrower pays, the lower the rate. A *temporary buy down* is the payment of points in exchange for a fixed-rate mortgage that starts at a reduced rate for the first period, then gradually increases to its final note rate. A temporary buy down for two years is called a 2-1 buy down. For three years it's called a 3-2-1 buy down.

Cash Out: Taking equity out of a home in the form of cash during a refinance. This is done by borrowing more than what is needed to repay the previous mortgage balance. Instead of just reducing your interest rate during a refinance and borrowing your closing costs, you borrow more, putting the extra money in your pocket.

Closing Costs: The various fees involved when buying a home or obtaining mortgage. The fees can come directly from the lender or may come from other entities required to issue a good loan.

Collateral: Property owned by the borrower that's pledged to the lender. The lender gets the collateral if the loan goes bad. A lender makes a mortgage with the house as collateral.

Comparable Sales: Part of an appraisal report, it lists recent transfers of similar properties in the immediate area of the house being bought. Also called "comps."

Conforming loan: A *conventional conforming loan* is a conventional loan that is equal to or less than the maximum allowable loan limits established by Fannie Mae and Freddie Mac. These limits change annually.

Conventional Loan: A mortgage made according to guidelines established by Fannie Mae or Freddie Mac.

Credit Report: A report showing the payment histories of a consumer along with his or her previous addresses and any public financial records.

Debt Consolidation: Paying off all or part of one's consumer debt with equity from a home. Can be part of a refinanced mortgage or a separate equity loan.

Debt Ratio: Gross monthly payments divided by gross monthly income. Expressed as a percentage. Lenders typically evaluate two debt ratios. The *housing ratio*—sometimes called the *front ratio*—equals the borrower's total monthly house payment (including any monthly taxes, insurance, private mortgage insurance, or homeowners association dues) divided by gross monthly income. The *total debt ratio*—also called the *back ratio*—is the borrower's total housing payment plus other monthly consumer installment or revolving debt as a percentage of the borrower's gross monthly income. Debt ratios are usually denoted as "32/38," for example; 32 is the front ratio and 38 is the back ratio. Ratio guidelines vary from loan to loan and lender to lender.

Deed: A written document evidencing each transfer of ownership in a property.

Deed of Trust: A written document that gives an interest in a home being bought to a third party, usually the lender, as security.

Delinquent: Being behind on a mortgage payment. Creditors typically describe delinquencies as 30 + days delinquent, 60 + days delinquent, and 90 + days delinquent.

Discount Points: Also called *points*, these are fees paid as a percentage of a loan amount. One point equals one percent of a loan balance. Borrowers pay discount points to reduce the interest rate on a mortgage. Typically, paying one discount point reduces an interest rate by one-quarter of a percent. It is a form of prepaid interest to a lender.

Document Stamp: Certain states call it a *doc stamp*, and it is evidence that the property owner has paid his taxes. It usually involves an actual ink stamp. Doc-stamp tax rates vary based upon locale. Some states don't have doc stamps, some do.

Down Payment: The amount of money the borrower gives the seller up front in order to close a mortgage. It equals the sales price less financing. It's the very first bit of equity the borrower has in the home.

Easement: A right of way previously established by a third party. Easement types vary, but they typically involve the right of a public utility to cross your land to access an electrical line, for example.

Escrow: This can mean two things depending upon where you live. On the West Coast, for example, the word refers to escrow agents, who oversee the closing of a home loan. In other parts of the country, an escrow is a financial account set up by a lender to collect monthly installments for annual tax bills and/or hazard-insurance policy renewals.

Escrow Agent: On the West Coast, the person or company that handles the home closing, ensures documents are assigned correctly, and ensures that the property has legitimately changed hands.

Equity: The difference between the appraised value of a home and any outstanding loans recorded against the house.

Fannie Mae: Federal National Mortgage Association. Originally established in 1938 by Congress to buy FHA mortgages and provide liquidity in the mortgage marketplace. Similar in function to Freddie Mac. In 1968 its charter was changed and it now purchases conventional mortgages as well as government mortgages.

Fed: Typically means the Federal Reserve Board. The Fed, among other things, sets overnight lending rates for banking institutions. It doesn't set mortgage rates.

Fee Income: Closing costs received by a lender or broker that are not interest or discount points. Fee income can be in the form of loan processing charges, underwriting fees, and the like.

Final Inspection: The last inspection of a property. It's intended to prove that a new home is 100-percent complete or that a home improvement is 100-percent complete. This lets the lender know that its collateral and its loan are exactly where they should be.

Fixed-Rate Mortgage: A mortgage whose interest rate does not change throughout the term of the loan.

FHA: Federal Housing Administration. Formed in 1934 and now a division of the Department of Housing and Urban Development (HUD), the FHA provides loan guarantees to lenders who make loans under FHA guidelines.

Float: Actively deciding not to "lock" or guarantee an interest rate while a loan is being processed. This is usually done because the borrower believes the rates will go down.

Float Down: A mortgage-loan rate that drops as mortgage rates drop. Usually comes in two types: one during the construction of a home and the other during an interest-rate lock period.

Foreclosure: The bad thing that happens when the mortgage isn't repaid. Lenders begin the process of forcefully recovering their collateral when borrowers fail to make loan payments. The lender takes your house away.

Freddie Mac: Federal Home Loan Mortgage Corporation (FHLMC). A corporation established by Congress in 1968 that buys mortgages from lenders made under Freddie Mac guidelines.

Fully Indexed Rate: The number equal to a loan's index rate plus a margin. This rate is how the interest rates on adjustable-rate mortgages are calculated.

Funding: The actual transfer of money from a lender to a borrower.

Gift: When a third party makes the down payment and pays the closing costs for the borrower(s). Usually such gifts can only come from family members or foundations established to help new homeowners.

Ginnie Mae: Government National Mortgage Association (GNMA). A government corporation formed by Congress to purchase government loans like VA and FHA loans from banks and mortgage lenders. Think of it as Fannie Mae or Freddie Mac only it buys government loans and guarantees its resulting mortgage-backed securities with the full faith and credit of the U.S. Government.

Good Faith Estimate: A list of estimated closing costs on a particular mortgage transaction. This lender or broker must provide this estimate to the loan applicants within 72 hours of receiving a mortgage application.

Hazard Insurance: A specific type of insurance that covers against certain destructive elements, such as fire, wind, and hail. It is usually an addition to homeowners insurance, but every home loan has a hazard rider.

HELOC: Home Equity Line of Credit. A credit line using a home as collateral. The customer writes a check on the line whenever he needs to and pays only on the balances withdrawn. It's much like a credit card, but secured by the property.

Homeowners Insurance: An insurance policy covering not just hazard items but also other things such as liability or personal property.

Impound Accounts: Accounts set up by a lender to deposit a monthly portion of annual property taxes or hazard insurance. As taxes or insurance premiums come due, the lender pays the bills using these funds. Also called *escrow accounts.*

Index: Used as the basis to establish an interest rate, usually associated with a margin. Most anything can be an index, but the most common are yields on certain U.S. Treasuries or similar instruments. See *Fully Indexed Rate.*

Inspection: A structural review of the house. The inspector looks for defects in workmanship, damage to the property, or required maintenance. It does not determine the value of the property. A pest inspection looks for evidence of termites, wood ants, etc.

Interest Rate: The amount charged to borrow money over a specified period of time.

Intangible Tax: A state tax on owners of personal property. An intangible asset is an asset not by itself but rather represents one. For example, a publicly traded stock is an intangible asset. The stock certificate itself has no value, but what it represents in terms of income has value.

Jumbo Loan: A mortgage that exceeds current conforming loan limits.

Junior Lien: A second mortgage or one that is subordinate to another loan. Not as common of a term as it used to be. You're likely to hear simply *second mortgage* or *piggyback*.

Land Contract: An arrangement where the buyer makes monthly payments to the seller but the ownership of the property does not change hands until the loan is paid in full. Similar to how an automobile loan works. When you pay off the car, you get the title.

Land-to-Value Ratio: An appraisal ratio equal to the value of a piece of land as a percentage of the total value of the entire property. If the land value exceeds the value of the home on the land, it's more difficult to find financing without good comparable sales. Also called the *lot-to-value ratio*.

Lender Policy: Title insurance that protects a mortgage from defects or previous claims of ownership.

Liability: An obligation or bill on the part of the borrower. Liabilities such as student loans or car payments can show up on a credit report, but liabilities can also be anything else that one is obligated to pay. They're the ones on the credit report that are used to determine debt ratios.

Loan: Money granted to one party with the expectation of it being repaid.

Loan Officer: The person typically responsible for helping mortgage applicants get qualified. The loan officer assists in loan selection and loan application. Loan officers can work at banks, credit unions, mortgage brokerage houses, or for mortgage bankers.

Loan Processor: The person who gathers the required documentation for a loan application. Along with the loan officer, the borrower works with this person quite a bit during the mortgage process.

Lock: The act of guaranteeing an interest rate over a predetermined period of time. Loan locks are not loan approvals; they're simply the rate your lender has agreed to give you at loan closing.

Margin: A number, expressed as a percentage, that is added to an index to determine the rate the borrower pays on a note. For example, an index could be the rate on a particular six-month CD (say, 4.00%) and the margin could be 2.00%. The interest rate the borrower pays is 4.00% + 2.00%, or 6.00%. A fully indexed rate is the index plus the margin.

Market Value: In an open market, the value of a property. Theoretically, it equals both the highest the borrower was willing to pay and the least the seller was willing to accept at the time of contract. Property appraisals help justify market value by comparing similar home sales in the subject property's neighborhood.

Mortgage: A loan with property pledged as collateral. A mortgage is *retired* when the loan is paid in full.

Mortgage-Backed Securities: Investment securities issued by Wall Street firms that are guaranteed, or collateralized, with home mortgages taken out by consumers. These securities can then be bought and sold in the open markets.

Mortgagee: The person or business making the loan.

Mortgage Insurance (MI): MI, also called *private mortgage insurance (PMI)* is typically required for all borrowers obtaining mortgages with less than a 20-percent down payment. MI is an insurance policy, paid for by the borrower, that covers the difference between the borrower's down payment and 20 percent of the sales price. If the borrower defaults on the mortgage, this difference is paid to the lender.

Mortgagor: The person(s) getting the loan. The borrower.

Multiple Listing Service (MLS): A central repository where real estate brokers and agents show homes and search for homes that are for sale.

Negative Amortization (Neg Am): An adjustable-rate mortgage that can have two interest rates, the *contract rate* or the *fully indexed rate*. The contract rate is the minimum rate the consumer may pay. The fully indexed rate is a loan's index rate plus a margin. The borrower has a choice of which rate to pay, but if the contract rate is lower than the fully indexed rate, that difference in the two payments is added back to the loan principal. For example, assume your payment using the contract rate is only $500, but the payment using the fully indexed rate is $700. If you pay only the contract rate, the lender adds $200 back to your original loan amount. Negative amortization is not for the faint of heart or for those with little money down.

Nonconforming: Mortgage loan amounts above current Fannie Mae or Freddie Mac limits. Also called *jumbo* mortgages.

Note: A promise to repay. May or may not have property involved and may or may not be a mortgage.

Origination Fee: Usually expressed as a percentage of the loan amount, this is a fee charged for costs associated with finding, documenting, and preparing a mortgage application.

Owner's Policy: Title insurance made for the benefit of the homeowner.

PITI: Principal, Interest, Taxes, and Insurance. These figures are used to help determine front ratios.

PMI: Private Mortgage Insurance. See *Mortgage Insurance.*

Points: See *Discount Points.*

Prepaid Interest: Daily interest collected from the day of loan closing to the first of the following month.

Prepayment Penalty: A monetary penalty paid to the lender if the loan is paid off before its maturity or if extra payments are made on the loan. Sometimes defined as *hard* or *soft.* A hard penalty occurs automatically if the borrower pays the loan off early or makes extra payments at any time or for any amount whatsoever. A soft penalty only lasts for a couple of years; the lender may allow extra payments on the loan if the payments do not exceed a certain amount.

Principal: The outstanding amount owed on a loan, not including any interest due.

REALTOR: A member of the National Association of REALTORS. This is a registered trademark and not all real estate agents are REALTORS.

Refinance: Obtaining a new mortgage to replace an existing one.

Sales Contract: A written agreement, signed by both the seller and buyer, to buy or sell a home.

Secondary Market: A financial arena where mortgages are bought and sold, either individually or grouped together into securities backed by those mortgages (see *Mortgage-Backed Securities*). Fannie Mae and Freddie Mac are the backbone for the conventional secondary market. Other secondary markets exist for nonconforming loans, subprime loans, and others.

Second Mortgage: Sometimes called a *piggyback mortgage.* It is subordinate to a first mortgage. If the home goes into foreclosure, the first mortgage is settled before the second.

Seller: The person transferring ownership and all rights for a home in exchange for cash or trade.

Settlement Statement: Also called the *Final HUD-1*, it shows all the financial entries for the home sale including the sales price, closing costs, loan amounts, and property taxes. The Good Faith Estimate will be the borrower's first glimpse of the settlement statement. This statement is one of the final documents put together before closing and is prepared by the borrower's attorney or settlement agent.

Survey: A map that shows the physical location of the structure and where it sits on the property. It also designates any easements that run across or through the property.

Title: Ownership in a property.

Title Exam/Title Search: The process whereby a title agent or other party reviews public records to research any previous liens on the property.

Title Insurance: An insurance policy that protects the lender, the seller, and/or the borrower against any defects or previous claims to the property being transferred or sold.

Underwriter: The person who physically approves the loan, makes sure the loan meets lending guidelines, and signs off on documentation submitted.

Verification of Deposit: A written form sent by the lender to a financial institution to verify funds in a borrower's account. Also called a *VOD*, this form also shows how long the account has been open, everyone who has a claim to the account, and any withdrawals from or deposits into the account.

Verification of Employment: A written form sent by the lender to an employer to verify the employment of an applicant. Also called a *VOE*, this form also shows how long the applicant has worked at

his or her job, how much he or she makes, and whether the applicant has had any recent raises or bonuses.

Yield Spread Premium (YSP): The difference in basis points from one
rate to another offered by a wholesale lender as a result of a higher
rate. The opposite of discount points, which are paid to get a lower
rate, YSPs are paid by the lender to get a higher rate. Often used
to offset borrower closing costs and to provide a no-point, no-fee
mortgage loan.

Index